Praise for

ALONE **ON THE WALL**

"Riveting." —*San Francisco Chronicle*

"*Alone on the Wall* . . . is set to inspire multitudes [of climbers]. With his off-the-charts abilities and laconic, whip-smart, no-B.S. persona, Honnold has made climbing cool." —*Men's Journal*

"Honnold's narrative describes his genuine passion . . . while revealing a personal humility that paints a clear and vivid picture of a likeable and unassuming, introspective young man."

—*New York Journal of Books*

Praise for

ALEX **HONNOLD**

"The closest thing to a celebrity that American rock climbing offers."
—*New York Times*

"The greatest feat of pure rock climbing in the history of the sport."
—*National Geographic*

"The moon landing of free soloing." —Tommy Caldwell, *Outside*

"[Honnold] is best known for his fearless ascents of the world's biggest cliffs. . . . He has traversed them all with his bare hands, fingertips jammed into crevices and clinging to half-inch shelves of protruding rock to hold his chiseled 5' 11", 160-pound frame."

—*Sports Illustrated*

"Honnold climbs longer and more difficult routes than anyone previously thought possible. . . . He also climbs them in record time."
—*Atlantic*

"Alex Honnold has become arguably the most well-known and widely respected climber in the world." —*Interview*

"He's utterly genuine. There's no bullshit there." —Jon Krakauer, mountaineer and *New York Times* best-selling author

ALONE ON THE WALL

ALONE ON THE WALL

Alex Honnold

with David Roberts

W. W. NORTON & COMPANY
INDEPENDENT PUBLISHERS SINCE 1923
NEW YORK   LONDON

*To my family, for always supporting me
along an unconventional path*

For information about permission to reproduce selections from this book,
write to Permissions, W. W. Norton & Company, Inc.,
500 Fifth Avenue, New York, NY 10110

For information about special discounts for bulk purchases, please contact
W. W. Norton Special Sales at specialsales@wwnorton.com or 800-233-4830

Manufacturing by LSC Harrisonburg
Book design by Lovedog Studio
Production manager: Julia Druskin

The Library of Congress has catalogued a previous edition as follows:

Names: Honnold, Alex.
Title: Alone on the wall / Alex Honnold with David Roberts.
Description: First Edition. | New York : W.W. Norton & Company, [2016] | Includes index.
Identifiers: LCCN 2015027977 | ISBN 9780393247626 (hardcover)
Subjects: LCSH: Honnold, Alex. | Mountaineers—United States—Biography.
Classification: LCC GV199.92.H67 A3 2016 | DDC 796.522092—dc23
LC record available at http://lccn.loc.gov/2015027977

ISBN 978-0-393-35614-4 pbk.

W. W. Norton & Company, Inc.
500 Fifth Avenue, New York, N.Y. 10110
www.wwnorton.com

W. W. Norton & Company Ltd.
15 Carlisle Street, London W1D 3BS

6 7 8 9 0

Contents

CHAPTER **ONE**
MOONLIGHT

I started up the climb shortly after dawn. I wasn't even sure I'd found the right start, since I hadn't been on these lower pitches for two or three years. The beginning of the route is kind of scruffy and ambiguous—ramps, traverses, and hand cracks angling up to the right—but it's not as difficult as the upper two-thirds of the wall.

Still, I was nervous, even a little giddy. It had rained pretty much nonstop the day before, and now the rock was sandy, slabby, and a lot damper than I'd hoped. I probably should have waited another day before heading up the route. But I was overpsyched. I couldn't bear the thought of sitting in my van another whole day, thinking the same thoughts I had recycled for the past forty-eight hours. I had to strike while the iron was hot.

Moonlight Buttress is a 1,200-foot-high, nearly vertical sandstone cliff in Utah's Zion National Park. It may be the finest—the purest and most classic—route among Zion's thousands of lines. It's also one of the most continuously difficult crack climbs in the world.

The first ascent of Moonlight Buttress came in October 1971, when Jeff Lowe and Mike Weis, two legends of American climbing, pioneered the route. It took them a day and a half, with an overnight bivouac on a ledge in the middle of the wall. They used a lot of aid, pulling or hanging on expansion bolts and pitons.

Nearly twenty-one years later, in April 1992, Peter Croft and Johnny Woodward made the first free ascent, as they took all the aid out of the route by finding sequences of moves they could climb without hanging on gear. They solved the route in nine pitches (rope lengths), but rated the climb a really stiff 5.13a (since downgraded to 5.12d). In 1992, that was near the upper limit of free-climbing difficulty anywhere in the world, and Croft and Woodward's feat was a brilliant one.

Peter Croft was already one of my heroes, because in the 1980s and '90s he had pushed free soloing—climbing without a rope or gear at all—to unprecedented extremes. Many of the routes he'd free soloed back then had never been repeated in that style during the decades since.

But as far as I knew, no one had even thought of free soloing Moonlight Buttress. That's what I was hoping to pull off on April 1, 2008.

In the back of my mind was a nagging worry about the feature called the Rocker Blocker. It's an ample ledge, about half the size of a queen-size bed, at the top of the third pitch. Because it's loose, somebody has chained it in place with a two-bolt anchor, but it actually makes for a good stance about 400 feet off the ground.

It wasn't the ledge itself that fueled my angst. From the Rocker Blocker, stretching on tiptoe, you can just reach a key hold above. Essentially you face a 5.12c boulder problem right off the ledge. You don't actually have to jump to make the move, but it's more like an upward lurch to a small edge. As I climbed the easy pitches down low, that move loomed over me. I was pretty sure I could stick the ledge if I fell off, but I'd sure hate to find out.

The day before, sitting in my van in the rain, I had deliberately visualized everything that might happen on the climb. Including breaking a hold, or just losing it and falling off. I saw myself bouncing off the ledge below and going all the way to the ground, fracturing most of my bones as I rag-dolled down the mountain. I'd probably bleed out at the base.

I hadn't slept very well the previous night. So I got the early start in the morning that I'd planned, hoping to beat the sun to the wall and get cool conditions on the route. To reach the base of Moonlight Buttress, you have to wade the Virgin River, which in early April was freezing-ass cold. I forded the stream barefoot. The rushing water came up above my knees. My feet quickly went numb, and my whole body went into mild shock. Plus I had to pay attention to my balance as I placed my feet carefully in the gaps between polished river cobbles.

At what I thought was the start of Moonlight Buttress, I cached my approach shoes and my daypack. I'd decided to carry nothing— neither food, nor water, nor spare clothes—up the route. I clipped on my chalk bag and laced up my rock shoes. My feet were still cold, but they weren't truly numb—I could feel my toes all right. I was wearing only shorts and a T-shirt. At the last minute, I put on headphones and turned up my iPod. I was shuffling through my own Top 25 playlist of tunes—mostly punk and modern rock.

It may sound lame, but I didn't have a watch, and I was pretty sure I was going to set the speed record for Moonlight Buttress. I could use the iPod to measure the exact number of minutes the climb would take. Music also has a way of helping you focus, although nowadays I prefer to climb without my iPod, because I consider it a bit of a crutch.

• • • •

For me, free soloing a big wall is all about preparation. In a real sense, I had performed the hard work on Moonlight Buttress during the days leading up to the climb. Once I was on the route, it was just a matter of executing.

Yes, I'd climbed the whole route only once before, with a philosophy professor named Bill Ramsey. In his midforties, he was still climbing really well, and he'd been working on freeing Moonlight. He recruited me to climb it with him for his free attempt, and we swung leads up the whole route. It was a great day as we both climbed the route clean with no falls.

But that was two or three years earlier. In the days before my free solo attempt, I'd focused on the upper 800 feet of the route. It's a mellow hike along a paved trail to the top of Moonlight Buttress, so I hauled up 600 feet of rope, rappelled down it, and practiced the moves on toprope. To self-belay, I used a device called a Mini Traxion, which grips the rope on a downward pull but slides effortlessly up the rope as you climb. If I fell or even rested, the Mini Traxion would hold me tight.

With my toprope, I climbed the upper 600 feet of Moonlight Buttress twice. The crux of the whole route—the hardest single passage, which is the make-or-break stretch of an ascent—is an amazing clean inside corner, 180 feet long. It's the fourth of nine pitches on the route, and it's what gives the climb its 5.12d rating. It's continuous and really strenuous, so your arms get pretty pumped by the time you reach the top of it.

Each toproped rehearsal of those upper 600 feet had taken me only about an hour. I felt super-solid. At no point did I fall off or even feel sketchy. But then I realized that the 600-foot rope didn't reach down to a crucial 5.11c rightward traverse on the third pitch. So the next day I went back up to the top with 800 feet of rope, rapped down again, and rehearsed the traverse moves until I had them dialed too.

I ran into a few other climbers on my practice runs. I even rescued an aid-climbing chick who didn't quite know what she was doing and had gotten stuck on her lead. I yelled, "Hey, grab this rope!" as I swung the tail of my fixed rope to her, so she could liberate herself from her trap. She was pretty grateful. It's not every day that somebody comes rapping out of the sky on a route like that.

Then came two days of rain. I sat in my van in a movie theater parking lot in Springdale, stared out the windshield, and thought.

I'd gone to a movie to pass the time, but the rest of the day, into the evening, and through most of the second day I sat in the van, just thinking. It's not like I had work to do. I didn't have anything to do except think. About the climb.

Sitting and thinking, hour after hour. Visualizing every single move, everything that could possibly happen. That's what it takes to wrap your mind around a challenge such as the one I was about to attempt.

That's what I mean by preparation. Now I'd find out if I'd prepared adequately—if I could simply execute what I'd visualized, every handhold and foothold on the long way to the top of the wall.

A T THE END OF MARCH 2008, Alex Honnold was little known beyond the small circle of his friends. Seven years later, at the age of thirty, he is probably the most famous climber in the world. That's not to claim that he's the best climber in the world—in fact, there's no such thing as the "best climber," because the sport has subdivided into so many genres, from Himalayan mountaineering to bouldering in indoor gyms.

The reason for Honnold's meteoric celebrity is that he's pushed the most extreme and dangerous form of climbing far beyond the limits of what anyone thought was possible. Free soloing means climbing without a rope, a partner, or any "hardware" (pitons, nuts, or cams) to attach oneself to the wall. In its stark simplicity, that pursuit can be understood by the most casual observer. The stakes are ultimate: *If you fall, you die.*

What Alex has done is to free solo routes both longer and of much greater difficulty than anyone before him has thought possible. So far, he's gotten away with it, though some of his closest friends are afraid that he's going to kill himself.

Free soloing is far more than a stunt. It amounts to reducing climbing to its most elemental challenge: a man (or woman), with only rock shoes on his feet and chalk on his fingertips for better purchase, against the cliff. It's climbing at its absolute purest.

This is not the only kind of climbing Alex does, however. His speed "linkups"—enchainments of two or three big wall climbs back-to-back against the stopwatch, with only a minimal reliance on ropes or protection—have rewritten the book in Yosemite. And since 2013, Alex has expanded his horizons to mountaineering, where he's already doing things no one else has managed to pull off.

Alex Honnold, in short, is a climbing visionary, of the sort who comes along maybe once in a generation. He's also smart, funny, a man with surprisingly little ego, and a person who wants to make the world a better place for people less privileged or talented than he is. Nearly everyone who knows or even just watches Alex likes him, because, as Jon Krakauer says, "He's utterly genuine. There's no bullshit there."

Again and again, whenever he speaks in public, Alex is asked the same two questions by everyone from little kids to graybeards. Indeed, they are the fundamental questions about what he's doing on rock. They are:

Aren't you afraid you're going to die?
Why do you do this?

In a sense, those questions are unanswerable. They lie in the realm of George Leigh Mallory's throwaway response in 1923 to the umpteenth journalist who asked him why he wanted to climb Everest: "Because it is there." (Though intended as an irritable jab by a man fed up with the question, Mallory's quip has become the most famous quotation in mountaineering history.)

Alex has come up with his own quips to answer the inevitable questions. About falling to his death: "It'll be the worst four seconds of my life." And: "I'm sure half the people will say, 'At least he died doing what he loved best.' And the other half will say, 'What a fucking douche!'"

Alex is unmistakably a driven, competitive fellow. Yet his modesty, born of an innate shyness, takes the form of radical understatement of his accomplishments, verging (like the quips above) on self-deprecation. His nickname among his closest climbing buddies is Alex "No Big Deal" Honnold.

In the last forty years, only a handful of climbers have pushed free soloing to the razor edge of risk. Half of them are dead. Some of those soloists have survived their decades of dancing above the abyss: they include not only Peter Croft but also Henry Barber, who crisscrossed the globe in the 1970s, blowing the minds of locals at crags from Wales to Australia by flashing their hardest routes.

Others died when a single mistake caught up to them. Among their number was Derek Hersey, a Brit transplanted to the States, who fell to his death in 1993 on the Steck-Salathé route in Yosemite, possibly because a rainstorm slickened the holds. Dan Osman, Charlie Fowler, and Michael Reardon also died in accidents related to their pursuit of extreme exploits on cliffs and mountains. But the demise that most shocked the climbing world was that of John Bachar, with Peter Croft one of the two outstanding soloists of the 1980s and '90s. After thirty-five years of climbing route after route without a rope, Bachar fell off a short climb he had done many times before, on a route near his home in Mammoth Lakes, California, in July 2009.

Alex points out that none of this group of elite climbers died while pushing their limits at free soloing. Hersey and Bachar fell off routes that would normally have been well within their capacities. (There was speculation that a spinal problem that caused his left arm and shoulder suddenly to weaken, the result of a recent car accident, might have caused Bachar's fatal fall.) Reardon was swept to his death by a rogue wave after he had soloed *down* to the base of a sea cliff in Ireland. Fowler died in an avalanche as he attempted an unclimbed mountain in western China. Osman met his end while pushing to new extremes a sport he had virtually invented— rope jumping, or deliberately leaping off a cliff to be caught by the rope or ropes he was tied into. Having set a record jump of more than a thousand feet, Osman died when his rope broke on a plunge off Leaning Tower in Yosemite.

Still, all five of those extreme free soloists were out there on the cutting edge of adventure when they perished. Osman in effect discovered the boundaries of rope jumping by paying for the experiment with his life. Though still alive and well at sixty-two, Henry Barber came perilously close to falling to his death in the early 1980s as he was filmed free soloing a British sea-cliff route for an American TV show. Distracted by a nearby cameraman's sudden movement, Barber lost his balance. As he later described that moment,

> It caught me the wrong way. . . . I was doing some stemming moves, pushing with both hands against the sides of the groove. I pushed just a little too hard and my left shoulder bumped the wall, so that I started to fall. Adrenaline shot from my toes right up to my head. . . . I was off and headed down. But the balance and flow of all the movement that had gone on until that point carried me through, keeping me on the rock and still moving.

With his sharp intelligence, Alex inclines toward a hyperrational take on life. He actually insists, "I don't like risk. I don't like passing over double yellow. I don't like rolling the dice." He distinguishes between consequences and risk. Obviously, the consequences of a fall while free soloing are ultimate ones. But that doesn't mean, he argues, that he's taking ultimate risks. As he puts it, "I always call risk the likelihood of actually falling off. The consequence is what will happen if you do. So I try to keep my soloing low-risk—as in, I'm not likely to fall off, even though there'd be really high consequences if I did."

Just as rational, on the other hand, are some of the arguments made by close friends of Alex who worry about the chances he's taking. Seven years Alex's senior, Tommy Caldwell has been his partner on marathon linkups and mountaineering expeditions. One of the best rock climbers in the world, as well as one of the role models Alex most admires, Caldwell said in 2011, "I've never tried to free solo anything really grand. I've fallen completely unexpectedly lots of times—maybe a dozen—on relatively easy terrain, when a hold broke off or the rubber peeled off the sole of my shoe, or something. If I'd been soloing, I'd have died.

"I really like Alex. I don't want him to die."

• • • •

By now, the audience Alex commands stretches far beyond the ranks of hardcore climbers. He's known, for instance, as "that kid Lara Logan interviewed on *60 Minutes*," or as "the guy in that amazing photo on the cover of *National Geographic*." But for nonclimbers fully to understand exactly what Alex is doing, a brief primer in techniques, gear, and grade ratings is necessary.

In conventional rock climbing, a pair of climbers is connected with a nylon rope usually about sixty meters (almost 200 feet) in length. One climber, anchored safely to the wall, belays the leader as he climbs above. To minimize the consequences of a fall, the leader places protection ("pro") as he goes.

Throughout most of the history of rock climbing, the leader would hammer a piton—any of an assortment of differently shaped metal spikes, first made of iron but now improved with chrome-molybdenum steel alloy—into a natural crack in the rock surface. Once the piton was firmly driven, the leader clipped a carabiner—an oval link with a spring-loaded gate—into the eye of the piton, then fed the rope through the 'biner. That way, if he fell, say, five feet above the piton, the belayer on the other end of the rope could stop his fall after a plunge of only a little more than ten feet—the additional footage due to the stretchiness of the nylon rope, which also cushions the jolt.

By the 1980s, pitons had become passé except in big-range mountaineering, because the repeated hammering as they were driven home and then pried loose damaged the rock, leaving ugly "pin scars." Instead, climbers started using nuts—variously shaped blobs of metal that could be slotted into cracks and wrinkles in the rock so they'd hold tight under a downward pull. Nuts, in general, are much less secure than pitons. In the late 1970s, Ray Jardine invented ingenious devices he called "Friends" (now more generically referred to as "cams"). They're spring-loaded gizmos with opposing semicircular plates. You pull a kind of trigger that retracts the plates, slot the cam into a crack that wouldn't hold a nut, then release the trigger. The spring allows the plates to grip the edges of the crack, and a well-placed cam can hold weights of thousands of pounds. Needless to say, cams have revolutionized rock climbing.

From the earliest days onward, climbers surmounted otherwise unclimbable stretches of rock by using their pro as artificial holds. This is called "direct aid," or simply "aid." Whole pitches of aid can be negotiated with *étriers* or aiders—nylon slings with three or four foot loops to make flexible ladders. The aid climber hangs an aider from a piton or nut or cam, then climbs the nylon rungs rather than the rock itself.

Eventually, expansion bolts enlarged the technical arsenal. In blank rock devoid of cracks, the climber bores a hollow sleeve, either by hammer or mechanical drill. Into that sleeve he then hammers the cylindrical bolt, usually made of stainless steel. A hanger, similar to the eye of a piton, is affixed to the head of the bolt. Then the climber attaches a carabiner to the hanger and clips in his rope. A good bolt is as strong as the best piton.

Free climbing, as opposed to free soloing, means that the leader uses his protection only to safeguard a fall. He does not slot a nut or cam and then pull on it to move upward. He climbs the rock with only his hands and feet, but if he falls on solid pro, he's not likely to be injured.

In the United States, rock routes climbed free are rated on a scale of difficulty, called the Yosemite Decimal System (YDS), that currently ranges from 5.1 to 5.15. The reason for the awkward numbering is that in the US experts long believed that no climbs harder than 5.9 would ever be accomplished. By the late 1960s, however, that limit had been transcended, and the classifiers felt they had no choice but to invent 5.10. The system is inherently conservative, so the higher grades, such as 5.13, have been subdivided into four classes of their own, ranging from 5.13a through 5.13d. Top-notch climbers recognize that there is as great a gap in difficulty between 5.13b and 5.13c as between 5.8 and 5.9.

At the moment, the hardest climbs in the world, of which there are only a handful, are rated 5.15c.

In the last twenty years, expansion bolts have given rise to the phenomenon of "sport" climbing—as distinguished from "trad" (short for "traditional"), in which climbers place and remove nuts and cams for protection. On a sport route, permanent bolts placed as closely as six or eight feet apart, often driven on rappel before the route has been attempted, allow climbers to get up very hard free routes on rock that won't take cams or nuts, with almost bomb-proof safety. The leader simply clips into one bolt after another as he climbs. For the belayer, catching the leader's fall is routine.

Sport climbing has skyrocketed in popularity in recent years. There are now hotshot teenagers who can climb 5.14 sport routes but who have never led a single pitch of trad, and wouldn't have a clue how to do so.

Because the YDS 5.1 to 5.15 system measures only the pure difficulty of the hardest move, nearly all the top-rated climbs in the world are on short sport routes on easily accessible crags. To put up a 5.15 route, an expert such as Chris Sharma or Adam Ondra will "work" the sequence of moves for weeks or even months on end, falling harmlessly hundreds of times, before he can complete the climb in one try without a single fall. That kind of climbing is so specialized that the Ondras of the world practice almost no other art.

Ironically, then, trad climbing is more "sporting" than sport climbing—and more daring and dangerous.

But free soloing is another whole game. When Alex Honnold performs one of his long free solos, he does away altogether with ropes, with a partner to catch his fall, with pro of any kind (no bolts, pitons, nuts, or cams) to use for artificial holds or to safeguard a fall. Because the chances of falling on even a 5.11 or 5.12 climb are considerable, only a few practitioners have dared to push free soloing beyond the 5.11 level—and then usually on short routes, and only after "rehearsing" the line by climbing it with a rope and a partner many times to memorize every hold and sequence. (For that matter, when you're climbing without a rope, you can fall off and die on a 5.4 route if a handhold or foothold breaks loose.)

Free soloing, then, is the most sporting—the purest—form of rock climbing ever devised. It's the ultimate adventure on rock—with the ultimate stakes if you make the slightest mistake.

People ask me all the time how I got into free soloing. But I don't think they quite believe me when I give an honest answer. The truth is that when I started climbing outdoors, I was too shy to go up to strangers at a crag and ask if they'd like to rope up with me.

I first started climbing at age ten at an indoor gym in my hometown of Sacramento, California, but I did very little outdoors before the age of nineteen. I was so antisocial and tweaky that I was actually afraid to talk to strangers. Though I was already climbing 5.13, I would never have gotten up the nerve to approach other guys at a crag like Lover's Leap near Lake Tahoe and ask if I could rope up with them.

So I just started soloing. The first route I did was a low-angle 5.5 slab called Knapsack Crack at Lover's Leap. Then I tackled a much steeper three-pitch route called Corrugation Corner, rated 5.7. I overgripped the shit out of it, because I was really scared and climbing badly.

But I quickly got better. I've always been a compulsive ticker. From the very start, I kept a bound notebook in which I recorded every climb I did, each one with a brief note. My "climbing bible," as I called it, was my most precious possession. In 2005 and 2006, I did tons of routes at Joshua Tree, on the granite boulders and pinnacles in the desert east of Los Angeles. I developed a voracious appetite for soloing. I'd do as many as fifty pitches in a day, mostly on short routes up to 5.10. A sample entry from my bible:

10/7/05

18 pitches—kind of a low-day

5.7 to [5].10b

I couldn't start the left Peyote Crack. Weird.

I soon got so that I felt pretty comfortable soloing. I discovered that if I had any particular gift, it was a mental one—the ability to keep it together in what might otherwise have been a stressful situation. By 2007, I had soloed a few pitches up to 5.12a in difficulty. I felt like I was ready for a big next step.

Still, back then I had no thought of becoming a professional climber, or even of attracting any attention for what I did. In September 2007, I went to Yosemite. I had my eye on two legendary routes—the north face of the Rostrum, a beautiful 800-foot granite pillar, rated 5.11c, and Astroman on Washington Column, a touchstone 1,100-foot route, also rated 5.11c.

Way back in 1987, Peter Croft had stunned the climbing world by free soloing both routes in a single day. No one had repeated that feat in twenty years. Of the two climbs, Astroman is significantly harder and more serious—more physically taxing and more insecure. Only one other guy had free soloed Astroman—Dean Potter in 2000. Still climbing hard at age forty-three, Potter has recently specialized in combining hard routes with wingsuit BASE jumping. He was another influential free soloist I looked up to as a role model.

On September 19, I free soloed both Astroman and the Rostrum. I'd climbed both routes before roped up with partners, but I couldn't say that I had either route dialed. I was glad that day to find no one else on either climb. I didn't tell anybody beforehand what I was going to try. I just showed up and did them. They went really well—I felt in control the whole way on both climbs. In my "bible," I noted only

9/19/07

Astroman—5.11c—solo

Rostrum—5.11c—" "

I added a smiley face after Astroman, but no other comments.

That evening I called a friend (it might have been Chris Weidner) and told him about my day. That's how the word got out. I'll admit that the double solo stirred up a certain buzz in the Valley (as climbers call Yosemite), but only among the hardcore locals. In my mind, the fact that I did both routes in one day, just as Peter Croft had, wasn't particularly significant. What was significant was committing to doing them at all. And succeeding gave me the confidence to start imagining even bigger free solos.

· · · ·

Five months later, in February 2008, I drove to Indian Creek in southern Utah. The Creek is a mecca of short, beautiful cracks on solid Wingate sandstone. I was in terrific form there, climbing roped up with various partners. I onsighted the hardest routes, getting up them on my first try without falling. Routes up to 5.13b or c. But I'd been climbing so much, I'd developed a bad case of tendinitis in my left elbow. At first I didn't even know what was wrong—I thought I'd hurt my biceps from sheer overuse. But at the Creek, after only two or three pitches, the pain was so intense I'd have to shut it down. One day on, then two days off. I'd go mountain biking with my friend Cedar Wright, just trying to mix it up. But it drove me crazy not to be able to climb more.

Weirdly enough, by contributing to my general angst, the tendinitis was good for Moonlight Buttress. It takes a certain hunger to be motivated to go do something big. At the Creek, I was so fit and climbing so well, but I was also hungry to do more, because I had to limit my days on rock to a lot fewer than I wanted.

And Moonlight Buttress was a project I'd been dreaming of for years, ever since Bill Ramsey and I had climbed it a few years before. Which is why I found myself in Zion, sitting in my van all day in the rain on March 30 and 31, 2008, visualizing everything that could possibly happen on that amazing route the next day.

All the soloing I had done during the previous several years had taught me the value of preparation. But I'd never prepared for a free solo as diligently as I did for Moonlight. Rehearsing the moves on toprope for two days until I had every sequence lodged in my memory was crucial, but so were those days of just sitting and thinking. Imagining every placement of each hand and foot all the way up the huge route. Visualizing everything that could happen. . . . In a real sense, I performed the hard work of that free solo during the days leading up to it. Once I was on the climb, it was just a matter of executing.

The dampness and sandiness of the lower part of the wall had addled me somewhat. And at first, I was confused as to whether I was actually on-route. I wasn't truly scared—just hesitant and uncertain. In retrospect, I think I projected my anxiety about the whole project, as I'd sat in my van visualizing it for two days, onto the start of the climb. Now I was driven upward by pure excitement, which always has an edge of anxiety about it.

The second pitch is a clean splitter crack, and once I got onto that, I knew I was on-route. There's really only one line to the summit. And after that second pitch, the rock dried out and the sandiness pretty much disappeared. As I climbed higher, I steadily gained confidence. The 5.11c rightward traverse on the third pitch went like clockwork. By the time I got to the Rocker Blocker ledge, it was "Game on!" I was making the moves with what felt like perfect execution.

As I started off the Rocker Blocker toward the tricky boulder problem, the scenario of coming off and trying to stick the ledge was in the back of my mind. But I was moving efficiently, and as soon as I made the little upward lurch and seized the crucial handhold, I knew I wouldn't come off. My confidence surged even higher.

Above the Rocker Blocker, I started up the 180-foot 5.12d

inside corner that's the crux of the whole route. That stern rating doesn't derive from any single particularly hard move, but from the strenuous continuity of the whole thing. And here's where my preparation paid off. I started up the corner stemming—placing the edges of my feet carefully on tiny wrinkles of sandstone on either side of the central crack, then moving smoothly upward from one hold to the next. The wall here is dead vertical, so you have to gauge those holds precisely. But I remembered every one from my toprope rehearsal. Also, as I had expected, the wall here, which is protected from the rain by a small roof far above, was totally dry.

I was able to rest here and there on small holds as I stemmed up the first eighty feet of the corner. But then I had to shift from stemming to liebacking. Now I grabbed the edge of the crack with both hands, leaned back to the left, and walked my feet up the opposite wall till the soles of my shoes were only two feet below my lower hand. Liebacking feels somewhat unnatural. The whole key to moving upward is the stability provided by the pull with your hands counterbalancing the push with your feet. The position you're in is almost like sitting in a rowing shell and pulling hard on the oars. You methodically alternate feet and hand movements as you inch up the crack. Yes, it's strenuous, but a clean lieback feels solid and secure. If the edges of the crack aren't sharp or are flared outward, though, or the wall you place your feet on is too slick, liebacking is pretty scary. You feel like you could pop loose and plunge toward the void in an involuntary backflip. But if you don't get your feet high enough, they can slip off and your hands holding the crack become worthless. Either way, you're headed down.

The trick of that last hundred feet in the corner is not to let the overall pump get to you. You can't lieback forever, because the strain on your arms keeps mounting. That's what "pump" is all about. If you get too pumped, you simply can't hold on any longer.

If I'd been climbing with a rope, or even with a harness and some gear, I could always have clipped in to something, hung for a while, and regained the strength in my arms. Bad style, of course, but better than coming off. But free soloing, I had no choice. I needed to get to the top of the corner before the pump took over.

By now I was in full game-on mode, so I scurried up the corner as well as I had on toprope rehearsal. Didn't even come close to losing it. My only concession to the airiness of being up there without a rope or gear was that I cranked my feet a little higher than I had on my two toprope rehearsals. That meant more arm-pump, but it felt a bit more secure.

The three pitches above the crux are rated 5.12a, 5.12a, and 5.12b—pretty darned hard, but well within my abilities. In fact, those pitches follow a perfect finger crack. It was here that the true glory of free soloing came home to me. Sticking my first digits into the crack, I turned them slightly into perfect fingerlocks, and I felt bomber. At any given moment, I had only a tiny amount of skin inside the crack—like half of two fingers—and my toes weren't on holds, but just pasted to the wall. So little of my body was actually touching the rock. There was air all around me. I felt like I was stepping into the void, and yet it was an amazing sensation. I was one hundred percent certain I wouldn't fall off, and that certainty was what kept me from falling off.

And here, though I didn't pause to look around and take in the view, the beauty of Zion came home. The whole world of the canyon is all red and green—red for the rocks, green for the forest. There's the Virgin River winding so far below. No traffic sounds, that far up. Just peace and quiet.

A final 5.10d pitch leads to the summit, tough enough in its own right. But I climbed it as smoothly as the pitches just before. All the feelings of vague doubt I had on starting up the route had vanished.

Almost before I knew it, I stood on top of the cliff. I checked my time against the iPod. One hour and twenty-three minutes. It was the speed record, as well as the first free solo ascent.

Standing there, as I unlaced my shoes, I was superpsyched. Though I still had to hike down barefoot (rock shoes are so tight that it's excruciating to hike in them), then circle back around and wade the river again to get my approach shoes and pack (it's never smooth sailing off into the rainbow), I was totally jazzed. During that hour and twenty-three minutes, I'd climbed as well as I ever had in my life.

O N APRIL 1, 2008, no one witnessed Alex's climb of Moonlight Buttress. As with Astroman and the Rostrum, Alex had told no one what he was planning to do, though he had confided in Chris Weidner that the free solo was something he'd *like* to do sometime. Now, after the climb, he called Weidner and told him about his glorious day. Weidner told others, and the news spread like wildfire.

Because the climb had taken place on April Fools' Day, a substantial portion of the climbing cognoscenti wondered at first whether the whole thing was a joke, or even a hoax. But within days, the tide had swung in favor of Alex's veracity.

On the website Supertopo.com, climbers who understood the magnitude of the ascent weighed in. "Holy living f#ck!" wrote one. "Unreal," blogged another. "Just the thought gives me chills." There were also commenters who saluted the climb as inspirational: "Amazing accomplishment, Alex. Reading this post motivated me to push way harder today than I would have otherwise." And those who knew about Alex's previous solos of the Rostrum and Astroman tipped their caps: "That is unbelievable. . . . I would have said

impossible, but since it has Alex's name on it . . . just insane." And:
"Congrats on the send. . . . keep crankin'!"

On April 6, Jeff Lowe, who with Mike Weis had made the first
ascent of Moonlight Buttress way back in 1971, posted on Supertopo that he had always known that the route would go free, and he
had attempted to free it before Peter Croft and Johnny Woodward
beat him to the prize in 1992. "But I never saw far enough into the
crystal-ball," Lowe added, "to foresee Alex's inspired leap of faith.
. . . Great job, Alex. Always take care, as I know you do."

Along with this encomium from one of America's stellar climbing pioneers, for the first time a larger media world, including the
directors at Sender Films, sat up and took notice. A new phenom of
the climbing world had emerged on the stage.

At twenty-two, Alex Honnold was just getting started.

CHAPTER **TWO**

A VERY PRIVATE HELL

Once I told Chris Weidner about Moonlight Buttress, I should have known the word would get out fast. He lives in Boulder, after all, right in the thick of the climbing scene.

I didn't anticipate, though, the explosion of postings on the Internet about the climb. I went online to check them out. My first reaction was surprise. Oh, wow, I'm in print! That's cool. Somebody had even dug up a photo of me climbing. That's my photo! I bragged to myself.

There was also, of course, the undercurrent of posters who wondered whether the free solo of Moonlight Buttress was an April Fools' joke. But one thing I've always appreciated about the climbing community, after so many of my climbs by now have gone undocumented by film or photos or unverified by witnesses, is that people have taken me at my word. In April 2008, no one on the Internet was accusing me of perpetrating a hoax. If the free solo of Moonlight Buttress was bogus, it was some poster who was lying about it—goofing on the credulity of the Supertopo audience, maybe.

I still could not have imagined ever becoming a sponsored professional climber. If I got a little notoriety, I just hoped that maybe some gear company would give me a free pair of rock shoes.

The tendinitis in my left elbow hadn't gotten any better. If anything, all the work I'd done rehearsing the moves on Moonlight Buttress and then free soloing it had probably made the condition worse.

I finally realized I had to knock off climbing for a while to let my elbow heal. That's how I ended up spending the summer in the Sierra Nevada, doing long hikes and loops on big mountains like the Evolution Traverse. It involved a lot of scrambling, but as long as I could do it in tennies, I figured it didn't count as real climbing. Meanwhile, I was getting into great shape.

Recently a journalist asked me if I could stop climbing for stretches at a time. "Sure," I answered.

"You mean you could go for, say, a month without climbing?" he asked.

"Hell, no!" I blurted out. "Not a month! I thought you meant three days."

That's just the way it is with me. No matter what else I've turned my attention to over the years, nothing seems as interesting as climbing. I can't do without it, even though by now I've been climbing in one way or another for almost twenty years straight.

That whole summer in the High Sierra, the idea of free soloing the Regular Northwest Face of Half Dome floated around inside my head. It's such an iconic formation, one of the most striking thrusts of sheer granite anywhere in North America, and I'd always loved the way it dominates the whole east end of the Valley.

By 2008, Yosemite had become my favorite climbing area in the world. Some climbers are drawn to towers and pinnacles, others to complex ridges. What I love is big, clean faces, and they don't get any better than the ones in Yosemite—especially El Capitan and Half Dome. You stand at the base of El Cap and look up its 2,700-foot precipice, and you just say, "Wow!"

Granite is also my favorite kind of rock. And that's what Yosemite is made of—more clean, sweeping walls of granite than anywhere else in North America.

The Regular Northwest Face route takes a pure line up the left-hand side of the nearly vertical wall. That summer as I got in shape making loops and traverses in the High Sierra, Half Dome became my muse, a random source of motivation that drifted through my thoughts while I strolled along one ridge after another. The notion of trying to free solo the route was intimidating, yet irresistible at the same time. In terms of sheer grandness, it would be a big step up for me—an even greater challenge than Moonlight Buttress.

THE REGULAR NORTHWEST FACE ROUTE was pioneered in 1957 by Royal Robbins, the finest American rock climber of his day, and two partners, Jerry Gallwas and Mike Sherrick. Two previous attempts, including one by Robbins, had gotten no higher than a quarter of the way up the 2,000-foot wall. The face, which inclines at an average pitch of eighty-five degrees, is intimidating in the extreme. As Steve Roper writes in *Camp 4*, the definitive history of early climbing in Yosemite, "The view upward [from the base] is overpowering. It doesn't seem possible that humans can climb such an enormous cliff with normal techniques"—i.e., ropes, pitons, and bolts.

It took the 1957 trio five days to complete the ascent, during which they pulled out all the stops: using their newly invented chrome-molybdenum pitons and expansion bolts for direct aid, lowering Robbins fifty feet so he could "pendulum" sideways across the blank granite to reach a chimney system, and enduring four bivouacs as they hung from slings and stirrups. The key pitch, led by Gallwas, involved strenuous aid on pitons and bolts that reached a "disturbingly narrow" ledge stretching across the face only 200 feet below the summit. Thank God Ledge today is one of the most famous features anywhere on American rock.

The YDS scale from 5.1 to 5.15 measures only pure difficulty, with no regard to danger. Another scale within the YDS, however, is grade ratings, which indicate the overall difficulty, danger, and required commitment of a long route on a big wall or a mountain—in short, the "seriousness" of a major ascent. Until very recently, the system ranged only from Grade I to Grade VI. A few landmark ascents in the last decade—nearly all of them in the remote ranges—have been tentatively rated as Grade VII, but by and large the pinnacle of the scale remains Grade VI.

The first Grade VI ever climbed in the United States was Robbins, Gallwas, and Sherrick's 1957 ascent of the Regular Northwest Face of Half Dome. At the time, it was matched only by a few routes in Europe.

In 1976, nineteen years after Robbins's team climbed the wall, Colorado-based climbers Art Higbee and Jim Erickson made the first free ascent of the Regular Northwest Face route, eliminating all the aid moves—almost. (It was Erickson's tenth try to free climb the route.) Roped together, belaying every pitch, using pitons, nuts, and bolts for protection, the duo required thirty-four hours of extreme climbing to reach a point only one hundred feet short of the summit. There, to their chagrin, they had to resort to aid to surmount the final obstacle. That glitch rendered the deed a "magnificent failure" in Higbee's and Erickson's eyes, but subsequent climbers, impressed by the achievement, have granted them the first free ascent. Higbee and Erickson rated the climb solid 5.12—close to the highest level of technical difficulty accomplished at the time anywhere in the world. The single passage on which they had to resort to aid would also prove to be the dramatic crux of Alex's 2008 climb.

By 2008, no one had ever attempted to free solo a Grade VI climb, let alone succeeded on one.

That September, my elbow seemed healed, and I was in top shape from all that cruising around the High Sierra. Dwelling on Half Dome for months had put me in a mental state where I felt I had to do it. Maybe I'd just spent so much time thinking about it that now I had to clear it from my mind.

I'd climbed the route five or six times before with different partners, but I'd freed all the moves, roped up and clipping pro in case I fell, only twice—most recently two days before my solo attempt, when I'd gone up there with Brad Barlage. There are three completely blank sections on the route that Robbins's team solved by going on aid as they drilled bolt ladders through the impasses. Almost everybody climbs the bolt ladders today—they're secure, and relatively easy for aid. But free variations have been worked out that bypass those blank sections. That's why it's possible to climb the whole route free, as Higbee and Erickson (almost) did, though they were roped up and using pro.

After Brad and I climbed the route on September 4, I spent the whole next day resting, sitting by myself in my van, thinking about the route. I was still somewhat conflicted about going up there alone: Do I really want to do this? I'd already made plans with different friends to climb a few days later in the Valley, so I felt some pressure to get my soloing done before any of them showed up. Ultimately I decided to go back up to the base of Half Dome the next day. I told myself that I could just hike back down if I wasn't psyched. I've done that a few times, or even started a route and then backed off. In 2006, on Royal Arches Terrace, a long climb in the Valley but technically a pretty easy one, I climbed a pitch and a half up the friction slab at the start of the route, then realized I just wasn't into it. I downclimbed, hiked back to the road, and hitchhiked out of Yosemite. I was done for the season.

This time, though, I knew that once I got up to the base of Half Dome, there was no way I was going to bail.

I didn't want to make a big fuss about my project, so I told only two people about it, Brad and Chris Weidner. Brad said, "What the fuck?" But then, "Okay, be safe. Text me when you're done." He was being a bro.

Chris tried to talk me out of it. "Dude, that's crazy," he said. "You should rehearse the hell out of it on a toprope before you try to solo it."

"Nah," I answered. "I want to keep it sporting."

"Are you crazy?"

When I look back on those exchanges, it sounds as though I was being flippant or arrogant. That's not what was going on. I just didn't want to make too big a deal about the attempt—especially in case I backed off low on the route. It's bad form to brag about a climb before you do it. And I didn't want my good buddies to get too alarmed—then I might start worrying about them worrying about me! I guess I was just trying to reassure them: Hey, guys, I think I can handle this. I'll be safe.

There was something else going on as well. Despite my emphasis on methodical preparation, I'd begun to think that maybe I'd rehearsed the moves on Moonlight Buttress so thoroughly that I actually took some of the challenge out of the climb. Half Dome was so much bigger than Moonlight that it would take forever to get all the moves dialed. I decided to head up the wall with a little less preparation—that's what I meant by "keeping it sporting."

As it would turn out, maybe too sporting. . . .

In September it's still pretty hot in the Valley. That meant there weren't likely to be many other climbers on the face, which is what I was hoping for. But because the wall faces northwest, in September it stays in shade the whole day, which meant I could climb without getting too sweaty or dehydrated. Sweaty hands make smooth climbing pretty dicey, no matter how much you chalk up, and dehydration not only saps your strength but also can interfere with your judgment.

So on September 6, I found myself at the base of the route again. With a much lighter load than I'd carried with Brad two days before, the approach hike had taken far less time, but the whole way I felt the face looming over me. I tried not to think about it too much. It was a bluebird day, a perfect, clear morning. Resting at the base, I felt completely detached from the rest of the Valley glowing in the morning sun below me. As I had hoped, I had the whole wall entirely to myself. For the next few hours I would be alone in a unique way, locked in a high-stakes game of solitude.

It's not much trouble to climb through a roped party when you're soloing—I'd done it before, and I'd do it again. But encountering others on the wall, especially if they express their incredulity that you're climbing without a rope, can make you self-conscious. And that can interfere with the absolute concentration you need to pull off a big free solo. Before such a climb, I have to get really psyched up. And once I'm off the ground, I'm totally fixated. I'm going to do this. It's the most important thing in life right now. That's not the kind of mental state I can share with random strangers.

I was wearing only shorts and a long-sleeved T-shirt. I had my Miura rock shoes on my feet, and my chalk bag dangling at my back, but no harness, and not even a single carabiner. In one pocket I put a few Clif Kid Zbars, my favorite multi-pitch snack, and I filled a collapsible flask with about a third of a liter of water. I put that in my other pocket, though it pulled my shorts down a little. But I knew it would take me a few hours to climb the route, and I didn't want to be parched by the time I reached the hard pitches up high. A pack was out of the question, partly because of all the chimneys in the middle of the route (it's almost impossible to chimney wearing a pack), but mainly because the climbing was hard enough that I didn't want any extra weight on my body.

Finally, there was nothing else for me to do but quit procrastinating and climb. I started up the first pitch.

• • • •

For years, the great Yosemite pioneers had been heroes of a sort to me. The guys from the "golden age" of the 1960s—Royal Robbins, Warren Harding, Yvon Chouinard, Tom Frost, Chuck Pratt, and the like—were almost too remote in history for me to appreciate, even though I'd read stories about their memorable antics. It was the self-described Stonemasters of the next generation, in the 1970s and '80s, that I most admired. John Long, Jim Bridwell, Billy Westbay, Tobin Sorenson, and their buddies. . . . But especially John Bachar and Peter Croft, because of their soloing and free climbing at the highest level. And Lynn Hill, the first person, male or female, to climb the Nose route on El Capitan completely free, in 1993. A year later, she freed the route in a single day. Those are still two of the greatest feats ever pulled off in the Valley. I was also fascinated by John "Yabo" Yablonski, to whom so many wild and crazy stories clung—about him falling off a free solo and saving himself by catching a tree branch, about his nude ascent of North Overhang, about his infamous "screamers" when he fell (roped) as far as a hundred feet, only to be caught by miracle belays. Yabo was evidently a tortured soul, for he committed suicide in the early 1990s.

A lot of the Stonemasters, though, were into drugs. Some of them even bragged about doing serious climbs in Yosemite while they were tripping their brains out on LSD. Their style was part of the counterculture movement of the day, but I just couldn't relate to it. I've never done drugs, and though I've tasted alcohol, I've never had a whole drink. I don't even drink coffee. I had a small cup once—it was like drinking battery acid. I had to poop all morning. I once had *a sniff of Scotch. I thought, I should be cleaning my sink with this stuff. It's not some moral objection—drugs and booze and caffeine just have no appeal to me.*

I grew up in Sacramento, California. Both my parents taught English as a Second Language (ESL) at a series of institutions in the United States and abroad. Eventually they landed more permanent jobs at American River College in Sacramento. My mom, Dierdre Wolownick, taught ESL, Spanish, and French at the college. Today she constitutes the entire French department for the school. She's a gifted linguist, fluent in three foreign languages (French, Spanish, and Italian) and competent in German, Polish, Japanese, and a bit of American Sign Language.

My dad, Charles Honnold, got a full-time job teaching ESL at American River College before my mom did. So I grew up in an intellectual, academic climate—for whatever good that did me.

Mom likes to tell people that on the day I was born, August 17, 1985, I could stand up, holding onto her fingers. Like a lot of her stories about me as a kid, I tend to think she made that up—or at least stretched the truth pretty far. She's told journalists that from the time I was two years old, she knew I'd become a climber. She also relates a story about taking me to a climbing gym when I was only five. According to Mom, she was talking to the supervisor, turned around, and found me thirty feet up in only a minute or two. She says she was scared to death I'd kill myself.

My sister, Stasia, was born two years before me. From our infancy on, Mom spoke only French to us. Her idea was to make us bilingual. She still speaks only French to us when we visit. But Stasia and I rebelled from the start—we'd answer her in English. Even so, I'll have to give Mom the credit for making me pretty fluent in French. My grasp of the language has come in handy on many trips to France and three to North Africa.

Mom may be right about me being an uncontrollable, hyper

little monster. At age five or six, I broke my arm for the first time. I'd decided it would be fun to run down the slide at Carl's Jr.—my favorite restaurant. I went over the edge. The docs called it a green twig radius fracture, whatever that is.

I broke my arm a second time at age seven or eight. This was a really pitiful accident—in fact, it's hard to describe how I fucked up. There was a big rope that was part of a play structure in our backyard. It was meant be a rope swing, but I rigged it as a tight-rope, then lay down on it as if it were a hammock. Fell off and broke my arm.

Dad took me to the local climbing gym when I was ten. It was just a random stab at another kind of recreation, but it "took" from the first day. For years thereafter, he would drive me to the gym and spend the whole afternoon belaying me—he wasn't interested in climbing himself. Later he even drove me to other gyms around California where I'd enter competitions.

He was a man of very few words. We'd drive for hours with almost no conversation. He wasn't comfortable expressing his emotions, but belaying me tirelessly and driving me all over the state was his own way of showing love.

From childhood on, there was an elephant in the room. It was that my parents weren't happily married. They didn't fight openly—it was more just a kind of chilly silence that filled the house. For Stasia's and my sake, they waited till after I graduated from high school to get a divorce. But we knew they were going to split up, because we occasionally read Mom's e-mails. The real bummer for them was that they were so much happier after they got divorced, and they stayed friends.

I'm sure a shrink would have a field day with the fact that, to this day, I have a hard time remembering the details of my child-hood. In 2011, when Alex Lowther interviewed me for a profile for Alpinist, he started quizzing me about the early years. I told him *that my memories were fuzzy and unreliable. "Ask Ben about this stuff," I said. Ben Smalley and I had been best friends since first grade.*

L OWTHER DID JUST AS Alex suggested, contacting Smalley, who by 2011 had become an air force lieutenant. Smalley's sardonic portrait of Alex as a kid and teenager rounds out the picture of the dorky misfit Alex genuinely considered himself, even after he started to attract the notice of the climbing world. According to Smalley, as told to Lowther,

> Alex wore sweatpants to school. Every day. There was a gray pair and a blue pair. He wore T-shirts that were two sizes too big, and they said things on them like, "I hiked the Grand Canyon," "Visit Yellowstone," or "How to Identify Deer Tracks." He was very good at capture the flag. Defensively. He could talk to you about the War of 1812 for an hour. It wasn't so much that he was shy, as he just didn't even bother to try. Like, he would speak to you if you spoke to him. He wore hoodies in class, always with the hood up, and he would just sit there, but he always knew the answer if a teacher called on him. He's got sort of a Holden Caulfield thing going on, maybe, in that he's always on the lookout for a phony.

When that passage was read out loud to Alex, he confessed, "Ben's got me down." All the details about his youthful persona, Alex confirmed. The passage stirred up other memories. "I still love sweats," he said. "I never wear jeans." And: "I had another T-shirt from Banff or Jasper, with a picture of a bear on it, but a bear with antlers. It read, 'I am not a bear.' It was part of some kind of don't-feed-the-bears campaign.

"About the War of 1812—my dad gave me a book about decisive battles in history. The *Monitor* and the *Merrimack*, Hannibal crossing the Alps, that kind of thing. I loved history. It wasn't that I hated school—just that I was an uncool kid. I had a hard time talking to strangers."

In Lowther's profile, Smalley went on:

His parents were not very happily married. His father would sit on the couch most nights, reading until he fell asleep. I would say [Alex] got worse in high school, actually. He withdrew further. He hung out with the kids who played Pokémon in the math room at lunch. During sophomore year, Alex got his first girlfriend. Her name was Elizabeth Thomas. She went by E.T. That should give you some idea of the social circle she ran in. I just don't think Alex thought the typical high school stuff was for him. He considered himself more of a loner.

Says Alex, "E.T. was cool. Ben didn't like her. She was half-Irish, half-Japanese. A nice girl, real smart. We were a couple for maybe three years."

In high school, Alex consistently scored high marks, finishing with a weighted grade-point average of 4.8. Yet he wasn't at all sure he wanted to go to college. At the last minute, he applied only to two branches of the University of California—at Davis and Berkeley. Accepted by both, he chose Berkeley.

The single year he spent at one of the elite bastions of higher learning was, Alex feels now, a waste of time. "I had vague plans to major in engineering," he says. "But I didn't make any friends at Berkeley. I can't recall a single student or a single professor. I should have lived in a dorm, instead of the two-bedroom apartment a friend of our family let me sublet. I spent a year basically in isolation.

"I did have a job as a security guard. For fourteen dollars an hour,

I'd walk around by myself all night. I had a police radio. Sometimes I'd escort girls back to their dorms.

"The second semester, I stopped going to classes. I'd buy a loaf of bread and an apple and go out to Indian Rock"—a diminutive crag in the suburban Berkeley Hills—"and do laps. I just couldn't hack college." That summer, like most freshmen, he moved back home with his mother.

Alex's parents' divorce became final in May of his freshman year. Two months later, on July 18, his father was rushing through the Phoenix airport, trying to make a tight connection, when he dropped dead of a heart attack. Alex got the news when he came home from a long hike. He recalled the event to Alex Lowther:

> The house was open, all the windows were open and stuff, but like, everything was dark; nobody was in the house. And, I was like, "Mom?"—"Mom?" And went and found Mom sitting outside in the pool. Sitting with her legs in the pool. Just sitting there crying. And she was just like, "Your dad died." I don't remember what she said, but basically like, "Your dad died," and then she went to bed.
>
> I don't remember disbelieving her. But for all I knew, he could still be alive. I never saw a body. There was never a real funeral. This little can of ashes showed up one day, and people said he was dead. I read all the articles about him. For a while I would see people on the bike path. People who looked like Dad, with a big beard and just all big, and I would be like, "Oh!" And then, "Oh, that wasn't him."

Ben Smalley told Lowther, "I kind of had to yell at him about it. 'Why aren't you upset?' I think deep down, Alex never did any mourning."

"Did you mourn at all?" Lowther asked Alex.

"I was too young and angstful," he answered. "I had too much anger."

Alex clarifies: "It wasn't that I didn't believe Mom when she told me Dad had died. It's that my family doesn't do funerals. Dad was cremated in Phoenix. There was a memorial service at Lake Tahoe. I thought, 'Huh, I'll never see him again.' But there was no closure."

Charles Honnold was fifty-five when he died. Alex was nineteen. The event crystallized Alex's decision to drop out of Berkeley. Supported by the interest from his father's life insurance bonds, he "borrowed" his mother's minivan and set out for various California crags and the life of a dirtbag climber. In 2007, he bought a used Ford Econoline van that he converted into a cozy garret-on-wheels. Eight years later, after many home improvements, and despite his fame and unexpected wealth, Alex still lives in the van. His default residence is his mother's house in Sacramento, where he spends a few weeks each year.

Whether or not he truly mourned his father's death, the loss had a profound impact on Alex's outlook on life. His mother's parents had been devout Catholics, and both Stasia and Alex attended Catholic services when they were young. The effect was to turn Alex into a confirmed atheist. As he sardonically commented in a 2012 YouTube video, "At no point did I ever think there was ever anything going on with church. I always saw it as a bunch of old people eating stale wafers. . . ."

His father's death brought home the *carpe diem* injunction to live the only life he has to the fullest. In a 2012 Q&A for *National Geographic Adventure*, Alex came up with a startling metaphor. He was asked, "If you don't believe in God or an after-life, doesn't that make this life all the more precious?"

Alex responded: "I suppose so, but just because something is precious doesn't mean you have to baby it. Just like suburbanites who have a shiny new SUV that they are afraid to dent. What's the point in having an amazing vehicle if you're afraid to drive it?

"I'm trying to take my vehicle to new and interesting places. And I try my very best not to crash, but at least I take it out."

The Regular Northwest Face route on *Half Dome* *begins with a 5.10c finger crack that happens to be one of my favorite pitches on the whole climb. The next two pitches are only 5.9 and 5.8. It was a good warm-up for the two thousand feet of climbing above me.*

But then, on what's normally the fourth pitch, I ran into the first bolt ladder. There are two variations that bypass that blank section on either side. I'd climbed first one, then the other, on my two roped free climbs of the route. On the left is the two-pitch Higbee 'Hedral, rated a stern 5.12a, first freed by Art Higbee on his 1976 ascent with Jim Erickson. On the right is the Huber 'Hedral, named after the German climber Alex Huber, full-on 5.11d. ('Hedral is slang for "dihedral," a vertical inside corner in the rock. Thanks to Art and Alex for the handy alliteration of their last names!)

Even though the Huber variation is one grade easier, it's less secure. You have to traverse across a wall that's so smooth it's like polished glass. I thought about what it would take, then told myself, Screw that, and chose the Higbee 'Hedral instead.

The crux 5.12a sequence comes in a short boulder problem off a big, comfortable ledge. It made, I thought, for secure soloing, since if I couldn't connect the moves I thought I could jump off and land on the ledge. But those are some of the hardest moves on the whole route, and I had to shift my mentality from cruising up fun cracks to actually cranking on small holds. I laced my shoes up extra tight, then powered through the six-move boulder problem without hesitating.

The rest of the pitch was quite dirty. Half Dome is so much

higher in altitude than the other walls in the Valley that it has
some of the feel of an alpine mountain. And with mountains, you
get loose holds that you have to test before pulling on them. (Pulling loose a single hold, obviously, can spell the difference between
life and death when you're free soloing.) You also get dirt and even
vegetation in the cracks. Because the free variations are tackled so
seldom, they don't get "gardened" by climbers the way the regular
pitches do. It's a scary business to be on rock that ought to be reasonable to climb, only to have your fingers scraping through wet dirt
or your toes jammed on clumps of moss or scrawny little shrubs.
But I followed the faint trail of chalk marks that Brad and I had left
two days earlier, and managed to avoid most of the vegetation and
dirt. As I rejoined the normal route, I relaxed and mentally shifted
gears back into cruise mode. I had about a thousand feet of climbing above me until I got to the next hard pitch. I wanted to go slow
and steady, so as not to get tired. A slow jog, rather than a sprint.

I had my iPod with headband ear buds so I could listen to tunes
while I climbed. When the going got harder, I'd knock one earbud
out. If it was really serious, both buds, so I wouldn't be distracted.
The headband then would just dangle from my neck. That day I was
cycling through some songs by Eminem, especially "Lose Yourself."

The beautiful day was holding steady, but I had no time to
look around and admire the scenery. Scenery is what you get to
enjoy when you're belaying your partner on a conventional roped
climb. When I'm free soloing, even on the easier pitches, I'm totally
focused on what's in front of me. The universe shrinks down to me
and the rock. You don't take a single hold for granted.

The sheer magnitude of the wall came home to me as I climbed.
I realized that this project was way more serious than Moonlight
Buttress, even though both routes are rated 5.12.

Pretty soon I was halfway up the route, a thousand feet off the
deck. Here the line, as first climbed in 1957, suddenly traverses to

the right to access an enormous chimney system. The final section
of blank rock before the chimney is normally tackled by a fifty-foot
bolt ladder. The previous time I'd free climbed the route, I circum-
vented the bolt ladder via a 5.12c pitch, using the bolts for protection but not aid. But now as I was approaching the ladder, I got
cold feet about soloing it. The pitch is extremely insecure: slopers
and scoops, shallow indentations you can barely hold with flat-
tened fingers, and which you have to "smear" with your feet, straining your ankles so that you can get as much friction as possible on
the holds with the soles of your shoes. Then those moves are followed by a down mantle. It's a tricky move, like lowering yourself
off a table with your hands extended downward, palms gripping
the edge of the ledge. Balance is everything, and it's hard to look
down to see where to place your feet. And the feet have to find a
narrow ridge of granite on which you step before you can let go of
the mantle and move on.

The free variation Higbee and Erickson worked out in 1976
breaks off to the left a pitch before the bolt ladder and circles
around this whole section of the wall, rejoining the route another
pitch above. I'd never climbed it, and I'd heard that it was loose
and dirty, but suddenly adventurous 5.10 seemed a lot more fun
than insecure 5.12c. The variation is a pretty devious line, as you
climb a long 5.9 gully straight up, followed by a meandering 5.10b
scuttle toward the right, after which you have to downclimb a hundred feet of 5.10 to get into the chimney system.

I broke off the normal route at a random point and started wandering upward, trying to find the 5.10 variation. But as I moved,
I started to get confused about the line. The bushes I was climbing through gave me pause. There were no real signs of human
presence here—no chalk marks from previous climbers, no fixed
pitons, or even scars where they might have once been driven and
removed. I started to worry that I was completely dropping the

ball. I was literally in the center of Half Dome, a thousand feet off the ground, possibly off-route, on dirt.

I said to myself, Holy shit! This is hardcore. I hope I can find my way back. It wasn't true panic that I felt—just an uncomfortable anxiety. It would have helped a lot if I had climbed this variation before. But I guessed this is what I'd bargained for when I told Chris Weidner I wanted to keep the challenge "sporting."

· · · ·

Fear. It's the most primal element in cutting-edge climbing, or indeed, in adventure of any kind. Even nonclimbers can recognize that fact, when they watch footage of me free soloing. That's why the first question out of their mouths is usually, "Aren't you afraid . . . ?" (They don't have to finish the sentence—"that you're going to die?")

I've done a lot of thinking about fear. For me, the crucial question is not how to climb without fear—that's impossible—but how to deal with it when it creeps into your nerve endings.

Interviewed later by Sender Films, my Valley buddy Nick Martino claimed, "Honnold's on another level than anyone else out there. It's like he doesn't feel fear or any of the normal emotions that anybody else feels. He has this ability to just shut his brain off and do the sickest climbs that have ever been done."

Thanks, Nick, but that just isn't true. I feel fear just like the next guy. If there was an alligator nearby that was about to eat me, I'd feel pretty uncomfortable. In fact, the two worst doses of fear I've experienced in my life so far—both the result of heinous misadventures that sprang from seemingly minor mistakes—didn't come when I was free soloing. If I learned anything from those two screwups, it's never to take for granted even a casual outing in the backcountry.

It was the day after Christmas, 2004. I was nineteen. My dad had died five months before, so I decided to hike up an easy peak that had been a favorite destination for both of us—Mount Tallac near Lake Tahoe. It's all of 9,739 feet above sea level, but it rises a respectable 3,250 feet from its base. I'd climbed it a ton of times, but never in winter. We had actually scattered some of Dad's ashes on the summit the previous summer, shortly after he died.

In Dad's closet, I found an old pair of snowshoes. I'd never snowshoed before—never even done much of anything in the snow. As it turned out, they weren't very good snowshoes for this sort of outing—they didn't have crampons attached to the webbing. But I didn't know any better.

As it also turns out, the snow had fallen about a month before, and it had been dry ever since. So the snow had turned to a hard, icy crust.

I didn't want to take the slower, circuitous normal trail, with its ups and downs, so I just headed up one of the couloirs. I was tramping along, but the surface underfoot really sucked. And there was a crazy wind that day. I got most of the way up the couloir before I said to myself, This is bad. I tried to turn around to descend, and I just slipped.

I remember sliding down the hill, whipping out of control. I went at least several hundred feet. I had time to think, Oh my God, I'm going to die!

I came to in the rocks. I'd been knocked out cold, whether for mere seconds or for longer, I couldn't tell. I think I must have hit the rocks with my feet, then rag-dolled over and crushed my face. I had a broken hand. I thought my leg was broken, but it turned out it was just badly bruised. I had a punctured sinus cavity in my face and several chipped teeth. I'd been wearing gloves, but the thumbs had torn off—I must have been trying to self-arrest with my hands. The skin on my thumbs was like raw meat, as if they'd been sliced with a carrot peeler.

My mom had given me a cell phone for Christmas. I got it out and managed to call her. I don't remember this, but Mom later claimed my first words were, "Who am I? Where am I? What am I doing?" Mom called 911.

The normal rescue helicopter couldn't get in to where I had fallen, so they brought in a California Highway Patrol chopper. It took a while. Pretty soon I was lucid again. I could see lakes in the distance that I recognized. But I was still asking myself, "Why am I here?"

I must have been in shock. All the fear had occupied those few seconds of whipping down the icy slope, in the form of sheer terror and the conviction that I was about to die, but now I felt a deeper sort of dread: How badly am I hurt? Am I going to get out of here all right?

There was an Indian family out snowshoeing who came along from below. Two strapping twenty-five-year-old lads and their parents. They helped load me into the chopper. Within minutes I was in an emergency room in Reno. It would take months for me to fully recover, especially because I kept climbing while my broken hand was healing. I still have scar tissue on my right thumb where the skin was scraped off.

This is still the only real accident I've suffered. And what a complete debacle it was, thanks to my ignorance of snow and snowshoes. If this happened today, I'd be mortified. But I'd also self-assess, then hike out under my own steam. It's embarrassing to have to be rescued by helicopter. When I tell the story today, now that I've done so much serious climbing, the only way to treat it is as comedy. Maybe farce.

I'd started keeping my climbing "bible" the previous month. That day, writing left-handed because I'd broken my right hand, I recorded

Fell, broke hand . . . airlifted.

Should have stayed more calm and walked off. Pussy.

• • • •

The most scared I've ever gotten while climbing came when I was twenty-one, a couple of years after my snowshoe fiasco. I was with my second serious girlfriend, Mandi (short for Amanda) Finger. She was a solid 5.13 climber I'd met at Jailhouse Rock, a sport-climbing crag near Sonora. She was five or six years older than me, but we hit it off. We climbed together at Joshua Tree and Red Rocks near Las Vegas. We even talked about going to Europe.

Anyway, on this particular day we decided to climb a three-pitch 5.12 route called the Nautilus, in the Needles, a range of granite spires near the Kern River. The routes are trad climbs with the occasional bolt anchor. The Needles as a whole have a well-earned reputation for being intimidating.

The Nautilus is actually on the east face of a formation called the Witch. It takes a long and tricky approach, winding between and around other towers, then scrambling up to the base, just to get to the start of the route.

I led the whole way. The first pitch is a classic 5.12b. I climbed it in style, thinking, "Ah, sweet!" According to the topo, or route diagram, that I had with me, the next pitch was 11+, followed by a 5.10 finish. I didn't have any major trouble with the second pitch, but at the top I saw that the bolt anchors were way out in space, on the blank wall to the right, away from the crack system I'd climbed. It looked like a 5.11 traverse just to get to the anchors to clip in and belay.

So I said, Screw that. I'll just keep going. Combine the third pitch with the second in one long lead. I had a seventy-meter rope, so I figured it would reach.

What I didn't know was that the last pitch was loaded with loose, refrigerator-size stones that you had to lieback past—"death blocks," as climbers call them. We were in shade, it was cold, and by now I'd developed serious rope drag from all the bends in the rope as it linked the pieces of pro I'd placed on the previous pitch. There I was, doing strenuous liebacking, trying not to dislodge any of the death blocks, and the rope drag was making it really hard to pull up any slack. On top of that, I couldn't get in any protection, as I'd used up most of my rack on the third pitch. All I had left was a Black Alien—the smallest cam anybody manufactures—a few nuts, and three carabiners.

The climbing just felt too hard. No way it was 5.10. Later I found another topo that rated the last pitch at 11+. Basically, I was getting gripped—grasping the holds too hard out of fear and uncertainty.

Mandi had been stuck in her belay way below me for about an hour. Now she yelled up encouraging comments, like, "I'm cold! I'm scared! Can we go down?"

If I could have gotten in an anchor to rappel off, I probably would have gone down. Instead, I kept fighting my way upward. I placed no pro in the last forty or fifty feet. If I came off there, I'd take a really long, bad fall, with all those big blocks to worry about pulling loose or cutting the rope. The dread was mounting. I was seriously scared.

The last pitch ends in a little roof that caps the whole route. I got to just below the roof, but here the rock turned all licheny and dirty. The rope drag was horrible. There was a last mantle move to get over the roof, but I couldn't figure out which way to do it. At last I found a crack to get the Black Alien in, and I just busted for the top. I did a really hard move, a full-on iron cross, crimping on tiny holds.

It was so fucked. As I sat on top, belaying Mandi, I had only one meter of rope left. I'd used up the other sixty-nine linking the last two pitches. And I could barely pull up the rope, the drag was so bad.

That's the most frightened I've ever been climbing, and it came not on a free solo but on a conventional roped climb. All because of an impulsive decision to skip the bolt anchor and an ignorance of just how difficult the top pitch was.

Today, I would have handled the whole thing better. I've got more tools in my tool kit now. Maybe I could have downclimbed, or placed less pro on the second pitch so I had more left for the finish.

But as I sat there, emotionally exhausted, hauling the heavy rope that was tied to Mandi, I thought I was ready to give up climbing for good. Maybe I should go back to college, I said to myself, and finish my education.

Of course, by the very next day, everything seemed different. I wasn't about to give up climbing. I'd just make sure to avoid getting stuck in cul-de-sacs like that last pitch on the Nautilus.

Easier said than done.

• • • •

On September 6, 2008, a thousand feet up the Regular Northwest Face of Half Dome, as I pushed through dirty cracks and vegetation, wondering if I'd gotten off route on the Higbee-Erickson free variation, I sensed the threat of another cul-de-sac. My anxiety wasn't ratcheted up to the level of genuine fear, but it got my attention. So I focused hard, took a deep breath, and sorted out my options.

I told myself it wasn't a do-or-die situation. Climbing down is almost always harder than climbing up, but I still felt that I could have downclimbed the whole route so far, all thousand feet of it, if I had to. For that matter, if I got into a truly nasty predicament, I could always sit and wait, even for a day or two, until some other climbers came along, ask to tie in with them, and finish the climb as their probably unwelcome guest. "Hitchhiking," I call it. Other climbers in Yosemite have chosen that means of escape, or even have had to be rescued by helicopter, but I've never had to resort to either gambit, thank God—except for my ignominious chopper rescue on Mount Tallac, but that wasn't climbing. On Half Dome, "hitchhiking" would have really sucked, and a helicopter rescue would have been even worse.

As I later realized, I had climbed too high before traversing right. For all I know, on that traverse I was inventing a new variation to the Higbee-Erickson free variation, charting new waters. The variation is supposed to end with a hundred-foot downclimb of a 5.10 finger crack. I actually had to downclimb 150 feet. Eventually, though, I found some old nylon slings hanging from pitons, and that bolstered my confidence. But then I found it hard to get my fat fingers into the 5.10 crack. I could only lodge the first knuckle in a crack where other climbers—Lynn Hill, for example—could have sunk all three knuckles on each finger. So the downclimb felt distressingly "thin," harder than 5.10, and the pitch took me a long time. In all, the variation cost me a ton of time—in actuality, maybe fifteen minutes, though it seemed an eternity—and a lot of stress, and I was relieved to finally get back onto the clean, well-traveled path.

I put on my headband iPod again and switched back into auto-pilot mode for the next five hundred feet of chimney climbing. It felt great to be in a clean, secure chimney. A pleasant routine of squirming my back, stemming my feet, palming, and repeating for hundreds of feet. I took it slow and steady, enjoying the climbing. And that brought me to Big Sandy, an enormous ledge system 1,600 feet up the wall.

So far, I'd eaten none of my food and drunk none of my water. Big Sandy isn't the only place on the route where you can sit down, but it's such a spacious ledge you could have a barbecue there with friends (if you could get them up there in the first place). I spent a few minutes taking off my shoes and relaxing. It had taken me about two hours of climbing to get here, and now I needed a breather. I ate my bars and drank the water, so I wouldn't have to carry the weight through the next hard pitches. Some climbers might have tossed the plastic flask once it was empty, but I've always believed in packing out your trash, so I stuck it back in my pocket. Soon enough, I retightened my shoes, set my iPod to repeat Eminem, and started climbing again.

The day was getting warmer, even though I was still in shadow. At some point I took off my shirt and wrapped it around my waist, cinching it with an over-and-under tuck of the sleeves. My short rest stop hadn't really felt like relief, because I knew the hardest part of the climb was still above me. That final challenge hung over me the whole time I sat on Big Sandy, ramping up my concentration and intensity for the crux to come.

Resting can be a double-edged sword. When you're free soloing, the pain in your feet and your fatigue just seem to vanish. When you rest, those annoyances come back. You have to snap out of it and get serious again.

The next three pitches above Big Sandy are called the Zig-Zags, presumably for the single, zigzagging crack/corner system they follow. Rated 5.11d, 5.10b, and 5.11c, they've always seemed harder to me. Maybe it's because I happen to have huge fingers, but the thin crack set in a steep, polished corner has always felt more like 5.12. Aesthetically, the Zig-Zags represent the best Yosemite has to offer, perfect clean corners with staggering exposure. But I wasn't thinking about the amazing view of the Valley as I carefully liebacked my way up the first tenuous pitch.

I climbed almost in a daze. I knew what to do; I just tried not to think about it too much. I didn't think about the next hard pitches above. I didn't think about the 5.11+ slab on top, a pitch above the Zig-Zags. I just moved steadily between small fingerlocks up the steep dihedral. The crux of the first Zig-Zag felt much easier than it had two days before, probably because now I had the sequence dialed. Every hold felt crisp and perfect, and I pulled really hard.

The second pitch of the Zig-Zags flew by in a frenzy of hand jams and hero liebacking. The climbing was secure enough that I could relax and enjoy it. With every zag of the crack, I found myself handjamming over big protruding blocks, the base of the wall almost 2,000 feet below me, the Valley floor itself 4,000 feet below. The pitch was a delight, compared to the thin liebacks above and below.

Handjamming is another essential technique for the rock climber, and it's surprising that it took many decades to invent. If a vertical crack is between about two and five inches wide, but there are no edges inside it to grasp with the fingers, you can still use it for a hold, by inserting the whole hand, then flexing it to fit the crack, either by making a fist or by arching the back of the hand against the straightened fingers. Your hand acts like a wedge that you can put your whole weight on. Jamming is tough on the knuckles, and guys bent on a hard day of crack climbing will tape their hands to minimize the damage. I've never been into tape myself, though, mainly because my skin is so naturally resilient— I don't tend to suffer from the little cuts and scrapes that other climbers do.

I stopped again for a minute below the last Zig-Zag. I felt good but wanted to be sure I didn't get pumped. On a rope, you're forced to rest at least fifteen minutes per pitch while you belay. But when you solo, you never have to stop, so I force myself to pause at stances and relax, just to make sure I don't get ahead of myself. After a two-minute breather, I set out up the undercling lieback feature, a slight variation on the original aid line. The undercling is somewhat pumpy but only 5.11c, not terribly difficult compared to the original corner, which is supposedly 5.12+ (though I've never tried it). The real crux of the variation is making blind gear placements in the flaring crack. But since I wasn't placing gear, I was doing the pitch the "easy way."

Still, it was another pitch of insecure liebacking, with both feet pasted against a smooth granite wall and flared jams for my fingers. Again, as on the whole rest of the route, the crux of the pitch was an extra-thin section. I knew exactly what to do and hurried through it. The nearly two thousand feet of climbing below me were beginning to take their toll. I was finding it harder and harder to give the climbing my complete attention. Part of me just wanted to get the climb over with.

With the last Zig-Zag below me, I was soon walking across Thank God Ledge, the amazing sliver of rock that traverses out from beneath the Visor, only about 200 feet shy of the summit. I could hear noises from above and knew lots of people would be up top on this perfect late summer morning. The easy Cable route up the other side of Half Dome is one of the most popular hikes in the Valley, culminating in a fifty-five-degree slab on which the National Park Service has installed a pair of metal cords to use like handrails. On a warm sunny day like this one, there's a nonstop procession of hikers lined up on the cables like airport travelers in a taxi queue.

I could hear the chatter of the tourists on top, but no heads peered over the edge. I was glad no one was watching.

I walked across Thank God Ledge as a matter of pride. I had walked its thirty-five-foot length before, but I'd also crawled or hand-traversed it. It's less than a foot wide at its narrowest, with the wall above bulging ever so slightly at one point. But I didn't want to taint my solo ascent—I had to do this correctly. (Incidentally, walking Thank God Ledge is another of those things that's quite a bit easier with no harness, rope, gear, or pack hanging off you. The balance is more natural.) The first few steps were completely normal, as if I was walking on a narrow sidewalk in the sky. But once it narrowed, I found myself inching along, facing out with my body glued to the wall, shuffling my feet and maintaining perfect posture. I could have looked down and seen my pack sitting at the base of the route 1,800 feet below, but it would have pitched me headfirst off the wall. The ledge ends at a short squeeze chimney that guards the beginning of the final slab to the summit.

I paused for a moment beneath the ninety-foot slab, looked up to see if anyone was watching (still no one), and started up. The first few moves are easy enough, on somewhat positive holds with good feet. As you get higher, the holds disappear and the feet shrink. Two days earlier, I'd considered two sections "cruxy." The first involved a step-through onto a miserly smear, while the second, thirty feet higher, involved a few moves of shitty hands and feet before reaching a "jug"—a big, positive edge I could wrap my fingers around that marked the end of the hard climbing, sixty feet up the pitch.

I also knew that it was this slab that had thwarted Higbee and Erickson's attempt to climb the whole route free. So close to the summit, they'd had to use aid to surmount the last obstacle. Perhaps that should have given me pause.

I hardly noticed the first crux. I cruised right through it, feeling pretty good about myself. Twenty feet of thin cord hung from one of the bolts. I very briefly considered running the cord under my thumb—not weighting it but having it there just in case. But that felt suspiciously like cheating.

I climbed into the upper crux, feeling good about doing things legit. And then I ground to a halt. I'd expected to find some sort of different hold or sequence from the one I'd used two days earlier, which had felt pretty desperate, but perhaps I'd done it wrong. This time, in the same position on the same holds, I realized there were no better options. I had a moment of doubt . . . or maybe panic. It was hard to tell which. Although I'd freed the pitch maybe two other times the year before, I could remember nothing of the sequence or holds, perhaps because there aren't any.

A gigantic old oval carabiner hung from a bolt about two inches above the pathetic ripple that was my right handhold. I alternated back and forth, chalking up my right hand and then my left, switching feet on marginal smears to shake out my calves. I couldn't make myself commit to the last terrible right-foot smear I needed to snag the jug. I'd stalled out in perhaps the most precarious position of the whole route. I considered grabbing the biner. With one pull, I'd be up and off.

Tourists' oblivious laughter spilled over the lip. Tons of people were up top. I was in a very private hell.

I stroked the biner a few times, fighting the urge to grab it but also thinking how foolish it would be to die on a slab, sliding and bouncing almost 2,000 feet to my death, when I could so easily save myself. My calves were slowly getting pumped. I knew I should do something soon, since treading water was only wearing me out. Downclimbing never occurred to me—I was going up (it was just a matter of how high) one way or another. But now, real fear seized me. Once again, I took a deep breath, studied the holds in front of me, and tried to think rationally about what I had to do.

Although I never wanted to be on that slab in the first place, I had to finish what I'd started without invalidating my ascent. Finally, I compromised. I kept my hand on the pathetic ripple but straightened my right index finger just enough for the tip of my last pad to rest on the bottom of the oval. My thought was, if my foot blew, I could snatch the biner with one finger and check my fall.

I smeared my foot, stood up, and grabbed the jug. No problem. I was delivered, free from my little prison, where I'd stood silently for a good five minutes. And I hadn't cheated by grabbing the biner.

I took the final 5.7 slab to the summit at a near run. Twenty or more hikers sat on the edge of the precipice, witnessing my final charge. But no one said a word. No yells, no pictures, nothing. Maybe they thought I was a lost hiker. Maybe they couldn't conceive of where I'd come from, or maybe they just didn't give a shit. When I mantled onto the actual top, I was met with a flood of humanity, a hundred-odd people spread across the summit plateau. Tourists ate lunch next to me. They made out, took scenic photos. People everywhere.

It was so weird. Like parachuting out of Vietnam into a shopping mall.

I was shirtless, pumped, panting. Psyched out of my mind. Flooded with conflicting emotions. I was embarrassed that I'd gotten scared on the slab. But I was thrilled beyond words to have finally done something that I'd been thinking about for months. Ashamed of myself for maybe pushing it a little further than I'd planned. Yet still proud of myself.

On the summit, part of me wished that someone, anyone, had noticed that I'd just done something noteworthy—though maybe it was better that I didn't have to talk to anybody. How could I have expressed what my last few hours had been like? It was enough that I knew.

I didn't make a sound. I took off my shoes and started hiking down the Cable route. It was only then that someone noticed. "Oh, my God," this dude blurted out. "You're hiking barefoot! You're so tough!"

DESPITE ASCENDING AT A "SLOW JOG" rather than a "sprint," Alex completed the 2,000-foot climb, which spans twenty-three pitches for roped climbers, in the unthinkably short time of two hours and fifty minutes. Seven years later, no one else has seriously contemplated, let alone attempted, a free solo of the Regular Northwest Face on Half Dome.

Along with the outpouring of incredulous and wacky shout-outs on sites such as Supertopo.com, there was praise of the highest order from the peers who could best appreciate the magnitude of Alex's free solo. John Long, one of the original Stonemasters whom a younger Alex had regarded as a hero, commented, "There isn't anything else I can think of that requires that level of concentration, for that length of time, with the penalty being certain death if you make the tiniest mistake."

Sender Films got in touch with Alex, proposing to craft a twenty-two-minute film around reenactments of the Moonlight Buttress and Half Dome solos. *Alone on the Wall* would win prizes at mountain festivals all over North America and Europe, and turn Alex from a climbing prodigy into a minor celebrity.

None of this, however, went to Alex's head. "In the days after Half Dome," he reported, "any huge sense of gratification eluded me. I felt like I had kind of botched the climb. I'd gotten away with something. It wasn't a perfect performance."

In his climbing bible, he jotted his usual laconic entry to document the trailblazing free solo, downgrading the route even as he recorded it.

9-6-08

Reg NW Face—5.11d? <u>solo</u> 2:50 [2 hours 50 minutes] on route.
Higbee, 5.10 bypass. Sketchy on slab.

Alex closed the note with a sad-face emoticon, and the query to himself: "Do better?"

CHAPTER **THREE**

FEAR AND LOVING IN LAS VEGAS

A S ALEX BEGAN TO WIN a small measure of fame for his bold free solos, he started to taste the rewards of sponsorship. The first company to put him on board, through the championing of his climbing buddy Brad Barlage, was Black Diamond, the Utah-based firm that manufactures high-tech climbing gear as well as ski equipment and outdoor apparel. In the years to follow, Alex would win sponsorship from La Sportiva, Clif Bar, New England Ropes, and, most important, The North Face, whose "dream team" (officially known as the Global Team athletes) constitutes a roster of stellar rock climbers and mountaineers that is the envy of young aspirants worldwide. In 2014, the Ball Watch company, whose wristwatches fetch prices upwards of $2,500, ran full-page ads in the *New York Times Magazine* featuring a photo of Alex standing on Half Dome's Thank God Ledge, accompanied by the claim, "With no ropes and no protective gear, there is simply no room for error. That's why a dependable timepiece like Ball Watch is important in an environment with truly adverse conditions." Alex endorsed the product with the pithy phrase, "The watch that rocks," even though he never wears a watch of any kind on his wrist when he climbs.

In 2008, Boulder-based Sender Films, founded nine years earlier by Peter Mortimer as a bare-bones do-it-yourself video company, took notice of Alex. By then, Sender was putting out adventure films that were as well crafted and authentic as anything of their kind produced in this country or abroad. As Mortimer recalls, "We were hanging out in Yosemite a lot. Alex's solos of the Rostrum and Astroman were on our radar. We always have our ear to the ground, hoping to find the next hot young climber. Then when he soloed Moonlight Buttress, he really got our attention."

Mortimer adds, "Everybody else in our business was cranking out films about bouldering and sport climbing. I wasn't so interested in that. What I wanted to film was 'danger climbing'—big walls, big-range mountaineering on the cutting edge, and of course free soloing." For a new film titled *The Sharp End*, Mortimer and partner Nick Rosen enlisted a corps of strong young American rock climbers and set out for the Adršpach, a massif of steep sandstone towers just inside the Czech Republic near the German border, where it merges with the legendary Elbsandsteingebirge. (The "sharp end" is climbing jargon for going first on the rope, as the leader typically takes all the serious risks.)

The Sharp End is a glorious smorgasbord of wild exploits performed by adventurers in the United States and Europe. The episodes include trad "death routes" (extremely deficient in protection) in Eldorado Canyon near Boulder; long and sketchy aid climbing routes in Yosemite; alpine ventures on untouched spires in the Shafat Fortress of India; wingsuit BASE jumping off precipices in Switzerland; and free soloing, though the star in the film is not Alex but Steph Davis, who solves the 5.10+ Pervertical Sanctuary on the Diamond on Colorado's Longs Peak. Alex's role in the film is little more than a cameo appearance, but it dramatically foreshadows the stardom toward which he was headed. In fact, Sender chose for its movie jacket a still photo of Alex leading a desperate-looking pitch.

The Adršpach and Elbsandsteingebirge thrust out of the forest along the river Elbe, southeast of Dresden, in a wild burst of dark gray pinnacles. There, during the first two decades of the twentieth century, a cadre of hard men whose climbing culture was utterly insulated even from their peers in the Alps put up the most difficult rock routes anywhere in the world. As they did so, they developed a local style bound by ironclad "ethics" unlike that of any other scene.

Americans and Western Europeans discovered the Dresden arena only in the late 1960s, and when some of the best outsiders ventured there to sample that scene, they were uniformly impressed—and intimidated. By 2008, some forty years later, the purism of the eastern German and Czech locals still ruled the crags. In the Elbsandsteingebirge, big ring bolts, drilled frighteningly far apart (as much as twenty or thirty meters), form the only fixed anchors and protection. Pitons, nuts, and cams are not allowed. The only removable protection a climber is allowed to place is knotted nylon slings jammed into cracks—a practice with which American, French, and Swiss climbers were wholly unfamiliar. To make matters worse—or purer—chalk for the fingers is not allowed. Lacking decent rock shoes, the Dresden climbers put up many of their hardest routes barefoot.

Mortimer and Rosen rounded up their team of American rock stars, including Cedar Wright, Renan Ozturk, Matt Segal, Topher Donahue, and Heidi Wirtz. Alex went along as the promising rookie. For the film, the directors lured sixty-one-year-old Bernd Arnold—the grandmaster of the Elbsandsteingebirge from the late 1960s through the '70s and '80s—to act as guide for the awestruck Americans. In the film, although Arnold speaks virtually no English, he gleefully shows his charges the ropes (as it were), encouraging them to take off their shoes and scramble barefoot to get used to the strange rock. Arnold's comrades blithely underscore the seriousness of the routes with gallows humor. As one of them says, in accented English, "If you fall, you can become legend."

The climactic scene of this episode in *The Sharp End* unfolds after the Americans have succeeded on some of the classic routes but now want to make their own mark to salvage a bit of pride. They gather beneath a sharp vertical arête, a route that even the locals declare too dangerous. The talk is ominous and fearful. Wearing a hoodie, looking like the antisocial nerd Ben Smalley remembered from high school, Alex is almost silent. But then he quietly spouts, "We've been here for an hour, talking about how hard and how scary this is. We should just go do it."

So Alex takes the sharp end. His progress up the terrifying arête, superbly filmed, uses his buddies' spontaneous comments as voice-over. Cedar Wright says, "He's hesitating there for ten minutes. He's looking at a ninety-foot fall. He could hit the ground." In the film, you can hear Alex's short bursts of panting breath. But the smooth, exquisitely calculated movement is a work of art. Fear for his safety transmutes into his comrades' praise. "Watching Alex is pretty inspiring," one says, "because he keeps it together so well." Another: "Alex is in a different head space—his ability to stay calm and not get pumped, all the way to the top." And after Alex finishes the climb, yet another: "That's not a pitch I want to lead." Cedar Wright: "I'm definitely a little jealous."

Wordless, Alex stands on the summit of the spire and grins.

• • • •

After Alex free soloed Half Dome in September 2008, Mortimer and Rosen decided they wanted to shape a whole film around the prodigy's extraordinary deeds. But no one had witnessed Alex's climbs on either Moonlight Buttress or Half Dome. The solution was self-evident: approach Alex and ask him whether he'd be willing to reenact passages on those two routes for the camera.

Mortimer remembers, "He wasn't reluctant at all. He was up for it. 'Yeah,' he told us, 'I love the idea of getting some footage on those walls.'"

The logistical problems of filming that footage, however, were monumental. By the spring of 2009, when Sender was ready to shoot Moonlight Buttress, there were several parties on the route, climbing it in old-fashioned style, with plenty of aid. Fortunately, those parties were toiling low on the route. Mortimer and still photographer Celin Serbo decided to rappel down some 400 feet from the summit, hang on parallel ropes, then film and photograph Alex free soloing the upper pitches close up with the aid parties well out of the frame. Alex would rappel down those 400 feet, take off his harness, and start soloing upward.

Mortimer had deep misgivings about what he was asking Alex to do. *What if he falls to his death,* he worried, *just for the sake of our film? I can't imagine how I could live with that.* His film crew was equally apprehensive. "As we gathered in Springdale the night before the reenactment," Mortimer says, "we were completely stressed out. We were at a pizza parlor. We waited until Alex went to the bathroom, then we said to each other, 'I don't know if we should do this.'

"When Alex came back, I started to ask, 'Alex, are you sure—?'

"He burst out, 'You guys are such pussies! You mean I'll have to call someone else to shoot this?'"

The passages Alex soloed for the camera were the 5.12 pitches above the crux 180-foot inside corner, where a perfect finger crack into which he locked his first digits had given him such exhilaration when he'd first soloed the route the previous April. Mortimer: "It was cold. And it was windy. The exposure up there at the top of Moonlight Buttress is crazy. It's as vertigo-inducing as anything on El Cap. While we filmed, just a few feet away from Alex, we were super careful not to move an inch, so as not to distract him. You don't want to drop a lens cap or knock loose even the tiniest stone."

Even so, Mortimer and his cameramen were gripped. The finger-locked digits, the feet pasted flat against the smooth wall, seemed to give Alex only the most marginal purchase on the world. Below him stretched an 800-foot void. If he fell, he might strike nothing before slamming into the ground at the base of the wall. At that moment, Alex turned to the camera and said, "So, do you want me to make this look like it's hard for me?" According to Mortimer, "Alex was actually thinking, 'Oh, those guys must be so bored.'" A little later, Alex jammed his knee into a crack, then suddenly let go with both hands. "No hands kneebar, baby!" he exulted.

A few months later, a slightly different crew, including Mortimer's directing partner Nick Rosen and cameraman Tim Kemple, gathered to shoot Alex reenacting parts of the Regular Northwest Face route on Half Dome. In the interim, two of America's best mountaineers, Johnny Copp and Micah Dash (both featured in *The Sharp End*, as they explored the Shafat Fortress in India and the Chamonix *aiguilles* in France), disappeared on Mount Edgar in western China, along with cinematographer Wade Johnson, who had worked on *The Sharp End*. Living in Boulder, all three were close friends of the entire staff of Sender Films. Not only that, but Sender was crafting a film around the attempt on the massive, unclimbed southeast face of Mount Edgar.

It was only when the trio missed a return flight out of Chengdu that a rescue effort was launched. Top climbers from Boulder and elsewhere, including Nick Rosen, immediately flew to China to initiate a search. They were aided by Chinese troops. On June 7, 2009, Copp's body was found at the base of the wall, Johnson's the next day. It seemed clear that a gigantic avalanche of mixed rock, snow, and ice had scoured the wall, engulfing the climbers. Dash's body was never found.

Remarkably, much of Johnson's footage was recovered intact at base camp. Mortimer and Rosen used it to put together a film in homage to their friends. *Point of No Return* is a haunting, unforgettable work. Knowing the tragic fate that awaits the three young climbers, you watch their tearful goodbyes to girlfriends at the airport, their boisterous antics at base camp, with a sense of mounting dread. But you also see the monstrously scary, nearly continuous barrage of falling rocks and ice that had made the trio decide to abandon the route even before coming to grips with it.

It's torturous to learn that the men's final mission was simply a scramble up to a cache above base camp to retrieve equipment they had stowed a few days before. Watching them head off to their doom, you want to scream at the screen, *Just go home! Leave the fucking gear!*

In the wake of the disaster, which shook the whole American climbing community, Mortimer and Rosen approached Half Dome with Alex in a somber, even psyched-out mood. "We had absolutely no stomach," says Mortimer, "for anything crazy or on the edge. We were going to restrict the filming to the easier pitches down low, then rap down a few hundred feet from the summit to film Alex finishing the Zig-Zags and traversing Thank God Ledge."

Despite the fears and sorrows of the filmmakers, *Alone on the Wall* comes across as a blithe celebration of climbing; it's even lighthearted in places. The film is a minor masterpiece. No one can watch it, even for the fourth or fifth time, without feeling palms turn sweaty as Alex performs his ropeless dance on vertical rock. And the film never fails to inspire a heated debate among climbers and nonclimbers alike over the ethics of free soloing. (Some nonclimbers simply cannot bear to watch the film.)

A testament to Mortimer and Rosen's cinematic skill lies in the fact that most viewers don't realize they're seeing a reenactment. Instead, the film looks and feels like a documentary of two of the boldest exploits of twenty-first-century climbing. For comic counterpoint, the film intercuts the footage on Moonlight Buttress and Half Dome with Alex giving a tour of the Econoline van that serves as his home (narrator Rosen: "Do you have girls in here a lot?" Alex, guffawing: "Do I look like I have girls in here a lot?"), and with a visit to Alex's childhood home in Sacramento, where his mother proudly shows off all the magazine covers featuring her son, while he cringes in embarrassment. The film closes lightheartedly, too, with Alex eating food out of a bowl with a twig in lieu of cutlery, as he riffs about being like a tool-using chimp using a stick to ferret out ants. "This is what makes us human," he cracks.

The heart of *Alone on the Wall*, of course, lies in the dazzling footage of Alex on his two big walls. Interspersed with this action are sound bites from Alex's peers. Says Cedar Wright, one of Alex's best friends, "When you meet Alex Honnold, you're gonna be like, 'Huh, this guy is a bumbling, dorky, awkward goofball.' Until he steps on the rock, and then he's literally a whole other person. He becomes this poised, graceful, calculated badass dude." John Long, the Stonemaster who shared in the first one-day ascent of the Nose on El Cap in 1975, marvels about Alex's free solo of Half Dome: "It took some vision to get up there, but it took some frickin' *balls* to actually do it." Climbing buddy Nick Martino declares, "Frickin' Honnold is walking on the moon, as far as I'm concerned."

As the footage of the actual climbing spools by, Alex comments in voice-over: "There's all the little things you have to think about, like left-right, which sequence you're doing, but there's nothing I'm really thinking about—I'm just doing it." And: "I love the simplicity of soloing. You never climb better than when you're soloing." And: "Doubt is the biggest danger in soloing. As soon as you hesitate, you're screwed." But even Alex seems at last to realize the magnitude of his deeds, as, standing on the summit of Moonlight Buttress, grinning with happiness, he utters, "When I think about it, it's frickin' rad!"

The climax of the film dramatizes the stall-out that gave Alex his five minutes of "very private hell" only 150 feet below the top of Half Dome. But Mortimer and Rosen were not about to ask Alex to repeat that terrifying sequence of "miserly smears" on the 5.12 slab above Thank God Ledge, where, on September 6, 2008, he had confronted the very real possibility of falling almost 2,000 feet to his death. Instead, in the film, Thank God Ledge itself serves as the locus for the freakout. As Alex sidles carefully away from the camera along the narrowing ledge, facing out with his back to the wall, he pauses. In voice-over, he narrates, "Basically, when I'm soloing, normally I have like a mental armor. You could say I'm in the zone. Something that's protecting my head from thinking too much. And for some reason"—he laughs at the memory—"on Half Dome I ran out of what armor I had. . . . I had a mini-nervous breakdown."

In the film, the invisible cameraman, Tim Kemple, tells Alex that he can traverse back to safety if he doesn't like the feel of this predicament. But Alex shuffles on—across ground that in reality was fairly easy for him. And then, soon, he's bounding across the summit, alone in his joy.

In only six years, that moment of film footage on Thank God Ledge became one of the most iconic images in climbing history. Sender Films put a still from the sequence on the cover of their boxed set *First Ascent*, which contains four other films besides *Alone on the Wall* and *Point of No Return*. A couple of years later, in its May 2011 issue, *National Geographic* ran a feature on the younger generation of Yosemite hotshots, for which photographer Jimmy Chin duplicated the shot. It made the cover of the magazine. In the 2014 Ball Watch ad, yet another version of Alex on Thank God Ledge illustrated the "truly adverse conditions" facing "the world's explorers."

Within the last year and a half, that image has spawned a craze of imitations, under the rubric "Honnolding," as climbers pose on their own ledges (much closer to the ground), their backs to the wall, feet together, arms stiff at their sides, blank looks on their faces—as well as a number of goofy parodies, in which subjects assume the same pose standing on toilet tanks, refrigerators, stepladders, and the like. The only comparable phenomenon in recent years was the vogue of Tebowing—kneeling in prayer, one knee on the ground, elbow on the other knee, closed hand pressed to bent forehead—in homage to the born-again NFL quarterback. After Tim Tebow moved off the field and on to ESPN, however, that craze waned fast.

Says Mortimer about the original photo of Alex on Thank God Ledge, "Something about that position brings home to everybody what the pros do on big walls, better than a conventional climbing shot does. It captures the vulnerability of it all. It's as if Alex is standing there, facing God. Completely vulnerable."

• • • •

Alone on the Wall promptly won grand prizes at film festivals ranging from Telluride, Colorado, to Trento, Italy, and Kendal, England. As perhaps the most dazzling presentation in the annual Reel Rock Tour, jointly sponsored by Sender Films and New York–based Big UP Productions, the film was screened in scores of venues all over the country in the fall of 2009. (By then, Reel Rock had already acquired a cult following.) More than the buzz about Alex's exploits humming on websites such as Supertopo.com, more even than a feature article in *Outside* magazine and the cover shot for *National Geographic*, the film put Alex on a map that covered far broader terrain than the insular world of hardcore climbing. (It's hard to think of a comparable case in the recent past of a young extreme athlete morphing from complete obscurity to considerable fame in only two years.) The film was the main impetus that convinced the CBS news program *60 Minutes* to film a profile of Alex, which aired on October 2, 2011. At the time of that widely watched TV segment, Alex was only twenty-six years old.

For several years, Alex had kept a Facebook page. Now, with this new explosion of media exposure, the page was inundated with shout-outs and queries from strangers. As Alex said in 2010, "I had to erase myself from Facebook. It was too crazy—I was getting twenty friend requests a day. Some kid would ask, 'Hey, what kind of chalk bag should I buy?' You hate to blow him off, but, like, what can you say?"

In September 2009, before Alex erased himself, a twenty-four-year-old woman attended the Reel Rock Tour at a Tucson screening. Stacey Pearson, who worked as nurse in a local hospital, was also a serious distance runner, having competed in four marathons, clocking a best time of three hours and twenty-five minutes.

As Pearson recalled in 2010, "I'd never heard of Alex Honnold. A friend invited me to Reel Rock, but I almost didn't go. We arrived late. Alex was just one of many characters in the films, but I thought, 'That guy is really cool.'

"I went home and Googled him. I discovered I could find him on Facebook. I wrote to him: 'I saw you on the film tour. I don't know anything about you, but I thought what you did was really respectful and cool.'"

Pearson got no answer for days, as Alex was in Siberia attending an international climbing meet. Eventually, however, he sent back a few words. "So I asked if I could friend him," said Pearson. "He accepted. He'd seen my picture and things about me, like my bio, where I called myself a 'future ultra-marathoner.' He wrote back, 'Are you really into ultra-marathoning?'

"We started e-mailing every few days," Pearson recalled. "Telling each other all about ourselves. Alex was in Spain, then he was in China, where they don't allow Facebook. So our e-mails grew longer and longer. Finally we did a video chat. It was nerve-racking. I was nervous, and I could tell he was, too. He had the hood on his sweatshirt up. 'Hi,' he said. 'What's up?'"

At the time, Alex had no steady girlfriend. There had been

occasional brief liaisons, including a fling with Katie Brown, who
a decade earlier had dazzled the climbing world as a teen prodigy,
winning the world junior championship in Quebec at the age of
fourteen. "Three weeks of wild torment," Alex later described his
affair with Brown. "I was over-eager and under-suave."

"Alex was coming home on December 4, [2009]," Pearson
recalled. "He mentioned that he was going to enter the California
International Marathon in Sacramento two days later, to test his
running capability. That seemed like a perfect excuse for us to meet
at last, so I tried to sign up for the marathon, but unfortunately it
was sold out. I decided to come to California anyway.

"I was a little nervous, but also excited—I was about to do something I'd never done before. I was waiting by the curb at the Oak-
land airport. Alex called to say he was fifteen minutes late. Finally
he pulled up in his van. We may have hugged. It felt awkward. I was
wearing a zebra print cardigan. Many months later, Alex told me
that what I wore that day matched up to his standards of 'a hot girl'!

"It probably helped that our first time together was in the context
of Alex's full-on family—his mom, Dierdre, and his sister, Stasia. It
made things easier. The first night Alex gave a slide show for a small
crowd at a pizza joint in Santa Rosa. I met a few of his friends. One
of them said, 'Alex is a great guy.' I answered, 'Yeah, I've only known
him for a day.'

"I waited at the halfway point of the marathon. When Alex came
by, he gasped that he was starving. We ran together for a while. As
we passed a guy carrying some food, Alex asked if he could have
the banana in his hand, which the guy gladly handed over. Then
we passed a small aid station with a few goodies. Alex's eyes grew
wide when he spotted a bowl of M&M'S. He grabbed a handful
and shoved them in his mouth. That's how I learned that his biggest
weakness—so he says—is that he has an incurable sweet tooth."

Pearson returned to Tucson, and two weeks later Alex arrived for an extended visit. During their time together, they got to know each other. After Christmas, however, fed up with her job, Stacey took another gig as a nurse in Dallas. Thus began a two-year stint of working as a traveling nurse, changing jobs every few months as she rotated through hospitals all over the country.

Meanwhile, Alex was climbing in Yosemite. The pair spent a month and a half apart, before Alex came to Dallas for a second prolonged visit.

"I missed Alex," Stacey remembered, "even though I had no trouble making new friends in Dallas. When he visited, I made him do urban things, like going to museums and eating in good restaurants. We also ran and biked together. We fell in love for the first time in Dallas. But it's a big deal to say, 'I love you.' I made Alex say it first."

Twenty-nine years old in 2015, Stacey is a very pretty woman with light brown hair, striking gray-blue eyes, and an infectious smile. Slender and extremely fit, she comes across at first as quiet and sweet-tempered, but on further acquaintance, she reveals a sharp intelligence and a stubborn will that are a match for Alex's.

In early 2010, even as they fell in love, certain conflicts and incompatibilities emerged. "I felt uncomfortable sleeping in his van," Stacey recalled. "I had trouble adjusting to it. I felt dirty, gross, and cramped." The two argued about lifestyle. Stacey drinks moderately, Alex not at all. She enjoyed a regular social life with friends, but Alex still felt ill at ease in such situations. In turn, Alex thought of Stacey as insufficiently outdoorsy, and he worried that her commitment to nursing might not blend with his nomadic lifestyle. A joking to-and-fro that had begun in their e-mails became a teasing conversational routine. Hanging over it all was the possibility that, as so many of his friends feared, Alex might kill himself free soloing.

According to Stacey, "I would say, 'If you die one day, I can fly to Europe and find my dream European guy.' He would fire back, 'If you're hit by a bus, I can go hang out with the French chicks.'"

During the next five years, Stacey and Alex remained a couple. They discussed marriage and kids but committed to neither. Along the way, they had their share of fallings-out, and even several break-ups that both thought were likely to be terminal.

The first bad patch came in April 2010, toward the end of what Stacey would later look back on as a three-month "honey-moon period" after they'd finally met in Sacramento the previous December.

Stacey was in Dallas, but her nursing contract had been terminated early, so she was planning to move to Los Angeles. We hadn't actually broken up, but I suspected she was getting into this other dude in Dallas. In Yosemite, I'd been hoping to climb something rad, but the weather was shitty, raining every day, everything wet. Meanwhile, I knew the weather was perfect in Las Vegas. So I thought I could try my luck at Red Rocks, the great massif of sandstone cliffs just a few miles west of the city.

Stacey and I had made vague plans to meet in Tucson, as she drove from Dallas to L.A. So for me, heading down to Vegas was a kind of move toward our rendezvous in Tucson and, I hoped, toward saving our relationship.

Because of the weather, I hadn't been able to climb anything super-exciting in the Valley, so I'd done nothing but boulder. And if you boulder too much, the skin on your fingers gets raw and tender—worthless for sustained climbing. So I was in an angst-driven mood anyway, on top of the angst about Stacey.

I grew up reading climbing stories by Mark Twight, aka Doctor Doom. He was famous for dwelling on pain and heartbreak and existential suffering as the spurs that drove him to tackle more and more out-there routes. It's not that he was suicidal—in fact, he called climbing "a tool to forestall suicide." A whole generation of young climbers, myself included, was inspired by the essays in his collection, Kiss or Kill: Confessions of a Serial Climber. (If I reread it today, I suspect I'd see the affectation behind the carefully constructed persona of Doctor Doom.) But Twight also wrote Extreme Alpinism, the manifesto that pretty much defined the new style of light, fast, go-for-broke ascents.

Still, there's a rich vein in mountaineering literature of climbers using dark thoughts and stormy moods to precipitate cutting-edge climbs, especially solos. Angst as a motivator. I think an old issue of Climbing magazine ran a long piece detailing how romantic breakups had prompted rad solo climbs. Nerve-racking tales about emotionally wrecked men risking it all in an effort to sort out their feelings.

It's not necessarily suicidal. It's about a guy suddenly losing the love of his life, caring a little less about danger, and so finally doing something that he's always kept tucked in the back of his mind.

I've never felt suicidal myself. But trying to save my relationship with Stacey that April was stressing me out. I was definitely in a dark spell in my life.

Anyway, at first I envisioned a quick stop at Red Rocks for some mellow soloing in dry, warm conditions, then on to Tucson for the mission that was the real point of my trip. But I was also thinking about a great classic line, the Original Route on Rainbow Wall. In fact, it's been called the finest of all the thousands of routes at Red Rocks. At the head of Juniper Canyon, the Original Route is fourteen pitches of sustained climbing up this massive, concave, amphitheaterlike face, lots of it on tiny holds, up to 5.12b in difficulty. And the crux comes high, on the tenth pitch.

The route was first climbed in 1973 with a fair amount of aid, and rated at 5.9 A2. (Traditional aid grades in the YDS system range from A0—easiest—to A5.) The first free ascent came in 1997

by Leo Henson and Dan McQuade. I'd onsighted the route three
or four years before with Josh McCoy, but that was my only previous trip up the route, and I certainly didn't have the moves dialed.

On the way to Vegas, I called up all the friends I could think of
to ask if any of them wanted to do the Rainbow Wall. Nada. They
were all busy with something or other. In my angst-driven mood, I
made a snap decision: Fuck it, I'll do it anyway.

All the way on the road from Yosemite across Nevada, I was preoccupied with thoughts about Stacey. But ever since I'd first seen
the route, even before I climbed it, Rainbow Wall had been embed-
ded in my consciousness. I'd dreamed for years about free soloing
the Original Route.

So, on April 28, I found myself at the Pine Creek parking lot,
the wall looming above me. My mind was jangling with a dozen
interwoven streams of thought. The wind was blowing at close to
gale force, and while that didn't help my confidence, a rational part
of my mind was grateful that my skin would stay dry and cool on
the wall. Then, with perfect timing, Stacey called me on my cell
phone. We had a very pleasant, if brief conversation. She tentatively reconfirmed our plan to meet in Tucson. Suddenly the desert
morning seemed rosier, and I almost thought I could see a rainbow.

Even at the time, I knew that it probably wasn't healthy to feel
such euphoria over a girl. But I embraced the mood and harnessed
it to my purpose, starting my hiking with determination and glee.
Alone in the canyon, I listened to the various bird calls and the
sound of water babbling through the boulder-strewn wash. Suddenly all those little things seemed so much more meaningful, and
I was overcome with gratitude that I could be having such a great
time in such a beautiful place.

I suppose I should have realized that I was becoming emotionally unhinged. But I wanted to maintain my elation as long as I
could, maybe even to the top of the route. I focused on how excit-

ing the climbing would be, how much I craved the challenge, how beautiful the whole region was. Behind all that sensory delight floated the real excitement, which was that maybe, just maybe, Stacey did actually care for me, and we might be able to make things work. My mind was layered like an onion, though I suppose at the core lay the deep sadness that things might be ending.

But I made it all the way to the base of the wall in my semi-blissful state, and once there my mind turned practical. Finally I could stop trying to control my mood and focus solely on the climbing. I knew that this would be where I really found peace, in the intricacies of 11+ stem corners and 12a liebacking. As usual, it took me a few pitches to find my groove, but once I got moving I really did feel peaceful. I flowed up pitch after pitch of perfect corners. The amazing flat edges that appeared from time to time were a delight to use, and I found my position on the cliff stunning.

Free soloing this route after only one previous roped ascent of it—and that several years earlier—amounted to the polar opposite of the kind of superpreparation I had applied to Moonlight Buttress a little more than a year before. In some sense, I had no idea what I was doing up there on Rainbow Wall. Some people might call this crazy. I prefer to think of it as badass. It definitely amped up the adventure. This time, it felt like I was onsighting again—only with-out a rope. I remembered the odd move here and there, but most of it felt like I was discovering the sequences for the first time. There's no question, though, that my impulsive push on Rainbow Wall had everything to do with what was going on with Stacey.

About halfway up the route, there's a stretch of easy pitches, ranging from 5.4 to 5.8, that wanders up and to the right through ramps to a cozy perch on Over the Rainbow Ledge. Here, my mind turned back to "real" life, with all the angst I had carried with me from the Valley, but fortunately, that "down" interlude was fleet-ing. Soon enough, I was facing the crux tenth pitch.

I was about 750 feet off the ground. I was palming and stemming up this corner on really small ripples in the sandstone. All of
a sudden, I realized what the crux required. You'd have to get your
feet as high as you could, then jump to grab a jug. A true "dyno"
move, but not such a big deal if you were roped and had placed
some solid pro nearby. Maybe that's why I didn't remember it from
my previous ascent. But now I got there, looked at the jug out of
reach, imagined jumping for it, and said to myself, Hell, no!

I could still have downclimbed to Over the Rainbow Ledge,
traversed right, and finished the wall by the indirect Swainbow
variation, which is only 5.10. But in the mood I was in, I wanted to
finish what I'd set out to do. Four or five times I climbed up those
ripples, surveyed the situation, and climbed back down. It was
simply out of the question to jump for the jug. If you don't catch the
hold, you're off and down . . . and dead.

Slowly an alternative dawned on me. Just in reach from the ripples was a tiny divot, a natural hole in the stone caused by a black
iron-oxide intrusion. I could sink only about a third of the first digit
of my left index finger into the divot, then stack my middle finger
and my thumb on top of it. It would be the ultimate crimp, and I'm
sure the divot had never been used before. Finally, I committed my
whole weight to the jammed tip of my finger, smeared an opposing
foot against the corner, and pulled. My finger in the divot held, and
I grabbed the jug with my other hand. Strangely, instead of fear, I
felt complete serenity as I made the move.

The next pitch was a 5.12 lieback. I thought it would be a lot
easier than the pitch before, but it was pretty gnarly in its own
right. Wait, I thought, this shouldn't be so hard. And now I had no
option of downclimbing, because there was no way I would ever
reverse that crimp on the divot. But I kept it together and finished
the lieback.

The last two pitches flew by in a blur. I finally felt completely warmed up and climbed with ease. But as soon as I topped out on the summit, the driving wind nearly knocked me over. On the wall, I'd been protected from the gusts, but here I was fully exposed to the brunt of the gale. When you're free soloing, of course, rappelling the route isn't an option, since you don't have a rope. Now I cowered in a little hole and changed out of my rock shoes into approach shoes that I'd carried in a small backpack, along with a little food and water.

The descents from Moonlight Buttress and Half Dome had been pretty routine, down trails that scores of hikers trod every day, and it wasn't a strain to go down barefoot. The descent from Rainbow Wall, on the other hand, was heinous. It's a series of technical scrambles on slick sandstone slabs, all the way back to the limestone mountains west of Red Rocks, to gain the upper drainage of Oak Creek Canyon. Then all the way down Oak Creek as you circle the peak of which Rainbow Wall is the northeast face. The whole descent is a bit of a bear, really heavy on the scrambling.

Then, hiking the flat desert back to my van, I felt like I was on a death march—no food or water. Just endless walking.

And now, in an instant, the sense of peace that had carried me up the climb vanished. Away from the tranquillity of the wall, my psyche started to fray. I was exultant at having soloed the wall but suddenly much less optimistic about my "real" life. As I thrashed my way down, I wondered if I really would be able to salvage my relationship with Stacey, and whether or not it was even worth the effort. As the canyon drew out in front of me and the afternoon heat bore down harder on me, the world seemed so much less beautiful than it had on the hike in. By the time I'd reached the flat desert and started circling back toward my van, I was much less pleased with my performance and fairly sure I would soon be single. My mind sank as low as it had gone high, and I seemed powerless to keep it under control. The whole experience had left me a little raw. The constant howl of wind, the crushing heat of the sun, hunger, thirst, mental fatigue—they all left me feeling vulnerable.

As soon as I reached the van, my first thought was to check my phone to see if Stacey had called. I think we'd made some vague agreement to chat later. I hoped she had left a message. But I knew that she hadn't. Unsurprisingly, no call, which I took to mean that Stacey just wasn't very psyched about "us."

The sandwiches I made helped ease my disappointment. I planned on soloing another route in the afternoon, just so I could finish all my business at Red Rocks in one day and keep on driving toward my real goal—Tucson.

. . . .

I was pleased with myself for soloing the Rainbow Wall. Maybe I should have called it a day, but I'd already decided I wanted to do more. My plan was to solo up Prince of Darkness, a seven-pitch 5.10 route that soars through a blank-looking face on Black Velvet Wall. Then I'd downclimb another 5.10 route, Dream of Wild Turkeys, which joins Prince of Darkness about 650 feet off the ground.

I chatted with some other climbers in the parking lot, joking about the terrible weather in Yosemite, then drove over to the trailhead for Black Velvet Canyon. But now the euphoria was long gone, replaced by lethargy and the deep fatigue of my worn-out mind. I'd always thought that Prince of Darkness would be a good challenge for me in dealing with the exposure of tiny holds on a smooth vertical wall. I never considered calling it quits, but on the way to the base I found that I didn't really care. I was sick of the unrelenting wind and my feet hurt from hiking and edging. The wall didn't excite me.

Since I was already warmed up and in a soloing mindset, I

expected the climbing to be smooth and effortless. But instead I felt jerky and slow. I wasted energy by overgripping the sandstone crimps and worrying about breaking footholds. I didn't want to be there. Instead of relishing the process, the whole experience of being on the wall, I just wanted to have it finished. I wanted to be back in my van, out of the wind.

I kept trudging upward, though I never got comfortable. My feet hurt more and more, but I never passed a good-enough stance to adjust my shoes. By the time I reached the top of the route— the large ledge where Prince of Darkness joins Dream of Wild Turkeys—I hated climbing, hated the wind, and wanted to go home. On the ledge, I took off my shoes for a while, trying to allow some blood to flow back into my toes. I didn't look around the canyon, I didn't admire the shadows lengthening across the desert, I just looked at my feet and waited to start the descent.

I downclimbed Dream of Wild Turkeys, which turned out to be a pretty fun route. Or at least it would have been fun in a different time and place. As I descended, I would occasionally find myself having a good time. And then suddenly the wind would pick up and I would realize that I had only been enjoying a brief reprieve. But I suppose that the wind and my fatigue combined to blunt all my other emotions. I just didn't care as much. Everything to do with "real" life, including Stacey, seemed a little less critical. What really mattered was sitting down in a sheltered place and eating. And maybe sleeping.

· · · ·

That evening, I met some friends for dinner in Las Vegas. In the bathroom of the restaurant, I washed my hands for the first time and discovered I had a blood blister on my left index finger, where I'd jammed it into the iron-oxide divot, stacked a finger and a thumb on top of it, and made that pioneering move up to grab the jug. I came back to the table and showed the blistered fingertip to my friends. It felt like a badge of courage.

That marathon day of veering emotions at Red Rocks was like a whole life in a nutshell. As it turned out, though, I didn't wait for the rendezvous in Tucson. The next day I flew to Dallas, ostensibly to help Stacey pack for her move to L.A. But I really wanted to win her back. I basically re-wooed her. And it worked . . . for a while.

Two months later, we broke up—for the first time.

CHAPTER **FOUR**
WORLD TRAVELER

ALEX HAD PULLED OFF his three-route tour de force at Red Rocks in the same purist, private style that he had wielded on Moonlight Buttress and Half Dome. No one had witnessed his climbing on Rainbow Wall, Prince of Darkness, or Dream of Wild Turkeys, and only the folks with whom he had chatted at the trailhead around midday had any idea that he was up to anything special. But the word got out quickly. On Supertopo.com, veteran Yosemite climber Peter Haan—who in the early 1970s had dazzled his peers with first free ascents and roped solos of classic routes (using a complicated self-belaying system)—reported Alex's Red Rocks feat on May 12, 2010, only fourteen days after Alex had battled his demons in gale-force winds on those sandstone walls.

The response was another medley of disbelief, astonishment, congratulations, and cautionary screeds begging Alex not to risk his life so cavalierly. "You messing with us, Peter?" wrote another Valley veteran, invoking the kind of incredulity that had led some to dismiss Moonlight Buttress as an April Fools' Day hoax. But a believer posted, "This fella should try walking on water." Another veteran weighed in: "Having done all 3 routes, this just makes me sick."

Many of the responders expressed simple admiration. "Long live Alex Honnold," cheered one. "Another amazing send by a super nice dude!" John Long, the Stonemaster who would bear on-screen witness to Alex's genius in *Alone on the Wall*, posted simply, "Alexander the Great."

The cautionary comments, however, verged on the avuncular. "I hope Alex is being careful, he's such a great kid," one observer ventured. "It seems that Alex has taken it to a new level only by cutting the safety margin drastically. I'd feel more comfortable if his solos were cracks [as opposed to small holds on otherwise blank walls]. One thing is for sure, he has courage beyond belief."

So far in his career, the climbs that have won Alex the greatest acclaim have come in even-numbered years. Moonlight Buttress and Half Dome in 2008, Rainbow Wall in 2010, then other incredible breakthroughs in 2012 and 2014. Alex is aware of this pattern, referring to the odd-numbered years as periods of "consolidation." But in some sense, this schema belies the nonstop virtuosity of Alex's approach to climbing in all its forms.

In April 2009, for instance, Alex joined a team headed for Mount Kinabalu, at 13,435 feet the highest peak in Borneo. By its easiest route, Kinabalu is a tourist-thronged walk-up, but the mountain is actually a gigantic monolith of granite soaring out of dense rain forest. Some of its earliest explorers got lost in the jungle just trying to find their way to the mountain, and even today, Kinabalu still has untouched walls that challenge the best mountaineers.

The trip was the brainchild of Mark Synnott. Thirty-nine years old at the time, Synnott was a veteran mountaineer with a record of bold first ascents all over the globe. By 2009, he had perfected the art of getting magazine assignments combined with corporate sponsorship (usually by The North Face) to launch exotic adventures in the far corners of the world, his teams comprising some of the top American climbing stars. For *Men's Journal* and Borneo, he recruited Conrad Anker (who found George Mallory's body on Everest in 1999), photographer Jimmy Chin, filmmaker Renan Ozturk, and Kevin Thaw—all four veterans of other landmark expeditions. Anker, who had become the team captain for The North Face, had recently anointed the wunderkind of Moonlight Buttress and Half Dome with TNF sponsorship.

Now Anker tried to convince Synnott to add the twenty-three-year-old Honnold to the Borneo team. Says Synnott now, "I was pretty apprehensive. I'd never met Alex. In general, I don't like going off with guys I don't already know. There's a big potential for personality conflicts. And Alex had never been on an expedition."

The team's objective was an unclimbed, nearly vertical wall on the north side of the mountain, rising out of a forbidding abyss called Low's Gully. The place had an evil reputation, cemented by a catastrophe in 1994 when a ten-man British army team out on what was supposed to be a six-day training mission got entangled in a thirty-one-day survival ordeal. That disaster was vividly recounted in the book *Descent into Chaos*, by journalist Richard Connaughton.

Synnott had another source for his misgivings. Aware of Alex's deeds as a free soloist, Synnott worried "what kind of insane stuff" the young hotshot "might pressure me into doing." As it turned out, the two got along well in Borneo. "We hit it off right off the bat," Synnott remembers. "Alex has a wide-open personality. He deals with people well. There's no pretense. No bullshit."

Still, there were "quirky little things" that caused minor disputes between the leader and the rookie. "On his rack," Synnott claims, "he set up all his cams the way he would in Indian Creek"—the crag in southern Utah famed for short, steep crack climbs. This meant that Alex couldn't free up carabiners to use in all the different ways mountaineering requires. "So I had to take his rack apart," Synnott adds.

"'What are you doing?' Alex asked me.

"'Dude, this doesn't work here.'"

According to Synnott, Alex "wouldn't use shoulder slings"—long nylon loops that minimize drag by redirecting the climbing rope as it zigzags from one piece of protection to the next.

"What do you do about rope drag?" Synnott asked him.

"I just skip pieces," Alex answered. (In other words, he runs out his lead much farther than normal between points of pro, risking much longer leader falls.)

"Alex didn't like to use little stoppers" (the smaller styles of nuts for protection). "He said, 'I don't need this shit.' Then he'd get to a place where there were only tiny cracks, and he'd say, 'Wow, nothing else fits.'

"Alex had been living in this Yosemite bubble, where you don't need to learn all the tricks of mountaineering."

Despite those quirks, on Kinabalu, Synnott admits admiringly, "Alex did some pretty sick stuff"—long, highly technical leads with a minimum of protection.

The deft, amusing piece that Synnott wrote for the March 2010 issue of *Men's Journal* opens with a scene at the base of the wall in which a priceless bit of repartee evokes the "Yosemite bubble."

"Where's your helmet?"

"Uh, I don't have one," Alex replies, looking me square in the eyes and without apology.

"What do you mean? You forgot it back in camp?"

Before I finish my question, I know the answer.

"Uh, no. I mean I didn't bring one on the trip."

"Intentionally?"

"Sort of."

But when Alex leads the terrifying, almost unprotected crux pitch of the long climb, before the two men settle in to bivouac on a suspended platform called a portaledge, Synnott hails the prodigy's accomplishment.

Two hours later he reached the shelter of a small roof, 150 feet above me. It was, hands down, one of the best leads I'd ever witnessed. . . .

[Conrad] Anker was right. I was learning things from Honnold. . . . He brought something to the expedition none of us anticipated. Every jaw-dropping lunge, every inhuman pull, even every rookie mistake—it all rekindled the fire that we had back when we were his age. And it showed me, at least, that the fire was still there. Later, as we settled into our sleeping bags in the porta-ledge, Honnold needed to get something off his chest. "You know, I'm kind of feeling like a pansy," he confessed. "How so?" I replied. "You just did the sickest lead I've ever seen." "I know," he replied, "but it scared me. I shouldn't have gotten so scared."

Conrad Anker was one of my first mentors. I'd always admired the guy, not only for his great climbs such as the Shark's Fin on Meru Peak in the Garhwal Himalaya and his first ascents with Alex Lowe of wild-looking towers in Queen Maud Land in Antarctica, but also because of the way he lives his life. Conrad calls himself a Buddhist, and he constantly preaches and practices kindness to others and doing good for the planet. The school in the Khumbu Valley he started years ago to train Sherpas in technical climbing is a prime example of Conrad's altruistic service to others.

And it was Conrad who convinced The North Face to sponsor me, which really improved my climbing opportunities. So even though I knew almost nothing about Borneo, I was psyched to be invited by Mark Synnott to go along on the Kinabalu expedition.

All six of us got along well during that trip, and it's true that Mark and I hit it off from the start. But it was a really long expedition—a full month from April 2 to May 1, 2009. I was used to getting things done a lot faster—one-day ascents of big walls in the Valley, for instance. There were times during the trip when our sluggish progress nearly drove me crazy. After five days in Low's Gully, we'd gotten nowhere on the wall. I kept saying to myself, Why is this taking so long?

The "quirky little things" that got between Mark and me had as much to do with our difference in age as with our climbing styles. Like when Mark tried to take apart my rack—that just sent me off the deep end. I liked to think I knew how to handle my own cams and biners.

As for skipping pieces rather than building up rope drag, I do that all the time. It just depends on whether the terrain is dangerous or not. And Mark's I-told-you-so about the stoppers isn't the way I remember it. On the whole route, I doubt that I placed a single nut, because the wall was one pitch after another of overhanging granite. He was just too old-school for my taste.

For instance, Mark led one pitch of pure choss—crumbly rock, loose holds everywhere. It was about 5.7, but Mark aided it. He even drilled a bolt. He took forever to lead the pitch. I said to him, "Dude, it's just five-seven. Why don't you just climb it? It's not really dangerous if you tread lightly." But he was going, "Oh, man, this is really sketchy!" Once he got his anchor in, I toproped the pitch in about three and a half minutes.

Mark later took me to task for an awkward moment when he wanted Jimmy Chin to shoot some film in which I would talk about what it was like to have Conrad as a mentor. I balked. Mark

thought this meant that I wasn't open to being taught by my teammates. But back then, it was a lot harder for me to perform in
front of the camera, especially with all the guys standing around,
including Conrad. It felt like, "Okay, Alex, talk about this. Dance,
monkey!" So I'd have to start dancing.

There was a slightly weird dynamic going on among us as a
team. I knew going into the trip that none of the other guys was
as good a rock climber as I was. But they were all badass mountaineers, and I figured I'd be learning a bunch of stuff from them.
Halfway through, though, I just felt, This isn't the way we should
be doing this climb.

The big problem on Kinabalu is rain. We'd been climbing low
on the wall for about a week before we committed to the full thrust,
leaving our base camp behind. On only the second day on that
push, a huge squall came over the mountain from the north. Mark
and I settled in to the portaledge, while Conrad tried to push the
route above. In his Men's Journal article, Mark played this up as
do-or-die drama—which is what the magazines want:

> Massive waterfalls were now pouring off the cliff, and the gully
> below started to roar as it transformed into a raging rapid. Even if
> we had wanted to bail, there was no way out but up. Above, I could
> hear muffled yelling, followed by an alarming amount of rockfall.
> Anker was somewhere above us doing battle in the chaos.

The truth of the matter, though, was that the Kinabalu climb
just wasn't that rad. I felt that we could always have rapped off the
route if we had to, and by 2009, Low's Gully didn't figure anymore
as the hellish abyss that had trapped the British army guys fifteen
years earlier. Still, we spent twenty-four hours on the portaledge
getting soaked. Since Jimmy Chin and Mark took up all the space
on the portaledge, as the rookie I got the shitty seat. I had to sling

a hammock beneath the portaledge, suspended from its corners, which made for a very awkward body position. The water dripped through the floor of the portaledge onto my hammock and sleeping bag. I sort of sat in a puddle for a whole day and night. It was all right as long as I didn't move and stir up the water. I was reading The Brothers Karamazov, which fit the dreary mood. I tore the paperback in half and gave Mark the first part to read. Pretty grim, but I guess it builds character.

The weather cleared off enough so that we could finish the climb the next day. The last pitches were actually easy. After a brief celebration on the summit, we rapped the whole wall with our bags and hauled them back out the other side of Low's Gully. It was an ordeal. I think the reason we did this is because we didn't want to haul everything to the top of the wall. We just left it all in the middle and then lowered it to the ground in one huge lower.

In the Men's Journal article, Mark wrote some really nice things about me, even if they were still tinged with paternalism.

> Sharing a rope with Honnold had made me think a lot about what I was like when I was his age, and I couldn't help but draw comparisons to myself. I was never close to as talented as he is, nor was I as bold, but I did have a youthful hunger and my tolerance for risk was more than a little excessive. Honnold reminded me that climbing without risk isn't really climbing at all.

And he ended the piece with this summit vignette:

> Looking over at Honnold, I couldn't help but wonder if he understood the arc that we all seem to follow as climbers any better after hanging out with a bunch of old-timers, if he understood that he would have to ultimately accept the fact that if you're going to climb as hard as he does now his whole life, and live to tell the tales,

he was going to need a little bit of luck. These days I've got kids
waiting for me to return from expeditions like these, and there's a
line I just don't cross anymore. The problem is figuring out where
that line is at any given moment. Honnold is one of the brightest
and most talented climbers I've ever met. If nothing else, I think he
knows that climbing is the kind of sport that will sort you out, one
way or another.

After the expedition was over, for all my impatience with the old-school style the other guys seemed to think the route required, I realized that I owed a lot to Mark. He was probably right about my "Yosemite bubble." In Borneo, I realized that climbing in remote ranges did entail all kinds of techniques I hadn't had to learn on Half Dome or El Cap.

Mark had truly broadened my climbing experience. His whole thing—exploring, traveling the world, having adventures in exotic places—was new to me, and exciting.

Because, when all was said and done, we'd forged a good friendship. Mark invited me on his next media- and sponsor-supported junket, a truly exploratory climbing trip to an untouched desert landscape full of weird pinnacles and arches in northeastern Chad, in Africa. The trip was planned for November 2010. Without a moment's hesitation, I signed on.

• • • •

Mark had discovered the Ennedi Desert by staring hard at satellite photos. On a previous expedition to Cameroon, he started wondering about the climbing possibilities in Chad, which borders Cameroon on the northeast. Civil war in the Sudan had provoked a refugee crisis in Chad, making it an inhospitable country for Westerners to visit, but Mark loves that sort of challenge. He knew that expeditions had been active in the Tibesti Mountains, near the northern border of Chad, but the much more remote Ennedi seemed untouched by climbers. And the satellite photos made it clear that the rock formations there were spectacular.

For his team, Mark put together two threesomes. What he called his "media team," whose main mission was to film and photograph (even though all three were good climbers), consisted of Jimmy Chin, Renan Ozturk, and Tim Kemple. The "climbing team" was Mark, James Pearson, and myself. James is a Brit who'd made quite a splash on the gritstone crags of his native country, then had taken his act abroad. He was about the same age as me. I'd climbed with James for a day or two in the U.K., but I didn't really know him. I sensed, though, that his outlook on climbing matched mine a lot better than the more old-school mountaineers I'd gone to Borneo with. By 2010, like me, he was sponsored by The North Face.

Sparsely inhabited today, the Ennedi had once been a thriving homeland to seminomadic pastoralists who herded everything from goats and cattle to camels. The vivid rock art of the region—pictographs painted in red, white, brown, and black—was first discovered in the 1930s. The human figures abound in archers leaping and dancing as they carry their bows. By now, archaeologists have been able to use the rock art to date and define a series of cultures ranging back all the way to 5000 BC.

We arrived in N'Djamena, Chad's capital, in mid-November. One thing Mark is really good at is arranging logistics in developing countries. For our excursion, he'd recruited an Italian expat named Piero Rava, who at the age of sixty-six ran a trekking company taking foreigners on ambitious photo tours of places like the Ennedi. Piero was a veteran mountaineer himself, having participated in a bold Italian expedition to Cerro Torre in Patagonia in 1970. An amazing spire of granite and ice, Cerro Torre had once earned the reputation as "the world's most difficult mountain." Another Italian, Cesare Maestri, claimed to have reached the summit in 1959, only to have his partner, the Austrian Toni Egger, die on the descent when he was avalanched off the wall. Other climbers doubted the ascent, and it is now generally regarded as a complete hoax, with Maestri and Egger getting nowhere near the top.

The Italian team in 1970 got to within 200 meters of the summit. Had they succeeded, they would have claimed the true first ascent, which was finally pulled off four years later by a team led by Casimiro Ferrari, who had been Piero's teammate in 1970. It was cool to have a Cerro Torre veteran leading our expedition, and even cooler to know that Piero had fifteen years' experience in taking trekkers to the Ennedi. He had checked out lines on the arches and pinnacles, but he hadn't climbed anything, and he assured us that no other climbers had touched the rock there.

Piero spoke almost no English but good French. So I ended up translating for the crew in the jeep. The whole process was kind of fun.

Borneo had been my first taste of a true Third World adventure, but Chad was far more intense. And the impact on me of those three weeks in Africa would be life-changing, in ways I never could have foreseen.

We set off from N'Djamena in a Land Rover and a pair of Toyota Land Cruisers. The Ennedi was 625 miles away as the crow flies, but a lot farther as we ended up traveling. In an essay about the trip, Mark later captured the surreal flavor of our drive:

> We had been traveling Chad's only paved road for less than an hour when Piero suddenly veered off into the sand. I assumed we were stopping, but Piero just pointed the vehicle northeast and kept going—for the next four days.
>
> Sometimes we followed rutted tracks in the sand, while other times it seemed like we were driving across areas that had never

*seen a vehicle. In the softer sand, the only way we could maintain
headway was to drive at 60 mph, with the vehicle skimming pre-
cariously at the limit of control. When we stopped to camp at night,
our Chadian mechanic would work on the vehicles, cleaning out air
filters and sometimes replacing or repairing various engine parts.*

*We put in long, grueling days of four-wheeling, sometimes going
from sunup to sundown seeing nothing but flat sand. The key was
to spend as much time as possible in Piero's lead vehicle, because
in the following vehicles you lived in a cloud of dust, which worked
its way into every orifice of your body. It was the beginning of the
Chadian winter, and the temperature hovered in the 90s during the
day. In summer, Piero explained, it got up to 140°F.*

The other guys tended to space out or try to sleep during this
endless, monotonous journey, but I was transfixed. With my face
glued to the window, I stared out at the emptiness, watching for any
change in the horizon. On our second day in the sand, we had an
encounter that turned into a minor epiphany for me.

Suddenly I saw two men riding camels in the desert ahead
of us. Piero slowed down for them and stopped a short distance
away. In retrospect, I wonder if he was stopping only because he
was used to his tourists wanting to take pictures of such things,
or if he was truly stopping out of courtesy to interact with them,
the way hikers do when they're out in the backcountry. Regardless, we piled out of the jeeps and approached the nomads, one
of whom dismounted and poured us a large bowl of camel milk.
Piero explained that nomads will always offer you something as
hospitality, even though they don't have much for themselves. We
declined his offer, taking a few pictures instead. Piero gave the
two men the leftovers from our breakfast, explaining to us that it
was normal for them to travel for days without any real food. They
mounted their camels and continued into the desert.

Later I asked Piero how those nomads could navigate so accurately in the desert, especially when the stakes were so high. A slight mistake in bearing would mean missing the next well and dying of dehydration in the middle of nowhere. Piero explained that they use the sun and the direction of the wind, which is constant in the winter, to navigate. When I protested that it seemed like too serious a situation to rely only on the sun and wind, Piero drew an analogy to climbing. Sometimes you find yourself in positions where falling would mean death. So you don't fall. It helped me understand. The nomads just don't make mistakes.

Occasionally, when we passed a small oasis, we'd run into native people, small clusters of men, women, and children living in mud huts or thatched dwellings. These were Toubous, so unused to seeing strangers—especially white-skinned Westerners—that Piero warned us not to approach them or take photographs of them.

Still, I stared in fascination at these seminomadic desert dwellers. And here I had another, more lasting epiphany. After the trip was over, it wasn't the climbing that stuck foremost in my memory. It was the days of driving across the desert to and from the Ennedi. My lasting impressions were of kids beating donkeys to make them haul water faster, or of men riding camels through the middle of nowhere, or of other men working all day to turn mud into bricks. I was seeing a completely different way of life from any I'd ever witnessed before, in a completely alien place. The simple facts of Chadian life—what it takes to survive in that kind of climate with nothing but a hut and some animals—stunned me.

And this made me realize, perhaps for the first time, how easy my life was compared to those of people in less privileged societies. That insight would lead me, a few years later, to redirect my goals toward something other than climbing. It took a while to sink in, but that was the epiphany.

Toward the end of the fourth day, we spied some rocks in the distance. We hadn't seen so much as a hill since leaving N'Djamena. Anticipation ran high. All of us were thinking, Will the rock be any good? When we got close enough, we piled out of the vehicles and literally ran over to the nearest formations.

We knew from Piero that the pinnacles and arches were made of sandstone. But would it be the sharp, clean sandstone of Nevada's Red Rocks, or chossy stuff like the Fisher Towers in Utah?

To our dismay, we discovered that the sandstone in the Ennedi ranged from terrible rock to truly atrocious, abominable rock. It was all bad. No matter what, however, the Ennedi was a photographer's and filmmaker's paradise, and the "media team" got images and footage like you see nowhere else in the world.

Our first major objective was a 200-foot-tall spire that we called the Citadel. As Mark described it, the tower was "shaped like a giant boxcar standing on end, featuring four distinct arêtes, one of which appeared to have decent holds. A rotten overhang guarded the bottom, but sported a crack that looked doable."

James Pearson was psyched to lead it. (I thought it looked like a death route.) He tied in and started up as Mark belayed, with the media team in rapt attention. I didn't want to just sit around and watch someone else climb—I hadn't come halfway around the world and four days across the desert just to spectate—so I wandered off and started soloing up a random nearby tower.

Before this trip, Tim, Jimmy, and Renan had seen me solo a little bit on solid rock, but Mark and James had never watched me solo at all. I think what I was doing now freaked them out a bit.

A CHARACTERISTIC HONNOLD understatement. In his essay about the Chad trip, Synnott wrote,

I heard a noise behind me and saw Honnold emerging, ropeless, from a bombay chimney 40 feet up a nearby tower. Above him rose an overhanging fist crack into which he set some jams, then swung his feet out of the chimney. Flowing like a snake up the rock, he was soon manteling over the lip. He built a small cairn and then down-soloed the tower via an overhanging face. On his way down, he broke off several hand and footholds, and I was barely able to watch. He later admitted that the downclimb had been a little more than he'd bargained for.

According to Synnott, Alex made some six solo first ascents of untouched routes during the time it took Pearson, climbing brilliantly, to get to the top of the Citadel.

Interviewed after the team's return from Chad, Jimmy Chin reported that when Alex was soloing, "It got so that we couldn't watch. And we also didn't want him to know we were watching, because we didn't want to give him any extra motivation to push it."

Several days after the Citadel climb, Alex started up—tied in, effectively toproping—on a beautiful sandstone arch. In his article, Synnott played this exploit up as zany hijinks:

We ended up one day sitting below a 100-foot-tall arch with a 180-degree rainbow offwidth crack splitting the underside of the formation. I had zero interest in climbing this heinous fissure, but Honnold was psyched. . . .

Ten feet off the ground, Honnold lunged for a basketball-sized hold that promptly exploded in his face, sending him winging across the arch. Once the route had spit him off, you could see in Honnold's face that it was "game on."

He jumped back on and for more than [an] hour, battled his way up, across, and then down the other side of the offwidth. He shuffled across the horizontal section by hanging upside down by

foot cams. "That was the most disgusting route of my life," Honnold exclaimed, panting, his body covered in dust and bat piss,
but with a huge grin on his face. He looked happier than I'd seen
him all trip.

Yet four years later, Synnott looked back on Alex's free soloing in Chad with lingering misgivings, verging on disapproval. "In
Chad," he says, "Alex was cavalier about risk. Over-confident. On
that first tower, what he was doing was just plain mind-numbing. As
he down-climbed, he broke loose three of his four holds, so he was
dangling by one arm.

"'What was that all about?' I asked him when he got down. He
didn't answer. He wouldn't cop to it.

"As far as I can tell, Alex came very close to falling off in the
Ennedi."

Yeah, I've heard those guys' comments, but only second-
hand. I think one thing that freaked them a little was the assump-
tion that if you're going to free solo, you should do it on routes
you've climbed before, even carefully rehearsed, so that there are
no unwelcome surprises. As I had on Moonlight Buttress. To free
solo rock that you've never touched before—a lot of it chossy and
loose—might seem too out there.

But what I was soloing in Chad wasn't that hard—maybe 5.7.
As for breaking off holds as I downclimbed that first tower, Mark's
got it wrong. Yes, it was an overhanging wall, and I was hanging
from two 5.5 mud jugs. Both my footholds broke off, but it wasn't
hard to hang on, and I definitely wasn't dangling by one arm.

On a route called Royal Arches in Yosemite, I once pulled off
a big hold on a 5.5 pitch I was soloing. My body swung backward,

but I was able to grab the hold, shove it back in place, and recover. It was scary, but it was like magic. On 5.5, it's easy to have magic. On 5.11, it's not as magical.

We climbed for ten days in the Ennedi. The poor quality of the sandstone meant that bolts, and, for that matter, any of our gear, wouldn't really hold, which added a lot to the adventure of the climbing. Mark and James had real fears about ripping all the pro on a pitch, including the anchors. I found myself retreating off as many lines as I finished, though it didn't matter as much because it's easier to bail when soloing.

In the end, as I mentioned, it wasn't the climbing that made the trip so memorable. It was having an adventure in a completely alien landscape, and witnessing a way of life that would have been unimaginable to me beforehand. In Chad, I saw extreme poverty for the first time. It was hard for me to imagine living your whole life and never touching anything but sand. What we saw there were people surviving in a full-on Stone Age culture.

The trip coincided with a time when my own life was getting easier, thanks to sponsorship and recognition. Nowadays I can film a two-day commercial and make more money than those people in Chad make in their whole lives. That's fucked up. And that discrepancy ultimately forced me to examine how I ought to live my own life, and what I could do for others who were less fortunate.

B Y THE TIME ALEX WENT to Chad, in November 2010, he and Stacey were back together. But there would be subsequent breakups in their future. Looking back in 2014, Alex commented, "I find it really hard to see six months into the future, let alone a year or more. Stacey complains that that makes it hard for us to talk about our future together. She wants to know where we might live, or whether she should continue to work as a nurse, or just live with me on the road.

"We've talked about having children. I sort of joke that I'd like to have grandkids some day, but the thought of raising an infant seems heinous. Probably has something to do with my own childhood, but I don't really want to go there.

"It bugs Stacey when I joke about dying. I might say something like, 'You better appreciate me now, because I may not be around very long.' I'm just goofing around, but Stacey hates it. I know that she believes that I won't fall off soloing. She has faith in my ability and judgment.

"Some of our breakups got triggered by my feeling that I needed to be alone, that a relationship interfered with my climbing. When I told her that, she got really mad. She told me bluntly, 'Okay, it's over. Don't talk to me. Don't even try to contact me.'

"Then a few weeks or even months go by, and I realize I miss Stacey. I'll get all sheepish and call her up. 'I know you didn't want me to contact you,' I'll say, 'but couldn't we meet just to talk? Maybe have lunch?' She gives in, because I insist that I've learned more about myself and have realized that Stacey does have a positive impact on my life. And after all, we really do love each other."

In an unguarded moment, Alex admitted, "I think Stacey has had a lot to do with humanizing me." What spurred that insight was a playback in 2014 of some comments that Alex made to this writer [David Roberts] in 2010, when I interviewed him for a profile published in the May 2011 issue of *Outside* magazine.

An example. In 2010, Alex referred to having to go to North Carolina for a North Face appearance as "a gong show." He added, "I see all this stuff as media b.-s." An upcoming appearance as the featured speaker at the Banff Mountain Film and Book Festival was "full-on b.-s. I mean it's okay, but it's time I can't spend climbing."

"You want this on the record?" I asked.

"Why not?"

"How are your Banff hosts going to react if they read that comment?"

Alex shrugged. "I just say what I feel. Maybe it'll come back to bite me in the ass someday, and then I'll just stop talking to people."

Other comments in 2010 sounded like nonchalant bragging. "Yeah," said Alex, "I crushed high school. I took a test once, and they said I was a genius."

Yet others sounded like cruel putdowns, as when Alex dismissed one of America's leading female rock climbers as "a bit of a puss," because she'd had to ask her partner to overprotect a scary traverse she was seconding. About this high-profile climber, Alex added dismissively, "She hasn't done anything I couldn't do."

In 2010, Chris Weidner, one of Alex's best friends, complained, "When we started climbing together, he was very polite, very safety-conscious. Now, he's more likely to bad-mouth you. About a year ago, I was trying to lead this pitch, and I kept falling off. Alex said, 'Dude, what's your fucking problem? It's only five-thirteen.' He may have been joshing, but it hurt my feelings. He's got a certain attitude now, like, unless you're a world-class climber, you suck.

"I finally said, 'Hey, give me a break. I'm trying as hard as I can.' He may have realized he was hurting my feelings, but he just doesn't want to deal with it."

When I reminded Alex of these comments in 2014, he was abashed. "That's not me anymore," he insisted. "I think back then I was pretty aggro. I thought I had something to prove."

By 2015, Alex Honnold evidently has little still to prove. Yet his intensity shows no signs of ebbing. Something still drives him to a kind of perfection on rock—and recently, on snow and ice—that goes beyond the frontiers established by his boldest predecessors.

No matter what the difference in our styles and approaches—old-school versus new-school, mountaineer versus rock climber—Mark Synnott and I always got along well. Today I consider him one of my mentors, as well as one of the teammates I'm most indebted to. After Chad, I signed up for yet another Synnott trip sponsored by The North Face and Men's Journal. This time, in July 2011, we headed off for Devil's Bay on the south coast of Newfoundland, where big granite cliffs rise straight out of the ocean. We hoped to put up some good new routes there and document everything with camera and film.

Two others of our gang from the Chad expedition—James Pearson and Tim Kemple—were returning, and it was good to renew our friendship in Canada. The other three were Jim Surette, Matt Irving, and Hazel Findlay. I'd climbed a bit here and there with Hazel and Matt but had never met Jim, though Mark spoke highly of him. Hazel is a really strong British chick who evolved from gym climbing (six times British junior champion in indoor competitions) to become—a rare thing for women—a very strong trad leader on dangerous runout routes. Sender Films would make a beguiling film about her called Spice Girl, and I would later climb with Hazel in South Africa for another film, called Africa Fusion, released in 2015.

The only problem with the Newfoundland expedition was that the weather didn't cooperate. It turned out to be a miserable washout. To kill the downtime, I jotted down notes almost like I was writing a diary. Some entries:

> It's been raining on and off for 10 days and everything in my small tent is getting a little damp. Though I'm the lucky one on the trip, everyone else on the team had their tents either destroyed or damaged in last night's freakishly strong wind storm. . . . So far we've

climbed one route and sat in the rain and brooded. Well, to be honest, I'm brooding and everyone else is drinking a lot and making the best of it.

Before coming on this trip I felt like I was in great shape, climbing my first traditional 8b+ [5.14a] and a few other hard sport routes. I was fresh off a good season in Yosemite in which I'd soloed some things I was proud of. . . . Things should have been going great for me, and yet all I could think about while I festered in my damp tent was that my fitness was slipping away and that I was wasting my time. I could be anywhere else in the world, climbing every day. Instead, here I was in a tent, in the rain, depressed out of my mind.

I try to make the best of it and go for hikes despite the constant rain, just because the landscape is so beautiful. But then days of whiteout fog descend and it seems too dangerous to go wandering away from camp. I'm locked in my tent with nothing to do but read and do pushups.

We spend most of the time in the communal mess tent telling stories and bantering. Not that there's anything in particular to say after a week of rain, yet Mark has a distinctly entertaining way of telling stories, even if I have heard them all at least twice before. In many ways our trip to Newfoundland is what people who work normal jobs do for vacation: go somewhere exotic with a group of friends and then hang out all day eating and drinking.

Several years later, looking back on our Newfoundland trip, Mark insisted that the expedition had been a success. He thought that we'd made a good short film by making "raininess" the central theme. It was titled Tent Bound in Devil's Bay.

Mark told other people that the rest of the guys had a running joke about me. That I would just sit in the group tent, muttering,

"This is the grimmest place on earth." Mark even called me a sort of Debbie Downer, almost a whiner. He thought I damaged the group's morale. He also thought that a route the team free climbed, called Leviathan, was "awesome."

Well, sorry, Mark, but that's not how I remember Devil's Bay. Tent Bound is a horrible little film, because the guys didn't have anything to work with. There was no story. James Pearson and I free climbed a route called Lucifer's Lighthouse, which was the hardest thing on the wall. But the whole trip was grim. Not just because of the rain. If you were in Patagonia, it'd be worth waiting out the weather, just to get a chance to climb on some of the most epic peaks on earth. But I'd just come from the Valley, and I was losing my fitness day after day. And this place sucked. Wet, slabby granite, not featured, not that tall . . . worse than the stuff in Tuolumne. I could have been doing this kind of climbing in Tuolumne and eating pizza every afternoon. Newfoundland just wasn't rad. It wasn't the future.

As for me being Debbie Downer, well, that's not entirely fair. Everybody was bummed and bored. I went on hikes, but then we'd get those impossible whiteouts. You could get lost in the fog. It was hard to find the latrine, a hundred feet from camp.

I was, I'll admit, the most vocal member of our crew, saying early on, "We should just leave."

But I don't hold any of this against Mark. Every trip I've gone on with him has been a life experience. I always learn something.

• • • •

Between my trips to Chad and Newfoundland, in the winter of 2010–11, I embarked on what I half-jokingly called my Sport Climbing Tour of the Antiquities. From Africa I went straight to Israel, then Jordan, then Turkey, then Greece. In Israel and Jordan, I stayed with a friend. Stacey joined me for Turkey and Greece.

It wasn't a true tourist vacation. I did all the hardest routes in Israel, and all the hardest routes at Geyikbayiri in Turkey. At Kalymnos in Greece, where the climbing is terrific, I got shut down somewhat because it had rained so much the limestone cliffs were seeping.

As for the antiquities, I actually read some books about the histories of the countries where I was climbing. I did all kinds of cultural stuff. Got a pretty legit taste of the past. Saw a lot of old things. Saw a lot of people in funny dress.

A trip like that serves as a kind of filler-in between real climbing adventures. I traveled, climbed, tried new things, learned new stuff, all while I was preparing for something big. Two thousand eleven, like 2009, was what I call a year of consolidation.

In Alex Lowther's profile of me for Alpinist (summer 2011), he writes about the pressure on me to keep upping the ante. He paraphrases the public's response to my big free solos: "What's next? Give us more!" And he adds,

Expectations can be dangerous, and they only become more so when what you are famous for is risking your life.

If he's not careful, we could admire Alex Honnold to death.

That's a fair concern, but it's not like I haven't dealt with this pressure ever since folks started noticing what I was doing. The pressure only nudges me if it's about a project I want to do anyway. Actually, a bigger motivator than any media attention would be a hot chick at the base of a wall who I could impress. Though she probably couldn't tell the difference between 5.10 and 5.13. But no matter how hot the chick is, say if I was standing at the base of El Cap, and she urged me to free solo some route, my answer would be "No way."

For example, I can't tell you how many people over the years

*have pressured me to drink alcohol. We'll be at a party, and some-
body will taunt me, "Alex, just try this beer, it's not gonna hurt you
to take a sip." I've never given in. Booze doesn't interest me.*

*Most of the media attention that has come my way so far has
been focused on my free solos. But that's not the only kind of
climbing that compels me. Just as rad, in my book, are the big-wall
linkups I've attempted, especially in Yosemite. And 2012 would be
another watershed year for me, as I went after speed climbs on the
big walls and linkups, both with partners and solo, of some of the
most epic routes in North America.*

CHAPTER **FIVE**
TRIPLE PLAY

Borneo, Chad, and even *Newfoundland were novel experiences for me, but throughout my still relatively short climbing career, I keep coming back to the Valley when I want to push myself. Because of the sheer scale and difficulty of its soaring, clean granite walls, Yosemite offers almost limitless challenges to today's best climbers—as it will, I'm sure, to the stars of the next generation. No one, for example, has yet attempted a free solo of any of the routes on El Capitan.*

One of the great landmarks in Valley history came in 1975, when three of the Stonemasters—Jim Bridwell, John Long, and Billy Westbay—pulled off the first one-day ascent of the Nose. The first route ever climbed on El Cap, the Nose was put up in 1958 in a monstrous siege effort stretching over forty-seven days by the legendary Warren Harding and a series of teammates. Bridwell, Long, and Westbay, climbing mostly free, surged up the route in about sixteen hours. There's a famous photo of the trio shot in the meadow below El Cap after the climb. To get the wall as well as the climbers in the frame, the photographer has hunkered down to the level of the guys' knees. Because of that angle, they seem to exude cockiness—gods sneering down on mere mortals. Cigarettes dangle from Bridwell's and Long's mouths. They're dressed like hippies, in loose-fitting vests and shirts, but they could just as well pass for Hell's Angels.

By the time I first hit the Valley, almost thirty years after that landmark ascent, climbing the Nose in a single day was still a pretty big deal. In 2010, I managed to do that three times, paired with Ueli Steck. We'd talked about trying to go for the speed record, which was then held by Hans Florine and Yuji Hirayama, at an amazing 2:37:05—yes, just a little over two and a half hours. But things didn't quite work out.

Instead, in early June 2010, I took a big step upward when I soloed the Nose, also in a single day.

As I mentioned above, no one has yet even attempted to free solo a route on El Cap. But there are other kinds of soloing that aren't quite so extreme. The distinctions may seem arcane to nonclimbers, but they're huge for those of us who go after big walls.

Rope soloing is a process in which you belay yourself, usually by tying one end of the rope to an anchor, the other end to your harness, then leading more or less conventionally, placing pro or clipping fixed gear as you go. Instead of a belayer to catch your fall, you minimize the potential plunge by using one of several different devices. I generally use a grigri, the same autolocking belay device that I use to catch a friend at the sport crag or gym, though in this case I'm using it to catch myself.

The trouble with rope soloing is that it's extremely tedious. You have to negotiate each pitch three times to make progress—leading it with pro, rappelling to "clean" (retrieve) the pro, then "jugging" back up the rope (climbing the line itself with ascenders, metal devices that grip the rope under a downward pull but slide *easily upward*). Way back in 1971, Peter Haan climbed the Salathé route on El Cap—along with the Nose, one of its two most storied lines—in a monumental rope-soloing effort spread across six days. Haan used some kind of combination of prusik knot and Jumar (then the most popular ascender) to belay himself. What's pretty amazing is that he had never done a big wall before. I don't know Haan, but I can appreciate how rad his exploit seemed in its day.

In 2010, when I soloed the Nose, I carried a thin sixty-meter rope in my pack only because I knew there were a few pitches that I'd have to rope solo. They included the King Swing, a massive pendulum that allows you to escape from the apparent dead end of the Boot Flake. I lowered myself from my anchor a hundred feet, then started running and scrabbling sideways across blank granite, so that I could build up longer and longer swings. Finally I was able to grab the edge of a crack far to the left that leads to the crack system that continues the route. It's quite a daunting maneuver to pull off solo. The King Swing is like the biggest pendulum in climbing. At least it's the biggest one I've ever done.

It was a tough trade-off to burden myself with the weight of a sixty-meter rope that I'd use only a few times on the Nose, but I doubt that I could have gotten up the route without it. Most of the time, what I was doing was daisy soloing.

A daisy chain is a loop of nylon webbing, a little longer than an arm's reach, that's sewn into as many as a dozen regularly spaced miniloops. You keep one end firmly attached to your harness, then you clip whichever miniloop is at the right length to a cam or nut you've placed or a piton or bolt that's already in place. Then you can hang safely on aid from the gear, or just use it as a handhold to get past a tricky move. I carried two daisies, so that I could alternate clips without ever interrupting the security of my static connection to good pro. On the very hardest aid pitches on the Nose, like the crux of a big overhang called the Great Roof (rated

5.13d), I used the daisies to hang from either cams I placed or fixed gear—some of it pretty old and nearly worthless.

During most of the climb on the Nose, however—all but the very hardest passages—I was truly free soloing. The transition from daisy soloing to free is scary. I have to constantly remind myself, Now I'm safe. Now I'm not. It's tough mentally. But you never forget, never think you're clipped to pro when you're actually attached to nothing. You're fully aware during those long stretches when only your hands and feet finding the right holds keep you from taking the big plunge.

Even though by 2010 I'd already free soloed Half Dome and Moonlight Buttress, the feats that seemed to put me on the climbing map, this daisy solo of the Nose felt like a big deal for me. I was proud of how efficiently I climbed, too, since the whole ascent took me only five hours and fifty minutes.

Still, I had even grander ambitions for Yosemite that season.

• • • •

When I was still a young gym rat in Sacramento, I saw a film called Masters of Stone 5. One episode covered the daisy-solo linkup by Dean Potter of the Nose on El Cap and the Regular Northwest Face on Half Dome in a single day—Potter's elapsed time was twenty-three hours and twenty-three minutes. I thought, That is fucking cool. Just the idea of climbing two big walls in a single day filled me with awe.

Dean has since become a friend of mine, but back then he was a role model and an idol, both for his speed climbs and his audacious free solos. He's thirteen years older than me. We've bouldered together a few times but never gotten to climb anything big. Unfortunately, the media have tried to paint us as rivals, with him as the aging guru being challenged by me, the young upstart.

Anyway, after climbing the Nose with Ueli Steck in May and June 2010, I had the moves pretty well dialed. And I thought the Regular Northwest Face on Half Dome should be pretty mellow if I used daisies to protect myself at the hard parts—the sequences that had scared me two years earlier, when I'd free soloed the route.

Late on June 21, I headed up the long approach to the base of Half Dome, planning to bivouac there and get started at first light. Somehow, though, I mistimed the sunrise, waking up at 4:45 a.m. and having to sit around waiting for the lights to come on. I had a minimal rack and a thirty-foot line that I use to tow my van, which I figured could work for the Robbins Traverse—the only time I expected to use a rope.

Once it got light, I scrambled up the huge snow cone at the base of the wall—still there in June, courtesy of an unusually heavy winter. Halfway up the first pitch, I changed into climbing shoes and switched to rock-climbing mode, after tossing down my jacket and headlamp. I had a small pack with my shoes, food, and water, figuring it was important for me to stay well fed and hydrated since I was going to have a long day.

The climbing itself was pretty uneventful. It felt mostly moderate, compared to my free solo two years before—especially since I used the bolt ladders to avoid the hard free climbing, the same bolt ladders I'd had to detour around in 2008 to keep my free solo pure. Farther up, I climbed the chimneys with my pack hanging down below me on a daisy. The only time I really had to pay attention was on the Zig-Zags, where I climbed with two pieces clipped to my daisies on all the hard parts. As it turned out, I never used my thirty-foot towline.

The final slab, which had been quite stressful for me free soloing two years before, felt totally casual. Instead of insecure friction moves on almost invisible footholds, I could just pull on the bolts and swing between them on my daisies when need be. It was an entirely different experience.

I topped out among a handful of hikers. It was about 7:00 a.m. and the summit was still quite peaceful, a pleasant change from the usual gong show. I savored my climb for a few minutes while eating some food, then started my descent.

I'd timed the climb at two hours and nine minutes, which made it a new solo speed record for the route. It's sort of funny, but I can convince myself that speed for its own sake isn't a high priority for me. On Thank God Ledge, for instance, I wasted ten minutes trying to "booty" a brand-new #4 Camalot that somebody had recently gotten stuck in a crack. Just the day before, I'd learned a trick about hitting the individual lobes a certain way and walking cams around. I wanted to make it work. But after a while I gave up. For all I know, the Camalot is still there.

On the way down from Half Dome, I stopped to look at two amazing birds. I hate to have to hurry. The whole timing thing, I've claimed in print, is not a strong point for me.

Yet if that were really true, why did I time my ascent? Why was it important for me—not only on that day, but on many climbs thereafter—to go after speed records? I suppose it all comes back to purism. A speed record on a big wall is the ultimate validation that I've climbed as efficiently as I know how. It's consistent with my philosophy of life, my emphasis on simplicity, on paring away extraneous stuff. I also like speed records because they give a baseline for improvement. It's nice to know that I can improve on a route. It's gratifying to find that I can go faster.

From the summit of Half Dome, I hustled down to Mirror Lake, where I'd stashed a bike, then rode it back to my van. I reached El Cap Meadow around 10:00 a.m. There I spent some time reracking and trying to eat and drink. I didn't really know what I would need on the Nose, so I went a little heavy on gear: pretty much a double rack of cams. I had a skinny rope that I'd borrowed from a friend, something like an 8.5 millimeter. I figured it would be enough for my purposes. I wasn't planning on whipping huge on it.

All told, my gear weighed more than I would have liked. I hadn't really thought about it beforehand, but the problem with soloing is that you carry everything, all the time. Climbing with a partner, normally you burn off the rack as you go, so by the end of the pitch you only have a little left. And conversely, the rope weighs nothing at the beginning of a pitch. But when you're daisy soloing, you have the whole weight of everything on you all the time.

At the foot of the Nose, there were a bunch of parties converging from different directions. Some Frenchmen who were hauling bags, some Russians who were only hoping to climb to Sickle Ledge (a mere four pitches up) to check it out, some Americans who were at the very bottom and said they were taking up a lot of beer. I was a little weirded out by the whole show and took off climbing as soon as I could. I felt super self-conscious to start free soloing up a crack that people were lined up to aid climb.

It was surreal to look up the Nose and think that I would be scrambling the whole thing by myself. I had a good supply of food and water as well as a headlamp. I was prepared for anything, though I was planning on climbing in the same style as I had on Half Dome. Free soloing everything I could and daisy soloing anything hard. I had the rope for a few pendulums, the King Swing, and the Great Roof.

Everything went smoothly on the first three pitches, which seemed easier than I expected. On the fourth pitch, I got a pleasant surprise. Someone had fixed an extremely bomber line up across the two tricky pendulums to Sickle Ledge. I could see that the rope was fixed to the bolt on Sickle and refixed to a half-dozen pieces along its way down, so I happily hand-over-handed up and saved myself a lot of ropework. I figured that something useful like that makes up for all the times that you go up on a pitch and discover that someone has cleaned all the fixed gear or ripped a crucial piece that's supposed to be left in place, either by falling and pulling it out or by deliberately scavenging it. And then sometimes you get lucky and find a rope left in place!

Dolt Tower, ten pitches up, was my first real stop. It was time to eat and drink again, and I checked my timer. It read something like 1:15, which was a pretty damn good pace. I realized that I wouldn't be needing a headlamp after all. I waved down to the meadow, knowing that my friend Tom Evans was probably watching on his telescope, and I wondered if any of my other friends were around. Then I took a leak and wondered if they watched that, too. I figured if they could see everything from down in the meadow, then I had nothing to be ashamed of. . . .

I rope soloed the short aid section up to the Boot Flake, but then I took myself off belay before I free soloed the actual Boot itself. It's simpler for me not to deal with a rope, especially on something secure like a hand crack. Still, it's exciting to take yourself off belay on El Cap.

Everything went uneventfully up to the Great Roof, which is where I planned to do my only full pitch of traditional rope soloing. I'd even brought a single Jumar for the occasion. This was one of my first real pitches of rope soloing ever, but it went smoothly. I started to notice how tired I felt as I jugged, so I told myself I wouldn't do any more rope soloing. From here to the top, I was going to daisy solo, even if it took longer. I couldn't bear to go up and down to clean pitches.

At the base of the Pancake Flake, I put my rope in my pack. That was one of the more memorable moments of the day. As I unclipped my daisies from the anchor and started free soloing the easy lieback above me, I felt absolutely heroic. The sheer exposure of twenty-three pitches dropping off beneath me filled me with glee. I'd spent a lot of the season posing for photos on various routes for a couple of different projects. Now I found myself doing the most exposed climbing of my life all alone. It was invigorating.

The last six pitches are mostly hand cracks, so I largely free soloed them, but I was getting more and more tired. I started grabbing fixed gear a little more—"French freeing," we sardonically call it, after the traditional style in the Alps. As I climbed into the Changing Corners, I passed into the shade, which brought me new life. Climbing in the full sun all afternoon had left me a little wilted, and my feet hurt from hot, tight climbing shoes. And then, on the last two pitches, I finally caught up to the parties I'd seen from the base. I stopped at an anchor to eat some food and chit-chat with a cute belayer. But as much as I felt like hanging out and chilling in the shade, I still had to get to the top. So I climbed through the leader, with permission of course, and didn't stop again until the summit.

I was massively psyched to reach the top. My timer said 5:50, but I rounded up to six hours, since I hadn't started it until the top of the first pitch. I'd been distracted by the mob at the base and hadn't remembered to start the timer.

Now I couldn't quite believe that I'd actually done the linkup, and in roughly half a day. Having thought about it with awe for so long, I found it a little surreal to actually do it.

Honestly, I don't remember anything about the hike down or what I did on the ground. I guess none of that stuff was as impor-tant to me as the actual climbing. Weird that I can remember individual placements I used on the Glowering Spot, but I can't remember where I went for dinner, or with who.

Alex's linkup of Half Dome and the Nose had taken him only a little over eleven hours, including hiking down from Half Dome and biking, driving, and hiking to the foot of El Cap. That was less than half the time of Dean Potter's daisy-solo linkup in 2002, the feat that had first inspired Alex to "go big" (one of his favorite mottoes). Of course a decade in Yosemite is an eternity in terms of speed climbing on the classic routes. Between 1991 and 2002, for instance, the speed record on the Nose—achieved by roped pairs simul-climbing, or moving at the same time without belays—dropped from six hours and one minute to two hours and forty-nine minutes.

Still, Alex was justly proud that on his June 2010 marathon day he'd set not only the solo speed record for both routes but also the speed record for the linkup, with or without a partner. Yet this formidable accomplishment didn't generate the kind of buzz that had greeted Alex's free solos of Moonlight Buttress and Half Dome. The climbing magazines paid him dutiful homage: *Alpinist* cadged what its editor called "a characteristically nonchalant e-mail" out of Alex, summarizing his big day in the Valley. Stewart Green, a prolific commentator on the climbing scene, tipped his cap: "It's hard to know what to make of Alex's astounding ascents. No words can describe the difficulty and dangerousness of these ascents. It's simply pure brashness. Let's face it—the kid has a lot of chutzpah. Climb high, Alex, and be safe."

Alex's Valley nickname—Alex "No Big Deal" Honnold—helps explain the muted response to his pathbreaking linkup. The narrative he wrote a few weeks after the climb for Black Diamond, one of his sponsors, is short on gee-whiz superlatives and long on phrases such as "pretty uneventful," "easier than expected," and "totally casual."

Throughout his career, it's been a source of mild amusement

to Alex that the public goes gaga over his free soloing but seems to undervalue his massive linkups on big walls at record paces. Of course, for a nonclimbing audience, the stark simplicity of free soloing—if you fall, you die—comes across instantly in a few seconds of video footage. It's a lot harder for that audience to grasp the rigors of daisy soloing, especially the way Alex performs it, with the grueling mental ballet of switching constantly, as he puts it, from *Now I'm safe* to *Now I'm not*. The unspoken fallacy beneath a casual observer's take on one of Alex's bold daisy solos is that because he clips in to fixed gear or to cams he places on all the hardest parts, he's taken the extreme challenge out of the game. Nothing could be further from the truth. And though he can say, "I hate to have to hurry," Alex strives for speed on the big walls, even as he has to make shrewd calculations as to which pitches he will free solo and which he will cruise with his daisy chains. For that matter, even trusting your life to a fixed piton can be a gamble, as some of the pro placed years ago has weathered out and can no longer safely support a climber's weight, let alone a leader fall.

After his record-setting double, Alex still wasn't through with Yosemite linkups. The ultimate prize, he knew, was the Yosemite Triple—back-to-back climbs not only of El Cap and Half Dome but also of the south face of Mount Watkins. Those three walls stand as the biggest trio in the Valley. To enchain them would require not only technical perfection but the stamina of a world-class distance runner.

Once again, the role model showing Alex the way was Dean Potter, who in 2001, climbing with Timmy O'Neill, scaled all three walls in a single day. On their linkup, Potter and O'Neill mixed free climbing with "French free," aiding on pro to surmount the hardest stretches. It was a landmark achievement, pushing the boundaries of what in 2001 was considered possible. (Even today, the authoritative site Supertopo.com lists "normal" times on the south face of Mount

Watkins as two to three days, three days for the Regular Northwest Face on Half Dome, and five days for the Nose on El Cap.)

By the spring of 2012, Alex was back in Yosemite. This time he would pair up with another of his role models, Tommy Caldwell. Despite Caldwell's being seven years older than Alex, the two would soon form one of those rare partnerships destined to make climbing history, like the French duo of Lionel Terray and Louis Lachenal in the 1940s and '50s or the German brothers Alex and Thomas Huber in the 1990s and 2000s. Each would bring out the best in the other, complementing one another's particular strengths as climbers. And they got along like great friends just hanging out and having a good time, even when they were in the midst of a serious battle.

Even as a teenager in Sacramento, I was aware of Tommy Caldwell's stellar record in big-wall climbing. He seemed to specialize in first free ascents of routes on El Cap, including the Dihedral Wall and Magic Mushroom, both rated 5.14a. Yet he'd also excelled as a sport climber, solving a short route called Flex Luthor at the Fortress of Solitude in Colorado—rated a possible 5.15a, which remained throughout my childhood the hardest single route climbed in the United States. And in 2006, on his first trip to Patagonia, Tommy and two partners made the first free ascent of a beautiful route on Fitz Roy called Línea de Eleganza. (The first ascent, with heavy reliance on aid and fixed ropes, took an Italian party nine days. Tommy's team onsighted every pitch and got up the wall in only two days.)

I think a big key to Tommy's success is his incredible work ethic. He'll hike four hours to a route, then spend eight hours working it in the rain. Or he'll haul huge loads to the top of El Cap, then rap down just to check out a potential project. By the fall of 2014,

Tommy had been trying for seven straight years to complete the first free ascent of the Dawn Wall on El Cap, which he knew would be the hardest big wall free climb in the world. I could only imagine the tenacity and drive it would take to work on a single route nearly every season for most of a decade. I don't think I'd have the patience for such a long-term challenge.

Tommy's also had some experiences you wouldn't wish on anybody. In 2000, at the age of twenty-three, with his girlfriend (and later wife), Beth Rodden, as well as two other climbing buddies, Tommy was forced off a big wall in Kyrgyzstan when terrorists shot bullets at the climbers' portaledge a thousand feet off the deck. Once on the ground, the four were taken prisoner and then forced for days to march and hide as their captors evaded army soldiers hunting them. An unfortunate soldier whom the terrorists had also captured was executed just out of sight of their bivouac. Tommy, Beth, and their two teammates believed they would be executed themselves. They succeeded in escaping one night when Tommy pushed off a cliff the sole terrorist charged with guarding them. (Amazingly, the guy survived, only to be captured by the army and imprisoned under a death sentence.) The four young climbers then ran for the government front line, coming close to getting shot at by mistake. The whole wild adventure is chronicled in Greg Child's dramatic book Over the Edge.

The very next year, 2001, Tommy accidentally cut off his left index finger with a table saw. That kind of mishap can end a climbing career. Tommy had the finger sewed back on, but when it simply got in the way of his climbing, he had it removed. Today, at age thirty-seven, he's climbing as well as he ever has, despite the missing digit.

So I had always admired Tommy from a distance, but when we started climbing together, it was a joy to discover what a kind, generous, unegotistical guy he is. Unlike some professional athletes,

Tommy never toots his own horn, and, as a result, I think he's gotten less credit for what he's done than he deserves.

In May 2012, Tommy's idea for the Yosemite Triple—the south face of Mount Watkins, a route called Freerider on El Cap that weaves in and out of the standard Salathé line, and the Regular Northwest Face on Half Dome—was not simply to pull off the linkup in a single day but to free climb every single foot of all three routes. I knew that would be a tall order, but I was psyched to give it a shot with such a strong and motivated partner.

We started up Watkins at 4:45 p.m. on May 18. It was already hot in the Valley, so we arranged our schedule to maximize time in the shade. The technique we all use nowadays for speed climbing big walls is called simul-climbing. It works like this. One guy takes the rack and leads continuously, not for a single pitch but for as much as 800 or even a thousand feet. He doesn't stop to belay. Once the rope comes tight to the second, he starts up, too. Both guys climb simultaneously—hence "simul-climbing." The leader places cams or nuts every so often, or clips fixed gear, so that if either guy falls, the gear catches them in a kind of yo-yo effect, when the rope comes tight between them. You can take some pretty horrendous whippers simul-climbing and still not get hurt, as long as the pro is good.

Ironically, the most dangerous situation in simul-climbing arises when the second falls. If the leader falls, the rope coming tight to the second arrests the plunge, the second acting as a kind of unwitting anchor. But if the second falls, he can pull off the leader. Not good if both guys are falling at once, no matter how good your pro!

But part of what allowed Tommy and me to climb the Triple was using devices like the Kong Duck or the Petzl Micro Traxion, single-directional pulleys that allow the rope to go one way but not the other. When placed strategically, they allow the second to climb through terrain that would otherwise be considered much too hard—too close to the edge of falling off. Tommy and I could climb such big blocks—sometimes over a thousand feet at a time—because the devices made it safe for the second to climb as hard as 5.12.

Tommy and I led in what we call blocks—big stretches covering as many as twelve or thirteen conventional pitches of, say, eighty to 150 feet each. It's inevitable that as the leader places pro, he's going to run through his rack at some point. That's when you change over and give the rack and the lead to the other guy. We planned beforehand the places where our blocks would end, on ledges where a pendulum or a downclimb or some other unusual maneuver meant you had to manage the rope more carefully than in normal simul-climbing.

We got up Watkins in the excellent time of two hours and forty minutes. Neither of us took a single fall, despite pitches as hard as 5.13a. From there, a combination of hiking, driving, eating, and rehydrating got us to the foot of Freerider at 10:45 p.m. As we'd planned, we hoped to cruise all of El Cap in the dark. That's not quite as hard as it might seem, as long as you have the route sufficiently dialed so that your headlamp illuminates all the sequences and you don't get off-route.

In some ways, Freerider on El Cap was the climax of our adventure. One of the most memorable moments came in the wee hours. Tommy was leading up one of the harder corners. As he left his anchor, he said, "I'm too tired to lieback it, I'm just going to stem it," and then he proceeded to just totally bust out the entire pitch. I didn't even think you could do that! It's the middle of the night and it's really hard to see your feet because it's dark, he has a headlamp, he's standing on tiny little footholds that you wouldn't even be able to see in the light, and he just stemmed it, one foot on each slab, trusting those minuscule holds.

Tommy's a technical wizard on that stuff. He's really, really good on granite, so it was cool seeing how he could improvise like that and get away with it.

We got to the top of El Cap just after 5:00 a.m., with the first light of dawn. We'd finished Freerider in 6:15, also a damn good time. Tommy fell twice on the crux face climbing section, but no harm done, since I was belaying him, not simul-climbing. I managed not to come off anywhere.

Our big enemy was fatigue, and it really hit us on Half Dome. Having to free climb 5.12+ after twenty-one straight hours on the walls takes it out of you. It's really hard, and the prospect of failure—even if it meant "cheating" and using aid or grabbing fixed gear—is always there. The 5.12c variations on the Regular Northwest Face gave us all we could handle.

Each of the three routes has a specific crux. When we got to them we would get all psyched up, but they were all reasonable. The real trial is an overall, cumulative ordeal. Your feet hurt more and more and you get more and more tired. Linkups aren't super fun. Once you hit hour twelve or fourteen, you aren't really thinking, "Oh! What a great time we're having!" You think it will be cool until it isn't fun anymore.

It was 2:00 p.m. on May 19 when we topped out on Half Dome. Our elapsed time was twenty-one hours and fifteen minutes. Not only a new speed record but also the first free linkup of the three great Yosemite faces.

I was pretty pleased that I had managed to climb 7,000 feet of steep granite—seventy guidebook pitches—without falling once. And I'm equally gratified that, as of 2015, nobody else had duplicated our free linkup, no matter how long they took to do it.

AS MONUMENTAL AN ACHIEVEMENT as Yosemite's Triple
Crown with Caldwell was, Alex regarded it in some sense as a
warm-up. His goal for months had been to try the Triple solo—not
free climbing every pitch, but rope soloing and daisy soloing. As he
would later claim, "Doing the Triple with Tommy, I knew, would
actually be physically harder than daisy soloing it. After all, climbing
5.12+ when you're tired is way harder than French freeing the same
pitch. By doing it free with Tommy, I learned just how tired I'd be
when I got to Half Dome on a solo linkup."

After the success of *Alone on the Wall*, Peter Mortimer and
Sender Films had stayed in close touch with Alex. Now, for a new
film, to be titled *Honnold 3.0*, the filmmakers offered to shoot Alex's
attempt on the solo Triple. For Mortimer and company, it would
present a new kind of challenge. They would capture Alex's climb
not in staged reenactments, as they had his free solos of Moonlight
Buttress and Half Dome, but "in real time," as he attempted the
linkup through a very long day and night. There would be no second
takes, no rehearsals. If the camera missed a crucial bit of action,
that would be too bad.

Logistically, such a shoot posed a fiendish challenge. The cameramen would have to rappel into positions on the three walls well
before Alex got there, then simply hang out and wait for his arrival.
To ensure Alex's comfort level, Mortimer chose shooters who not
only were top-notch climbers but also were good friends with Alex.
They included Ben Ditto, Cheyne Lempe, Mikey Schaefer, Sean
Leary, and Mortimer himself.

Yet in Mortimer's view, such a project was actually less stressful than the shooting of *Alone on the Wall* had been. As he reflects
today, "There was a cleaner ethical boundary for me. Worst-case
scenario: If Alex wants to climb something and he falls off and dies,

that's still his choice. But if he dies during a reenactment, then in some way I'd feel that I killed Alex. I'd have to live with that."

Even so, every shoot with Alex took its toll on the filmmakers. In June 2011, to provide footage for the *60 Minutes* interview with Alex, Mortimer had agreed to film another free solo in Yosemite. As a side project, the day before the big show, Alex chose to go after the Phoenix, a single 130-foot pitch, but one rated a solid 5.13a. It's a climb you have to rappel to reach the start, since it hangs over a sheer precipice looming more than 500 feet above the valley floor.

Mortimer had misgivings. As he recalls, "I was almost at the point of telling Alex, 'No more reenactments.' But he said, 'I'm gonna fucking do the Phoenix tomorrow morning. You wanna come?'

"'Do you want me there?'

"'Sure.'"

The next day, Mortimer got in position. "I zoomed in on him with my camera," he remembers. "What I saw brought home the reality of what he was holding onto. It was incredibly stark. The rock was overhanging, his feet were on nothing. The granite looked slippery from spray from a nearby waterfall. He had only three fingertips in shallow cracks.

"I was terrified. It was the scariest thing in my life. I couldn't handle watching up close, so I had to zoom out."

Alex cruised up the Phoenix in eight minutes flat. It was the first 5.13 route ever free soloed in Yosemite.

Mortimer tells another story, this time about cameraman Brett Lowell shooting Alex on a free solo on a route on Liberty Cap, a dome also in the Valley, for Sender's film *Valley Uprising*. "Brett had a fancy new camera. He was all set in position. Alex climbed up to him, then, only a few feet away from the camera, he set out from a locker crack onto a steep slab. Normally child's play for Alex. But he botched the sequence. Went up, downclimbed, went back up.

"Brett came close to losing it. He thought, *I'm going to film this guy falling to his death.* He turned white as a ghost. Alex noticed Brett's distress, and, in the middle of sorting out the moves, said, 'Hey, no big deal. This is what you do when you're climbing.'"

Yes, the logistics of filming my Triple solo for the Sender guys were supercomplicated. But their presence actually made it easier and more pleasant for me. Daisy soloing requires a way lower commitment than free soloing, so it didn't really matter to me if other people were around, because I have a harness and a rope and I can just hang out. If I was free soloing and there was a cameraman next to me, it would be harder to focus. But it's nice to have friends around when you're climbing through the night.

Also, the crew made my own logistics a lot easier. If I was alone, I'd have to figure out car shuttles between the climbs—a big hassle. But with the filmmakers, I had rides already set up. And they could give me food and water on the summits. If I was doing it alone, I would have pre-stashed food and water at various places along the route.

I started up the south face of Mount Watkins at 4:00 p.m. on June 5, 2012. The first pitches were a little wet and buggy, because it had rained the day before, but I felt pretty smooth. Finished the wall in 2:20, twenty minutes faster than Tommy and I had done it two weeks earlier.

It was kind of chaotic driving down to the start of El Cap. There was all this shit on the floor of the van—the filmmakers' Pelican cases, assorted gear of my own, since I'd use a different rack for El Cap, and I'm trying to eat and hydrate. And it was dark by now. I started up the Nose at 9:30 p.m. I got 150 feet up and realized I'd forgotten my chalk bag. Must have left it among the debris on the floor of the van. Oh, shit, I said to myself. I considered scrambling back down to get the bag, but by then the van had left. So I just climbed on without chalk. The lower pitches were wet, so I found it a little bit hard and weird.

Climbing in the dark is quieter and lonelier than in the daylight. In some ways, there's no exposure. You're inside this little bubble with your headlamp. A fifteen-foot beam of light is the whole universe. There was no danger I'd get off-route, since I knew the sequences so well by now. And yet, you still sense that there's this void below you, somewhere in the darkness. It's like swimming in the ocean and realizing there's a bottomless abyss below you.

When I got to the Dolt Tower, about a thousand feet up, I met two parties: one was a pair of guys bivouacking, the other two were cooking a meal. We exchanged pleasantries, then I asked, a bit sheepishly, "Do you guys have a chalk bag I could borrow?" This guy named Steve Denny unhesitatingly handed over his. It was a new felt bag, and it was full of chalk. Putting my hand into it felt orgasmic. I thanked Steve and told him I'd tie the bag to a tree on the summit, so he could retrieve it later. Then I headed on.

A strange thing about climbing in the dark is that all these creatures come out. Bugs, mice, bats, even frogs that live in the cracks. And these giant centipedelike insects. I've always worried that I'd step on one and splooge off. Then, all of a sudden, I heard this loud "whoosh!" and a scream. I nearly peed my pants. It took a moment to realize it had to be a BASE jumper. In fact, it was a friend of mine—I won't name him here, since BASE jumping is illegal in the park, which was why he flew at night.

At the Great Roof, I met up with Stanley—Sean Leary is his real name, but everybody calls him Stanley. After filming me on the roof, he climbed with me the rest of the way up the Nose, Jumaring next to me as I daisy soloed. We actually chatted about other things, such as the speed record on the Nose, which he was keen to go after. I didn't have to concentrate too hard, except for spots here and there where I'd say, "Hold on a moment. I need to focus."

Finished the Nose at 3:30 a.m., still in pitch dark. Six hours for the climb, fifteen minutes faster than Tommy and I had climbed Freerider.

The psychological crux of the whole linkup was actually on the grueling hike up to Half Dome, where I started to bonk. I felt agonizingly slow on the route, but I knew I was in the home stretch. Near the top, I ran into Mike Gauthier, who was chief of staff in the park and, unlike most of the rangers, a good climber. (Traditionally, in Yosemite there's been a constant antagonism between rangers and climbers.) He was roped up with a guy from the Access Fund—a nonprofit devoted to preserving access to climbing areas across America. We sort of climbed side by side a couple of pitches together. I hadn't met Mike before, but he seemed like a really nice dude. I thought it was cool—an NPS bigshot who was a serious climber, an Access Fund partner, and all that. Then I pushed on.

I topped out at 10:55 a.m. to a whole gong show of hikers on the summit. I was really tired, and the scene felt weird, out of control. My total time was 18:55. It was another speed record, but mainly I just felt psyched to have done it.

Four days later, when he topped out, Steve Denny recovered his chalk bag, which I'd tied to a tree.

*H*ONNOLD 3.0, WHICH SENDER packaged with four other films for its Reel Rock 7 anthology, released in 2012, is every bit as skillful and impressive as *Alone on the Wall*. The Yosemite Triple solo takes up only a little more than half the film, but it forms its inevitable climax. Picking up where the earlier feature ended,

and segueing through Alex's appearance on *60 Minutes* and his role
in a clever Citibank commercial, in which he belays Katie Brown (a
former infatuation of Alex's) on a sandstone tower in Utah, the film
poses the question of whether fame might corrupt or endanger Alex.
As his good friend Cedar Wright puts it, "How do you do this when
it becomes a public spectacle?"

The footage covering the Triple solo smoothly intercuts action
sequences with friends as talking heads and Alex's own voice-overs.
Anticipating the linkup, Wright pronounces, "If he pulls it off, it's
the most monumental feat of soloing in Yosemite history."

On Watkins, the camera powerfully captures the scary dance of
switching from daisy solo to free solo, especially where the bolts are
far enough apart that Alex must unclip and climb a stretch without
a safety net before he can clip in again. The alternation of "Now I'm
safe. Now I'm not" comes across vividly. In voice-over, Alex says,
"I guess I should have a disclaimer on this, because basically you
should not do this, even though I love it and I think it's so fun." He
grins at the paradox.

A thousand feet up the south face, there's a film moment that's
already become as famous as the freakout on Thank God Ledge in
Alone on the Wall. Free soloing, Alex traverses toward the camera,
which is less than a dozen feet away. There's a bolt he hopes to
clip. In the frame, you can't see either Alex's feet or the fingers that
clasp a sloping ledge high above his head. He lets go with his left
hand and reaches toward the bolt to measure how far away it is. His
fingers stop an inch or two short of the bolt, but he knows he can
clip it with a daisy. Carefully he reaches back to his harness, seizes
the daisy, and puts the middle loops of it between his teeth as he
reaches down for the biner.

All at once Alex's whole body jerks downward several inches. It's
obvious that his foot has slipped off its hold. How had he kept his
purchase on the wall, with only the fingers of his right hand gripping

the out-of-sight sloping ledge? How close had he come to the fatal fall everyone worries he'll someday take?

Audiences invariably gasp, or even shriek out loud, at this moment. But on film, Alex's face registers nothing. He reaches down again, clasps the biner, clips it to the bolt, then swings across with his weight on the daisy. *Now I'm safe.*

When asked how Alex had felt about that terrifying close call, Mortimer later reported, "He didn't even remember it. But later, he gave me grief about it. He said, 'How come with all the great footage you got on the Triple, you put that single clip up on YouTube?'"

According to Alex, "In that moment, I wasn't even close to falling off. I had a really good handhold. The foot that slipped was not on a weight-bearing hold. I didn't want to lurch for the bolt. That wouldn't look good on camera."

Yet in the film, Alex's voice-over immediately after the slip on Watkins seems to acknowledge a close call. "Having little things go wrong," he says. "That's just part of the game. Those kinds of things shake you for a second, but then you just keep climbing."

Of necessity, because of the widely scattered positions where the cameramen had stationed themselves on the three walls, the film could not cover all the highlights of the linkup. Because there was no way cinematically to recount the drama of the forgotten chalk bag, Sender simply ignored it—even though there's footage of Alex gearing up with rack and rope in the dark as he heads toward El Cap.

Some of the best footage documents Alex climbing up the Nose in the dark, with the cone of his headlamp bathing the microworld of hand- and footholds, the void an inky blackness all around him. And fortuitously, at the Great Roof, the audio captures the "whoosh!" and joyous shout of the BASE jumper. A voice-over about the crux moves on the Great Roof perfectly complements the visuals. "The fixed nuts are hanging half out," Alex comments, "and they pull straight down, so it looks like it's all going to fall out. There's always running water, and slime coming out of [the crack]. It's a pretty intimidating position."

By accompanying Alex not only to the top of El Cap but also on the arduous approach up the "Death Slabs" to the foot of Half Dome, Sean Leary captures the extreme fatigue and dispirited mood of Alex as he gets ready for the last wall. He complains about the cold and looks as though all he wants to do is go to sleep. In voice-over, Alex admits feeling out of it on the "trudge" up the first half of the route. Then, miraculously, he finds his groove again. The last few hundred feet of climbing look effortless and triumphant.

The film ends with the "gong show" on top. Dozens of hikers, knowing he's near the top, lean over the edge of the precipice. "He's coming," one voice intones, and another, "That's so sick."

As Alex sits exhausted on the flat bedrock summit, hikers ask to take his picture and shake his hand. If he thinks the scene is weird, it doesn't show. Gracefully, he assents to their requests, shakes their hands, poses for a group photo with four awestruck teenage girls.

The final voice-over is a winning one. "I think of all the people who inspired me as a kid," Alex reflects, "and I sort of realize they were all normal people, too. I just do my normal life, and if people choose to be inspired by the things I'm doing, then I'm glad they're getting something out of it."

• • • •

In the short span of two months, 2012 had already become a breakthrough year for Alex. But even after the Triple Crown solo, he still had one more project in his sights for Yosemite that season. Less than two weeks after topping out on Half Dome, Alex would enter the fiercest Valley competition of all—the race to set a new speed record on the Nose.

CHAPTER **SIX**

THE SPEED RECORD

THE ONE-DAY ASCENT OF THE NOSE in 1975 by Jim Bridwell, John Long, and Billy Westbay dazzled the climbing world. Their time on the wall—a shade under fifteen hours—shaved an astounding twenty hours off the previous record, set just the year before.

It was inevitable that someone would show up and climb the Nose even faster than the trio of legendary Stonemasters. In 1979, a French ace, Thierry Renault, came to the Valley and surged up the route in under thirteen hours. His ascent was notable in view of the fact that most European climbers get shut down cold on their first visits to Yosemite, either because they're unused to severe crack climbing or because they're simply intimidated by the sheer, sweeping granite walls. Renault made so little fuss about his deed that the name of his climbing partner seems lost to history (the compendia of speed climbs simply cite "Thierry 'Turbo' Renault + other").

Five more years passed before Renault's time was bettered. Again, the new record was claimed by climbers from abroad. On the summer solstice in 1984, the Brit Duncan Critchley and the

Swiss Romain Vogler pulled off the ascent in the remarkable time of nine and a half hours.

Then along came Hans Florine.

An All-American pole vaulter in college, Florine started climbing in his native California at the age of nineteen and almost at once realized that his forte was speed. Early on, he won virtually every speed competition on artificial walls that he entered, including three gold medals in the X Games. It was logical that Florine would turn his attention to the Nose.

In 1990, at the age of twenty-five, Hans paired up with Steve Schneider to lop nearly an hour and a half off the Critchley-Vogler record. Their time on El Cap, from base to summit, was eight hours and six minutes. But the new record didn't last long, as Peter Croft and Dave Schultz cut the mark to 6:40.

As mentioned in previous chapters, Peter Croft was one of the climbers a young Alex Honnold most admired, because of the bar he set with his solo climbs. Alex's free solos of Astroman and the Rostrum in a single day in 2007 gained him his first fame in the Valley, since no one had dared to try to repeat Croft's blazing feat during the previous twenty years. Six years older than Florine, Croft was a creaky thirty-two when he set the new record on the Nose.

With that, the race was on. Times were now clocked to the minute, not the more casual "slightly under X number of hours." Unlike most of his peers, who tend to minimize the role that competitiveness plays in their lives, Florine has always unabashedly confessed to relishing head-to-head combat. In 1991, with Andres Puhvel, Florine took back the crown with a time of 6:01—only to have Croft return with Schultz and reduce the record to a mind-boggling 4:48.

It was always, however, a friendly competition, so it was apropos that the two masters paired up and went for an even faster time. In 1992, Florine and Croft set the mark at 4:22.

That record stood for the next nine years. Perhaps no one in the

Valley could imagine improving on such a stellar performance, or perhaps the speed record simply fell out of vogue. It was not until Dean Potter emerged on the scene that Croft and Florine saw their record challenged. In October 2001, climbing with Timmy O'Neill, Potter broke the four-hour barrier—just barely. Their time was officially noted as 3:59:35. For the first time, seconds, not minutes, were required to measure the race up the Nose. And for the first time, the rules were codified. The stopwatch started when the first climber left the triangular ledge at the bottom of pitch 1 on the route topo. It clicked off only when the second climber tagged the "official" tree about forty feet above the topmost anchors on the route.

By 2001, at the age of forty-three, Peter Croft was no longer keen to compete for the Nose speed record. Instead, he turned to the mountains, blithely putting up severe new technical, multipeak routes in the High Sierra. But Florine felt the burr under his saddle. In the same month as Potter's breakthrough, he teamed up with Jim Herson to knock exactly two minutes and eight seconds off Potter's mark. Florine was now thirty-seven years old, but apparently fitter than ever. Undeterred, Potter came back in November and, climbing with O'Neill again, blew the record out of the water with a time of 3:24:20.

Florine bided his time for eight months. In September 2002, paired with a new speed demon, the Japanese Yuji Hirayama, Florine trumped Potter's feat. The duo not only broke the three-hour barrier: their time of 2:48:55 bested Potter and O'Neill's mark by 34.5 minutes.

The race was now a pitched battle. Out of nowhere, it seemed, the German brothers Alex and Thomas Huber jumped into the fray. In October 2007, they lowered the mark to 2:48:30—a mere twenty-five-second improvement on the Florine-Hirayama watershed. Only four days later, the Hubers improved their own record by two minutes and forty-five seconds.

All this rivalry only served to wave a red flag in Florine's face. Pairing again with Hirayama, he improved on the Huber brothers in July 2008 with a time of 2:43:33. Three months later, the duo broke their own mark, lowering it to 2:37:05.

Hans Florine, then forty-four years old, had held the speed record on the Nose seven times, losing and regaining it five times, and capping his amazing run by trumping his own best time by more than six minutes. Had the ultimate limit been reached? Dean Potter didn't think so.

At this point, Sender Films decided to document the whole show. Their twenty-two-minute film *Race for the Nose*, appearing as part of the Reel Rock Tour in 2011, captured the outlandish characters of the leading competitors and covered the action in scintillating you-are-there footage.

I really liked Sender's Race for the Nose *when I first saw it in 2011. Besides all the great action footage, which vividly captured just how hairy simul-climbing against a stopwatch can get, the film pitted these two great climbers—Hans Florine and Dean Potter—against each other in a classic mano-a-mano duel. They have such different personalities that the contrast only enhanced the drama.*

Dean likes to insist that he's not competitive, that he climbs for the spiritual rewards of perfecting his craft. Whereas Hans just lays it out there. The film billboards one of his pronouncements: "I love competition and I'm blatant about it. If it's something that makes me climb better than before, if it pushes me to do my best, then I see it as a good thing."

It's to Sender's credit that they get Dean to admit that the challenge of Hans's speed records brings out the competitiveness in him that's just beneath the surface. "He was like this little dog humping my leg," Dean says of Hans, "and so it brought out the little dog in me." Classic Dean!

The film focuses on Dean's attempt with Sean Leary to break the record on June 11, 2010. By then, Hans and Yuji's mark of 2:37:05 had stood for a year and a half. Before launching on the Nose, Dean announced, "I think it's possible to break the record by a large amount." But when Sean, coming second, tagged the tree on top of El Cap, the stopwatch clicked off at exactly 2:36:45. They'd broken the record, but only by twenty seconds. That didn't dampen their wild celebration on top.

Dean and Sean had considered their first attempt only a practice run, so their time was impressive. But before they could push the route to their absolute limits, winter storms hit the Valley and shut down the climbing season.

Watching that film made me want to give the record my own best shot. And I thought it would be really cool if I could do it with the old master, Hans. At the end of my great season in the Valley in 2012—climbing the Triple with Tommy Caldwell, then climbing it solo—I was in such good shape that I thought I should go for the Nose. By then, Hans was forty-seven years old, but I knew that he always stayed in tremendous shape. And I knew that he'd love nothing better than to take the record back from Dean.

Hans is a super straight-up dude with everybody. Like the way he makes no bones about loving competition. To me, he epitomized the successful older climber. By 2012, he had a wife he loved and kids he loved, but the fire was still in his belly. He didn't hesitate to accept my invitation. He lives in the Bay Area, so he wouldn't be acclimated to Yosemite. He just came up and took on the challenge as a weekend warrior.

The one thing Sender may have overemphasized in Race for the Nose is the ruthlessness of the rivalry. All the guys who are interested in the speed record are friends of mine, and of each other. I even gave Sean some beta—route-finding advice—before he and Dean went up to break Hans and Yuji's record. Some climbers look askance at speed records—they even criticize us for (so they think) corrupting the purism of ascent. My answer is simple: I do it because it's so much fun.

The whole thing started, I suppose, with the cachet of "Nose-in-a-day," which has bloomed as the acronym NIAD. That's still a cherished goal for many climbers. Of course, the whole in-a-day thing is arbitrary. Twenty-four hours is an arbitrary measure. If it had taken me twenty-five hours to do the Triple Crown solo, I'd still have felt pretty good about it.

Going for the Nose speed record is simply a fun game. All this stuff is a game.

Hans and I started our stopwatch on June 17, 2012, the day before his forty-eighth birthday. And I'll have to say, we climbed the route about as efficiently as is possible. Our teamwork was perfect. The only glitch (if you can even call it that) came in the Stove Legs, on pitches 8 and 9, when Hans slowed down a little. When Hans tagged the tree at the finish line, we stopped the watch. Our time was 2:23:46. Pretty rad, we both thought. We'd knocked thirteen minutes off Dean and Sean's record. Hans was overjoyed. I was surprisingly pleased myself.

After the climb, as we were walking down the backside of El Cap, I asked Hans, "Hey, what happened there in the Stove Legs?" He said, "I was catching my breath." "What do you mean 'catching your breath'?" I needled him. "We were going for the speed record!"

It's now been more than three years since Hans and I broke the record and nobody has bettered our time. Of course, that's mainly because no one has tried. We'll see how long it takes for someone to get properly motivated to go after it.

All the same, someday I'd like to try to break the two-hour frontier. I think it's possible. It's a huge psychological barrier, like the sub-two-hour marathon, but sooner or later, I'm convinced, somebody will do it. If I'm right, that you can't climb any more efficiently than Hans and I did that day in June 2012, then the only way to do the Nose faster is to get fitter. The upper part of the route is really steep and pumpy. When you're climbing fast, your forearms get superpumped. The burn is intense. That's where fitter might mean faster.

That said, and as gratifying as setting the record was, I don't see speed climbing the Nose as the same kind of major accomplishment that the Triple solo was. It's on a much smaller scale, much lighter, and two and a half hours of any kind of climbing doesn't take the mental and physical stamina of linkups on big walls. Or of free soloing.

In the spring and early summer of 2012, I'd had my best season ever in Yosemite. I wasn't sure what I'd do next, though I had plenty of projects jotted down in "to-do" lists in my climbing and training journals. Would 2013 be another year of consolidation? Not in the ways I might have anticipated. . . .

· · · ·

The revelation that had first come to me on our endless drive across the desert in Chad in 2010—that, compared to the men I saw spending all day turning mud into bricks, or the boys beating their donkeys to make them haul water faster, I had it pretty easy in life—had stayed with me. The eternal question was how that revelation should dictate the way I lived, especially after sponsorship made my life even easier.

One answer had to do with lifestyle. Ever since 2007, I'd lived out of the Ford Econoline van I had bought cheap as a five-year-old used car. By 2010, it was still pretty ghetto, but a friend of mine had installed industrial carpeting, side panels, finishing work, and sturdy insulation. I cooked my meals on a two-burner Coleman stove, slept in my sleeping bag with a bouldering crash pad for a mattress, and read by headlamp.

By 2012, I could easily have rented an apartment or a condo to live in, but I decided to stick with the van. One reason was that it gave me the ultimate freedom—a kind of traveling base camp as I drove from one crag to another, following the changing seasons. A permanent residence would have felt like an annoying anchor. Living in a van reflected my ideals of simplicity, frugality, and efficiency.

Instead of trading in the old Econoline for a spiffier model, I decided to refurbish the vehicle. Now it's a really well-crafted van, even though it's got 180,000 miles on it. Between climbing trips in 2013, I left my van with John Robinson, a seventy-year-old retired friend from Sacramento, who had built out his own van. He made all kinds of improvements to mine. In my kitchen area, there's a five-gallon water tank and, instead of the Coleman two-burner, a built-in range connected to propane tanks. All enclosed in nice, custom-made cabinets.

In back, where I sleep, I have to lie a little bit diagonal, because I'm slightly taller than the van is wide. I've put in a sliding curtain for privacy, or to keep the light out when I stop over in a well-lighted parking lot. Instead of the industrial carpet, I've now got a linoleum floor—Home Depot's finest.

What I call my foyer—where the side door opens into what used to be the back seats—is where I take my shoes off. It's also my bathroom, where I pee into a bottle.

Under the bed platform, John built a big sliding storage drawer where I keep all my climbing gear, just the right size for my bouldering crash pad. Side chambers for other stuff. I even haul around my baseball glove, in case somebody wants to play catch—it's a good way to limber up the shoulders.

Goal Zero, a solar company that sponsors me, was kind enough to install two sixty-watt panels on the roof of the van. They in turn power an inside battery, which I use to charge my phone and laptop—though it also powers the LED lights in the ceiling and the carbon-monoxide detector that John insisted on installing, saying, "If I'm going to do this, it's gotta be up to code!"

The Econoline is a full-size van, but I've got the smallest engine Ford offers—a 4.2-liter V6. It might not be a powerhouse, but it manages pretty well. And, to be honest, I don't know anything about cars. I think of mine more as a tiny house that moves.

There are of course drawbacks to living in a van. One is getting hassled by security guards. A few years ago, when I was climbing at Red Rocks, I went to sleep in the parking lot of Caesar's Palace in Las Vegas. I was awakened from a deep slumber by a loud knock on my window. I had no idea what hour it was. I opened the front door a crack to talk to the guy.

"You can't camp here like this," he said irately, as if I was doing him personal harm. "Oh, sorry," I said, "I thought it was all right since I was in the casino last night."

"You have to leave," he went on, with enough disdain in his voice for me to know what he thought of anyone who would dare to desecrate the sanctity of his Palace.

Groggy and irritated, I got in the driver's seat and took off. It certainly wasn't the first time I'd been harassed like that, nor would it be the last. But for some reason the exchange stuck with me, grating on my nerves. I think it was because I could tell how much he looked down on me, how disgusted he was that someone would consider living in a van. In retrospect, I wish I'd laid into him, asking how someone who spends forty hours a week riding around a parking structure on a neon bicycle has any right to look down on my lifestyle choices.

During that Vegas outing, I used the Whole Foods parking

lot for my Internet service. Their free Wi-Fi was strong enough
to cover the whole surrounding lot, so I would park as close as I
could to the building and settle into the back of my van for e-mail
sessions. In fact, I used the Whole Foods bathrooms at least once
a day as well, though I also bought a lot of their organic food, so I
felt like it all balanced out.

There's no convenient camping around Vegas (the Red Rocks
campground is ridiculously overpriced and underwhelming), so I
split my nights among various hotel parking lots, twenty-four-hour
grocery stores, and some of my friends' streets. Each venue was
well-lit and loud with the sound of traffic. Getting rousted by security and told to move along was just part of the game, and being in
a place like Vegas for a month or more really made me appreciate
moving on to Indian Creek in Utah—at the other end of the car-
camping spectrum.

Where Vegas is annoyingly bright and bustling, the Creek is
almost oppressively dark and sometimes lonely. The night sky is
full of stars and the only sounds are the animals (and occasionally drunk climbers). The word quiet doesn't really do justice to
the deep, peaceful calm that settles over the desert at night. The
camping is unregulated, so you basically just find an empty spot
that suits your fancy and you post up for as long as you'd like. I've
spent weeks at the Creek and marveled each day at how beautiful
the landscape is—it really never gets old.

But what did get old was having no showers, no cell service, and
no food. A lot of people, especially Americans, get all excited about
"going camping," about how cool it is to be out in nature with nothing around you. But I think that camping holds a special appeal
for those who don't do it routinely. I like showering, I like eating
out, I like being able to call my friends or check my e-mail. And as
beautiful or romantic a place like the Creek might be, I eventually
tire of camping—even if it's in a van.

The whole thing is a trade-off. But as of 2015, I still have no plans to buy or rent an apartment anywhere. In my newly spiffed-up van, solar panels and all, I'm pretty content.

• • • •

Making a lifestyle choice, of course, is merely a personal matter. What I'd taken away from Chad was a certain feeling that I had an obligation to do something for others, for those with fewer choices in life and fewer means to accomplish them. By 2012, thanks to sponsorship and commercials, I had more money than I needed to live comfortably. So I established the Honnold Foundation. Its motto is "Helping people live better, simply." The mission statement I posted on my new website read, "The Honnold Foundation seeks simple, sustainable ways to improve lives world-wide. Simplicity is the key; low-impact, better living is the goal."

Three years into its operation, the foundation is just getting started. But already we've funded projects that I'm excited about. One involves supporting SolarAid, a British nonprofit that runs a campaign to provide solar lamps to four countries in Africa—Kenya, Malawi, Tanzania, and Zambia—to replace the ubiquitous kerosene lanterns that are both costly and toxic. SolarAid's ultimate goal is to abolish the use of kerosene lanterns in Africa by the year 2020. Some folks might think that's a pie-in-the-sky dream, but it's sure worth trying to make it happen.

Another nonprofit we support, called Grid Alternatives, aims to provide solar energy for low-income housing in the United States. So far we've focused on California and Colorado. In the spring of 2014, we moved into the Kayenta region of the Navajo Reservation to start providing solar energy to traditional Navajo families, many of whom have spent their whole lives without electricity or even running water.

Some years ago, I went on what I called my God-hating kick,

as I read all the major manifestos arguing against the ideas of religion and an afterlife—Richard Dawkins, Sam Harris, Christopher Hitchens, and the like. During that period, I sometimes referred to myself as a "born-again atheist."

More recently, my reading kick has been focused on clean energy. I'm deeply worried about the future of the world in the face of climate change, the unbridled use of fossil fuels, and so on. It's this passion, as much as anything, that led to the idea of the Honnold Foundation.

CHAPTER **SEVEN**

ALASKA AND SENDERO

WHEN I INTERVIEWED ALEX in the fall of 2010 for *Outside* magazine, one thing he was adamant about was that he'd never take up mountaineering. Rock climbing was the be-all and end-all of his outdoor existence. "I read every issue of *Alpinist* cover-to-cover," he quipped, "but I flip right past all the pictures with snow in them."

Nonetheless, his natural curiosity had at times driven him to probe the literature of mountaineering. On an extended trip to England, he claimed, "I read all the classic British climbing books, but I could never remember them afterward. They were all the same, slightly different casts of characters, vaguely different mountains." Pressed on the issue, Alex waffled slightly. "Sure, I'd accept a free trip to Everest," he admitted. "Who wouldn't want to take a free hike to the top of the world?" And, "Maybe when I've got nothing left to live for, I'll climb real mountains. I can see myself at seventy-five, hunkered down in a cabin, going out on hikes, playing with my grandkids."

Thus it came as a complete surprise to learn in the spring of

2013 that Freddie Wilkinson and Renan Ozturk, two of the best young big-range mountaineers in the United States, had persuaded Alex to join them on an expedition to Alaska. Their objective was the Great Gorge of the Ruth Glacier, southeast of Denali—a stunning corridor of flowing ice surrounded by sheer granite walls soaring as much as 5,000 feet from base to summit.

In late May and early June, the trio assaulted three long routes on Mounts Barrille, Bradley, and Dickey. I took a keen interest in their progress, for the route they tackled on Dickey was first climbed way back in 1974 by Ed Ward, Galen Rowell, and me. Ours, in fact, was the first big-wall climb completed in the Great Gorge.

It was Renan who talked Alex into going on the trip. Longtime friends, both sponsored by The North Face, they had not only climbed together, but Renan had filmed some of Alex's free-soloing exploits. As Alex recalls, "I just thought it was a great opportunity to learn. I was single, had nothing to do myself, and two friends who are really good at what they do were willing to teach me something. I couldn't pass up the opportunity."

The previous year, in May 2012, Renan and Freddie had completed the Tooth Traverse, one of the greatest challenges in Alaska mountaineering, as they made a five-day enchainment of five savage spires linked by knife-sharp ridges, culminating in the Mooses Tooth, a dramatic monolith of granite and ice that stands like a sentinel guarding the northeast corner of the Great Gorge. The traverse required three bivouacs in wildly exposed positions and culminated in a nonstop thirty-eight-hour push on the Mooses Tooth itself.

Despite having fulfilled a dream that was four years in the making, Renan and Freddie were still drawn to the Ruth Gorge. For 2013, the men decided to explore the western side of the great glacial corridor. And instead of an all-out commitment like the Tooth Traverse, they set their sights on routes that had already been climbed by others, hoping to apply a pure, fast alpine style to test their own finely honed skills against those of their predecessors. "We decided to go after classics," says Freddie, "rather than one massive time-consuming project like the Traverse. Alex was our hired gun. We figured he could lead the long rock sections as efficiently as anybody we knew.

"We weren't trying to set record times per se. But we had a goal to try to do those routes in one long day each. Alex was coming off his big-wall Yosemite climbs where almost everything he did was within the confines of twenty-four hours."

At only 7,650 feet, Barrille is dwarfed by its neighbors, the Mooses Tooth at 10,335 feet and Mount Dickey at 9,545. Still, it has serious rock and ice routes on its eastern and southern faces that rise a full 2,500 feet from base to summit. In late May 2013, Freddie and Alex climbed the Cobra Pillar on Barrille. Nursing a cold, Renan sat this one out, as he had climbed the same line in 2009. The route had been put up by two legendary American alpinists, Jim Donini and Jack Tackle, in 1991. The first ascent had required a five-day push, of which two and a half days were spent marooned in a bivouac during a typical Alaskan storm. Now Alex and Freddie bombed up the route in a mere nineteen hours, in a relatively straightforward ascent.

Next the three men turned to a more serious, longer route on Mount Bradley, the impressive 9,104-foot peak just south of Dickey. The Pearl, a long, zigzagging, committed route on the mountain's south face, had been established in 1995 by a trio of Austrians—Helmut Neswadba, Arthur Wutscher, and Andi Orgler. The alpine-style ascent had taken five days to complete.

Making the Pearl's second ascent, Freddie, Renan, and Alex dispatched the route in forty hours round trip, including a complicated descent of the mountain via its southwest ridge. On the crux A3 aid pitch, Alex came into his own. According to Freddie, "There were some fixed copperheads on the pitch [nuts that are hammered into cracks, rather than slotted]. Alex stood on two or three of those pieces, which weren't very secure. We were halfway up the route, and because of the traversing down low, retreat would have been desperate. Alex was facing an ankle-breaker for sure if he came off."

Says Alex, "From the two fixed copperheads, the only pro on the whole long pitch, I made a few 11-plus or 12-minus free moves— which was very scary—until I got to a more continuous crack. So it was only a small section of hard free climbing, but it was actually pretty heroic. If I hadn't been psyched to free climb, we would have been pretty fucked. Rapping off from there would have been horrendous."

If Alex was indeed the hired gun on crux rock pitches in the Gorge, he was the acolyte on snow and ice. Says Freddie, "Renan and I gave him a pretty good intro to alpinism. He was a bit uncertain with the ice axe, and I don't think he ever got really comfortable wearing crampons." Alex concurs: "I didn't feel comfortable on skis, in crampons—even walking around camp felt wrong. I had no idea what I was doing."

In fact, growing up in balmy California, Alex had spent so little time in the snow that a glacier whose icy depths plunged invisibly 4,000 feet below his feet to bedrock was so novel that he treated it at times like a playhouse. According to Freddie, "At base camp we built a snow kitchen. Alex couldn't get enough of the shoveling, as he crafted benches, shelves, nooks and crannies. He has this frenetic need to exercise. Renan and I were happy to turn him loose on the shoveling. It was a real Tom Sawyer moment."

Yet Alex's manic impatience came to the fore during a five-day storm the men endured after Bradley. Freddie: "There was this typical Alaskan low-grade scud day after day. Alex was jumping out of his skin. He kept saying, 'What are we gonna do today?' He was like a golden retriever—we had to give him a job to do. So I told him, 'Today we're just going to lie in our sleeping bags. Your assign-

I can only guess what's going on here, but I look like I'm having a good time.
(Credit: Dierdre Wolownick)

Just playing around at the Gunks, when I was still predominantly a gym climber. I didn't yet know what climbing outdoors meant.
(Credit: Dierdre Wolownick)

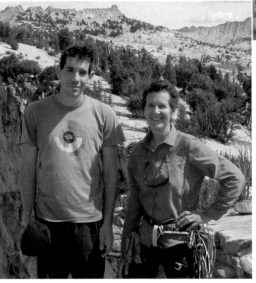

With my mom on the summit of Tenaya Peak in Tuolumne Meadows, to celebrate her birthday. I look like I have a paunch, but that's only because of the afternoon updraft filling my shirt.
(Photo credit: Sean McCartney)

On top of Mount Whitney with my sister, Stasia, during *Sufferfest 1*. I soloed a route up the Keeler Needle while she scrambled up the Mountaineers Route, and we met on top. *(Credit: Cedar Wright)*

Soloing splitter finger cracks up high on Moonlight Buttress. Don't worry, this is easier than it looks. *(Credit: Sender Films)*

High on Half Dome, re-creating my free solo of the Regular Northwest Face. *(Credit: Jimmy Chin)*

Walking face-out across Thank God Ledge is surprisingly scary. Normally, walking across a ledge is trivial compared with actual rock climbing, but in this case it's quite an experience. *(Credit: Jimmy Chin)*

I remember almost nothing about this route except that it was fun and mellow. One of the few really nice cracks at Smith Rock. *(Credit: Jimmy Chin)*

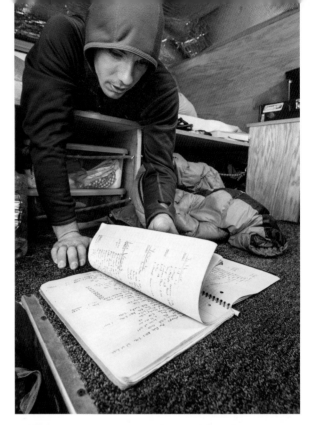

Flipping through my old climbing journal while lounging in my van.
(Credit: Ben Moon)

Home life in the van in 2010. This was the second-generation interior, pretty rustic compared with the way it looks now.
(Credit: Ben Moon)

Leave two men alone shooting portraits in a house and pretty soon it devolves into seminude feats of strength. *(Credit: Ben Moon)*

Just fun crack climbing.
(Credit: Dawn Kish)

Taking it easy between climbs at Smith Rock.
(Credit: Dawn Kish)

Dynoing between crack systems while trying to free climb on our new route on Mount Kinabalu in Borneo. The mist below was a constant threat—it would rise up and engulf the wall, making everything too wet to climb.
(Credit: Jimmy Chin)

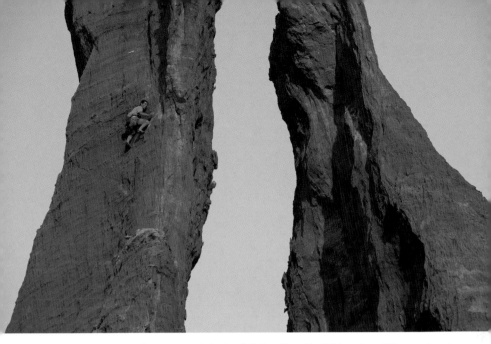

Mark Synnott and James Pearson were trying to climb the other side of this arch, and I became bored waiting, so I quested up the opposite pillar to try to beat them to the summit. But I had to downclimb after being turned around by bad rock and scary conditions. *(Credit: Jimmy Chin)*

Climbing on very soft sandstone high above Chad's Ennedi Desert. Adventure climbing at its finest. *(Credit: Jimmy Chin)*

ABOVE Normally a photographer shoots top down, hanging from a rope. In this case, Andrew Burr had to wait for me to get the rope up to the top, so he spent his time trying to create art while I climbed. Squamish has big ferns! *(Credit: Andrew Burr)*

BELOW My van, before I had cabinetry! Home sweet home. *(Credit: Andrew Burr)*

ABOVE Deep-water soloing in Oman. We would just stop wherever it looked interesting and put up new routes. Exploratory climbing at its best. And the snorkeling was even better than the climbing. *(Credit: Jimmy Chin)*

BELOW Soloing the Phoenix in Yosemite (5.13), with Cascade Creek raging below. This was one of my more intense solos, partly because you have to rappel in to get to the start. As soon as I started climbing, I was massively exposed and on difficult terrain. *(Credit: Sender Films)*

My first attempt at alpinism. Notice how awkward and uncomfortable I look compared to Freddie and Renan. Snowy mountains are scary! *(Credit: Renan Ozturk)*

Near the summit of Mount Dickey, approaching midnight in Alaska. *(Credit: Renan Ozturk)*

Base camp below Mount Dickey on my first trip to Alaska's Ruth Gorge. It's hard to tell how huge the walls are, since the glacier offers no perspective, but this face is almost twice as big as the biggest walls in Yosemite. *(Credit: Renan Ozturk)*

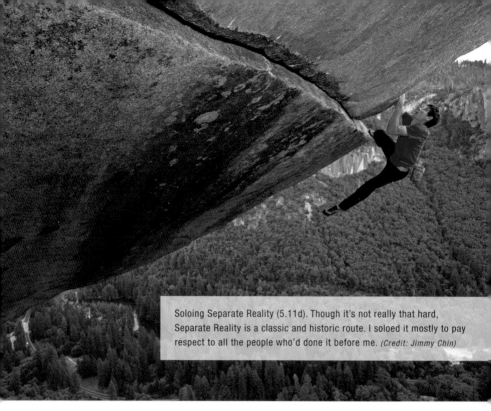

Soloing Separate Reality (5.11d). Though it's not really that hard, Separate Reality is a classic and historic route. I soloed it mostly to pay respect to all the people who'd done it before me. *(Credit: Jimmy Chin)*

Soloing one of the upper pitches of El Sendero Luminoso. Technical 12a face climbing. Good times! *(Credit: Renan Ozturk)*

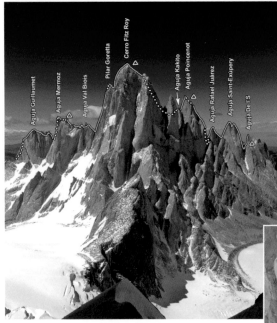

The Fitz Traverse, with route and camps marked. *(Credit: Rolando Garibotti)*

Our bivy on the first night of the Fitz Traverse, a little way past the summit of Aguja Mermoz. Tommy and I felt like this was the most scenic camping trip of our lives. The tent added some major comfort, since we were sharing a sleeping bag with no pad. *(Credit: Tommy Caldwell)*

On the Fitz Traverse, it was hard to take photos of each other, since we were mostly climbing at the same time. But on the north pillar of Fitz Roy, I ended one block and Tommy took the lead, so we were right next to each other. *(Credit: Alex Honnold)*

Tommy rapping off the summit of Aguja Rafael, after we climbed Blood on the Tracks, a 12ish pitch. Everything felt hard. *(Credit: Austin Siadak)*

Mountaineering makes you manly! Or maybe just worked-looking. *(Credit: Austin Siadak)*

Sean "Stanley" Leary and I were heading back up to El Cap while climbing it three times in one day in 2010. Sean was the most motivated big-wall speed-climbing partner anyone could ask for. On easy terrain, he would practically run uphill. He was amazing. *(Credit: Tom Evans)*

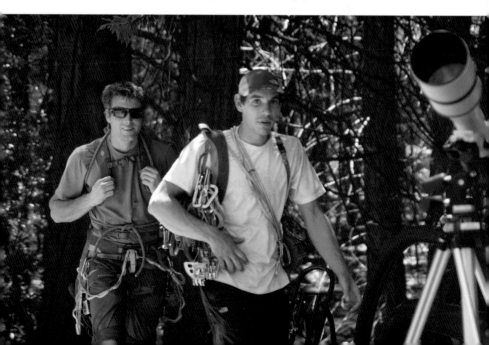

That's me atop the Cobra during *Sufferfest 2*. Disconcertingly, the tower fell over not long after our trip. Soft sandstone is such an impermanent thing. *(Credit: Cedar Wright)*

Having learned nothing from our previous follies in the High Sierra, Cedar and I launch *Sufferfest 2* among the sandstone towers of the Southwest. *(Credit: Cedar Wright)* ment is to read a book.' He finally settled in. Read *The Prize*, this nine-hundred-plus-page book by Daniel Yergin about oil and power, cover-to-cover.

"We basically got along great," adds Freddie. "But during those down days, Alex could become a bit of a whiner. He was always comparing everything to Yosemite. 'God,' he'd say, 'I could be wearing shorts, sport climbing at Jailhouse.'" (Jailhouse Rock is one of Alex's favorite crags, near Sonora, California.)

At last the weather cleared, and with only a couple of days left in their Alaska "vacation," the trio set their eyes on the southeast face of Mount Dickey.

Ed Ward, Galen Rowell, and I had been proud of the fact that in 1974 we got up the 5,000-foot wall in only three days, as we accomplished one of the first alpine-style ascents in the Alaska Range. The second and third ascents of our route, three decades later, also took parties of crack climbers three days. Alex, Renan, and Freddie would be attempting the fourth ascent.

On Dickey, Renan led the first pillar, steep and beautiful climbing on decent granite. Then he turned the lead over to the team's hired gun on the giant headwall. The insidious potential trap posed by the southeast face lies in the fact that about two-fifths of the way up the wall, the granite turns into horrible "brown sugar." On our second day of climbing in 1974, as the weather started to deteriorate, we had pushed up into that potential blind alley, not at all sure that we had enough hardware to rappel off should we run into a dead end.

Our crux came on the thirty-second pitch, where Galen, improvising wildly, drove a couple of baby angle pitons directly into the crackless brown sugar, then drilled a dubious bolt into the junk— the only bolt we placed on the route. It was obvious that there was no way to scale the blank cliff above the bolt. Instead we lowered Ed, who pendulumed to the right. Out of sight of our partner, Galen and I waited anxiously. At last Ed yelled, "It goes!" He had found the good granite again in a series of chimneys and cracks, the key to our upward escape.

On June 6, 2013, Alex surged up the wall in the lead, dispatching one difficulty after another, fixing the rope so that Renan and Freddie could follow on their ascenders. Alex climbed in rock shoes, while his partners followed in mountain boots. According to Freddie, after several hours Alex said, "I can't believe how easy this climbing is. But why am I so tired?"

Freddie reflects, "That crappy rock in the middle of the face would have freaked out most climbers. But Alex had plenty of experience with bad rock in places like Chad."

Both the second and third ascent parties had thought they were off-route in the middle of the face, until they ran into Galen's bolt. As we had done, they used it to lower one climber, who pendulumed to the right to reach the good chimney system. But Alex thought the bolt, which had now been in place for thirty-nine years, looked, as he put it, "pretty terrible." As he recounts, "Instead of rappelling, penduluming, and then aiding the chimney, I face climbed sideways across the rock and effectively skipped that pitch."

Alex, Freddie, and Renan took most of the aid out of our route. We had rated the climb 5.9 A3. They graded it 5.10c A0, meaning that what little aid they resorted to was as easy as aid climbing gets—little more than pulling on gear from time to time. Most of that 5.10 free climbing—child's play for Alex—would have been beyond our abilities in 1974.

According to Alex, "I led about a thirty-pitch block without really stopping. I kept thinking, *One more pitch, then I'll turn it over to Freddie*, but then I'd make an anchor, look up, and decide that I could climb at least one more pitch before I gave up the lead.

"Freddie led the last five hundred feet on scary mixed terrain. He was our ice ninja!"

The trio's elapsed time—nineteen hours—made a hash of our

three-day push in 1974. On the other hand, those three climbed
Dickey on a perfect, windless, sunny day—the finest during the previous several weeks. In 1974, we had finished the climb in a raging
storm, with snow lashed by a forty mph gale, and we were glad to
have survived our ascent.

A few weeks after their climb, I sent Alex a congratulatory e-mail.
His return message was a model of magnanimity. "Your route on
Dickey was awesome," he wrote, "and I can only imagine how crazy
it would have felt to set out up a wall that big so long ago. I come to
walls like that having soloed bigger linkups in a day, but back then
it must have been truly grand."

In a Q&A with his friend Jimmy Chin, Alex was asked what had
been the most "eye-opening experience" during his Alaskan sojourn.
"I learned tons of little things," Alex answered, "like how to put my
crampons on and how to use my ice tool, but in a general sense it
was still just climbing. I guess the thing that surprised me the most
was how much shit—rock and snow and ice—is constantly falling
down the faces. Alpine climbing is dangerous!"

Even after the expedition to the Ruth Gorge, Alex insisted that
he had no intention of becoming a mountaineer. "Climbing a peak
like Ama Dablam," he says, referring to a stunning 22,349-foot
mountain rising above the Khumbu Valley near Mount Everest, "has
absolutely no appeal to me." On the other hand, in his e-mail to me
after Dickey, Alex confessed, "Anyway, I'm psyched to go back to the
Ruth Gorge someday. Such massive walls. But I'm trying not to get
too sucked into alpine climbing."

Toward the end of 2013, however, Alex turned his rabid attention to a climbing objective that stood at the polar opposite of big
walls in Alaska. It was a route on a limestone cliff in the Mexican
state of Nuevo León. By 2013, Cedar Wright and Alex had become
close friends and frequent partners on the rope, even though Cedar
was eleven years older. They had met by accident on El Capitan in

2006, before Alex had won the fame he garnered from his one-day free solos of Astroman and the Rostrum. Cedar remembers being impressed by the shy young climber who seemed to come into his own the moment he started up a cliff: *Who's this kid?* he wondered to himself.

The two were together on the trip to the Czech Republic that fueled Sender's seminal 2008 film *The Sharp End*. Later, after Alex got sponsored by The North Face, their bond intensified. "We hit it off," Cedar recalls. "We shared the same sardonic sense of humor." And Cedar detected the modesty beneath Alex's sometimes "aggro" exterior. "It's just that Alex can't understand why anybody would have trouble climbing anything," he says.

Cedar was developing a career as a filmmaker himself, just as Renan Ozturk was doing at the same time, so it was almost inevitable that the three would collaborate on a major project. It all came together on El Potrero Chico.

Before January 2014, *except for Moonlight Buttress, nearly all of my big free solos had been on granite walls in Yosemite. But I'd first climbed on El Potrero Chico—"The Little Corral"—in 2009 and immediately enjoyed the highly technical style demanded by its gray limestone. It may be the best crag in Mexico, and it's certainly the best known. The whole ambiance of the place is congenial. There's a website devoted to singing the praises of Potrero, which offers "a lifetime of well-bolted, multi-pitch sport routes with ratings from 5.7 to 5.14 and routes with up to 23 pitches. The climbs have very easy access with only a 5-minute walk from most campgrounds, eliminating any need for a car. The cost of living is very low and the friendly people wonderful." Sounds like tourist hype, but those words match my own experience there.*

*Of all the routes on Potrero, the gem is a fifteen-pitch route
that arrows right up the middle of the face, called El Sendero
Luminoso—"The Shining Path." The first ascent was put up by
Jeff Jackson, Kevin Gallagher, and Kurt Smith in 1992. Two years
later, Jackson, Smith, and Pete Peacock freed the whole 1,750-foot
climb. They rated it 5.12d. But the climb is quite sustained, eleven
pitches of 5.12 and four of 5.11. Jeff is the editor of* Rock and Ice,
*and we've corresponded quite a bit over the years, including when
I wrote for the magazine or its website.*

*I first climbed Sendero in 2009, and I'd immediately fantasized
about soloing it. But when I came back in the winter of 2013–14 to
revisit the route, I realized that it would take a concentrated effort
for me to feel comfortable on it. Sendero climbs a north-facing wall
with a lot of vegetation, and since the climbing is sufficiently difficult
to keep the crowds away, there's not enough traffic to keep the route
buffed clean. Holds were full of dirt and plants, and even though I
could climb around them or avoid the particularly prickly cactuses,
it's hard to commit when in the back of your mind you're wondering if
there's an easier way. Potrero also has a reputation for being chossy,
but I think that's overrated. Yes, there are a lot of loose blocks on the
wall, but you just have to avoid grabbing or standing on them. The
smooth limestone texture of the wall is actually pretty nice.*

*Part of the appeal of Sendero for me lay in the technical com-
plexity of the climbing. Potrero is made of slabby, gray, water-
runnel limestone. It's full of small holds and solution pockets.
Really subtle features. All the holds tend to face the wrong directions. You get into tricky body positions that require real precision.
It's so stylish—such an old-school climb.*

*Of course limestone is more porous than granite. Holds just
break off unexpectedly. It's less predictable than granite. There are
holds that are sort of "glued" to the wall. You have to trust that the
one time you hold it is not the time it rips off the mountain.*

The plan that winter was for Cedar and Renan to come down to Mexico to make a short film if I decided to solo Sendero. Almost at once, however, I had my qualms about the project. Ever since my "epiphany" in Chad, I'd agonized over the environmental impact of my climbing. To fly the three of us down to Mexico—not to mention other crew members to operate automated drones to capture footage high on the wall—would be to leave a sizable carbon footprint. Could I really justify burning all that jet fuel and using pricey high-tech hardware just to capture my several hours of play on Portrero Chico? What if we got everybody down there, ready to film, and I chickened out because I decided I wasn't comfortable going up on the wall without a rope?

In my mind, our Newfoundland trip in 2011 was a classic example of waste. Both a waste of our time and a waste of natural resources. We all flew to Newfoundland, drove to Devil's Bay, and rented a boat to cruise around the fjords, and we didn't climb shit. We made a huge impact on the environment—for nothing.

There was no guarantee I'd be up for the free solo. I've had other projects I set my eye on—notably Romantic Warrior in the Needles of California, a nine-pitch 5.12b route on a steep granite crack system—that I rehearsed, planned, and then backed off. It was too hot that June, my shoes didn't feel quite right, I felt rushed by other engagements I'd committed to in the upcoming days, so I realized I wasn't ready for it. Actually, there are tons of solos that I haven't done! In such a situation, I have to pay attention to my feelings and my judgment, not to outside pressures. So there was a real possibility in January 2014 that I might be dragging Cedar and Renan and the other guys down to Potrero Chico for nothing.

Starting on January 9, Cedar and I spent four days (with a rest day when it rained) climbing, fixing, and cleaning the route, using ropes and belaying to get the moves down pat and grigris to hold us in place while we cleaned. To get all the dirt, twigs, grass, and shrubs out of the cracks, we scraped away with our climbing brushes. They're like toothbrushes with extra-stiff bristles. If we'd really been serious, we would have used something more heavy-duty, like a big scrubber.

Each day, we worked from sunrise to sunset. The more vegetation we pulled off the upper pitches, the more dirt rained down on the lower ones. The more big plants we removed from the route, the more the small ones stood out. Once we started, we couldn't stop until we saw a perfectly clean slab of limestone. Some of the plants were particularly tough to get out, adapted as they are to rugged conditions. For a week after I returned to the States, I had thorns growing out of my hands. But Jeff Jackson e-mailed me, "God smiles every time you uproot a lechuguilla."

Purists or nonclimbers might think that by removing natural vegetation from a cliff, you're altering or even trashing the land-scape. I'll confess to faint qualms along those lines. Cedar and I knew that plants grow back quickly on Potrero, and that the wall would eventually revert to a hanging garden. I didn't worry much about our impact while we swung around plucking cactuses and ticking holds. I just felt a vague sense of unease that we were put-ting so much work into something that's supposed to be so pure and simple.

But at the end of the fourth day, as we rapped down a smooth, clean face, I couldn't help feeling a giddy excitement. At some point, a switch had flipped from "Maybe I'll solo it eventually" to "So psyched! Must solo immediately!" I have no idea what flipped that switch, though the climbing did look more inviting without the dirt and plants obscuring the holds. For whatever reason, I was ready, and I knew that I would solo the route the next morning, if the conditions allowed.

That's the strange paradox, for me at least, about free soloing. It's the waiting beforehand that's anxiety-producing. The vacillating over "Should I do this?" When I finally commit, the stress goes away. It's actually a big relief to go up there and do it.

January 14 dawned clear. I wasn't going to delay any longer. I wanted to go up on the route alone, which is sort of the point of soloing. I was seeking out a personal adventure, and the filmmakers knew that any intrusion would fundamentally alter the experience. Renan took up a position far out in the desert at the base so he could get a long shot. Cedar spent several hours guiding the drone pilots up to the summit of El Toro so they could meet me on top and film some summit footage.

I was and felt completely alone. I didn't know where the other guys were positioned or if they were even watching. I just went climbing, knowing that we could go back up on the route during the next few days to get all the filming done.

The high-tech gear was brought to Mexico by a Boulder-based firm called SkySight. The drone was a small octocopter, maybe half the size of a coffee table, with a super-expensive gimbal that held a RED camera steady. Between the high-quality drone and the top-of-the-line cinema camera, and the fact that the guys at SkySight are among the best in the industry, we were pretty sure we'd capture some amazing scenes. The drone was flown by a pilot using a big controller—a lot like a toy truck. The camera was operated by the pilot's brother. And they brought along their sister as an assistant to help carry gear and catch the craft on landing.

Renan was there shooting for Camp 4 Collective, which had been hired by The North Face to make a film of the ascent. Camp 4 owns a RED camera, so Renan had been shooting with it for years. And Renan had brought his girlfriend to be a camera assistant, so that brought the filming crew to a total of five people. And then Cedar and me as climbers.

The morning of the solo, nobody said much of anything, because they didn't want to influence me one way or another. Ear-

lier, though, everybody had assured me that I should climb only
what I felt comfortable with, and that they could shoot any other,
easier route if I changed my mind. But it was hard not to feel a
little pressure.

We'd rented a small casita sitting atop a hill above one of the
many camping areas, which provided a glorious view of the whole
area. That morning I opened my eyes lazily, gazing up from the
pile of jackets I was using as a pillow through the worn, faded
blinds to see the tops of the mountains just catching some morning
sun. Despite the pressure, I'd slept well. I almost always sleep well,
even before big solo climbs. From the sofa I used as a bed I could
easily see Sendero weaving its way up the wall. There was no way
of escaping. I followed my normal routine—cereal poured into the
yogurt tub, news on my phone. But I lingered, trying to stay patient
and let the morning humidity burn off. I focused artificially on my
phone, using it to ignore the people around me with cameras and
questions, but not really understanding what I read. The only thing
that mattered was Sendero, just coming into the light.

Finally, I made the fifteen-minute stroll over to the base of the
route, weaving through scrubby, prickly bushes and struggling up
a loose scree slope. My light backpack made me feel buoyant as I
scrambled up the hill. My shoes, chalk bag, energy bars, and water
felt weightless compared to the 600 feet of rope and full rack that
we'd been carrying the past few days.

One of my favorite aspects of soloing is the way that pain ceases
to exist. The previous four long days of climbing and cleaning had
worn out my fingers and toes, but now, as I pulled on the first few
holds, I felt none of the soreness. Each edge seemed perfect and
crisp, each fingerlock felt like an anchor. Foot jams that had been
hideously painful the previous afternoon felt rock solid. Hold after
hold, I worked my way up the wall, smoothly and perfectly.

What seemed to me to be the crux of the route came at the top

of the second pitch, maybe 250 feet above the ground. The standard sequence involves opposing side pulls with small and slippery
footholds, but I'd found a small two-finger pocket out to the side
that felt slightly more secure. As I chalked up, I felt a little nervous.
Or maybe just excited. Or maybe just my awareness was height-
ened. It's hard to untangle the various feelings, but I definitely felt
alive. I knew that this was the only moment on the route where I'd
have to try really hard. And that's exactly what I did, completing
the sequence exactly as I needed.

Once I calmed down a little from overgripping, I knew I'd finish
the route, even though there were still thirteen pitches to go.

A second crux comes on the fifth pitch, about 600 feet off the
ground. The pitch ends in a huge ledge where you can stop and
take a breather. On the crux sequence, I was connected to the wall
by only a small, sharp limestone undercling above my head. Trusting a tiny smear for my left foot, I raised my right foot almost to
my waist, and I levered off it to reach my left hand to a distant jug.

It was by no means the hardest climbing on the route, but the
stark simplicity of the movement stayed with me long afterward.
To me, that is soloing at its finest: to be nearly disconnected from
the wall with the air all around. There's a certain purity to that
kind of movement that can't be found with a rope and gear. But for
all my love of simplicity, it's not always simple to get to those positions. Here on Sendero, everything came together—a perfect mix-
ture of aesthetics and challenge, hard enough climbing to demand
total concentration and commitment on a line of strength that
goes straight up the biggest face on the massif.

From there to the top, I climbed easily, trusting my feet more
with each step. I used new sequences on a few pitches, trusting
myself to find the easiest way through the seemingly blank sea of
limestone. On the midway ledge, I popped my shoes off, and again
five pitches higher, just to let my toes relax after hundreds of feet of

technical slab climbing. But all in all, I'd found exactly the experience I was looking for: I was only a small dot on a vast, uncaring wall, but for those two hours, I got to taste perfection.

• • • •

We spent the next two days reclimbing and reshooting various pitches of the route. It's anticlimactic to go back up a route to pose all over it. The triumph of the actual achievement gets lost in what follows. But as I slithered in and out of my harness on various ledges, climbing different sections for the camera and clipping into anchors in between, I tried to remind myself that I wouldn't have the opportunity to climb a wall like this one without doing some work, and at least I was having fun with my friends.

From the start of our trip, Cedar had wanted to try to redpoint Sendero—lead it free but roped, with no falls. I owed it to my buddy to be his belay partner on such an effort. The trouble was, we had return flights booked for the following morning. So we set out on the evening of January 16 to try to climb the route in the night.

The full moon rose as he started up the first pitch, casting a pale glow across the whole wall. There's something eerily calm about moonlight. I left my headlamp off, and I fed out slack in the darkness, pondering the last week. Was it worth it? What had we really done?

For the first five pitches, Cedar moved steadily up the wall, the silence punctured only by the occasional "I'm off belay. Line's fixed!"—my cue to start jugging as fast as I could up the rope he'd tied to his anchor. That way, Cedar could conserve the energy he otherwise would have wasted on belaying and rope management. I tried to jug each pitch in four minutes flat.

It was at this point, however, that the ethical dilemma of my little "project" started to nag at me. Traveling to places like Chad has made me acutely mindful of my own impact on the world around me. At first, I'd assumed that my carbon footprint would be much lower than that of the average American, because I lived in a van and didn't own many possessions. But as I read more about the issue, I realized that the amount of flying that I did still left me near the highest percentile of environmental impact. My next thought was to buy carbon offsets—until I researched them and discovered that they weren't the cure-all I was hoping for. Paying someone to plant trees in the First World seemed far less beneficial than providing clean energy in the developing world, though both could be considered to be offsetting carbon emissions. The first basically pays the rich while the second not only reduces fossil-fuel use but also improves standards of living by saving people money and reducing the health problems associated with burning things for fuel.

I've tried to approach environmentalism the same way I do my climbing: by setting small, concrete goals that build on each other. That was the idea behind starting the Honnold Foundation. I also worked on smaller projects, such as setting up my mom's house with solar panels and giving up meat in an effort to eat lower on the food chain. In some ways it might seem silly even to make the effort, since the environmental problems facing our world are so much bigger than any one person's actions. But some walls also seem so huge and impossible that it appears pointless to work toward them. The beauty of climbing has always been the reward of the process itself.

While Cedar struggled through the intricate slabs, I couldn't help wondering whether making a whole production out of climbing went against all the environmental principles I wanted to stand for. Could radio-controlled heli shots and minimalism really go together? Was it worth the impact of flying a whole crew down to Mexico for me to enjoy one three-hour climb? Or could I possibly use the climbing to do more good than harm? Might the platform I've gained through climbing be harnessed toward more useful things?

The problem with worrying too much is that it can be crippling. Somehow, I thought, it must all come down to balance—finding that line between minimizing impact but still maintaining an acceptable quality of life. But who's to judge an acceptable life? I don't even know what I truly require to be happy. Do I have to be traveling all the time? Or soloing walls? The circle of Cedar's headlamp drifted slowly away, leaving me alone in the moonlight to swim with my questions.

Then, when we were halfway up the wall, a mariachi band started playing loudly just down the road from the cliff, filling the still desert night with the blaring sounds of horns and accordions. We couldn't help laughing. I told Cedar they were rooting for him. The moon tracked across the sky as I jugged to the rhythm of live music. At the belay, I pulled my hood closer against the cool night air. The summit loomed hundreds of feet above, silhouetted against the starry blackness. Though it seemed impossibly far off, there was nothing to do but carry on. Cedar continued tiptoeing up into the night, savoring the voyage.

T HE CAMP 4 COLLECTIVE FILM that Renan Ozturk crafted to feature Alex's solo of El Sendero Luminoso, a mere six minutes and twelve seconds long, is a minor masterpiece. If it lacks the gonzo zaniness of the Sender Films celebrations of Alex's deeds, as well as the humorous riffs in van or campground, it captures the grace of Alex's movement on rock better than any previous footage has. The camera work, zooming fluidly in and out, or floating gently through space (thanks to the SkySight drones), paints a lyricism that mirrors Alex's state of mind and body when he's doing what he does best.

There are moments in the film that bring home the seriousness of free soloing in novel ways, such as a bit when Cedar Wright, in the days of cleaning the route before the climb, says, "It's kind of weird, helping your friend do something that you know could potentially lead to his death"—this, as the camera pans over the graveyard in the nearby town of Hidalgo. But the closing footage captures Alex standing on what look like "nothing" holds, his hands dangling free at his sides, as a slow grin takes over his face.

Shortly after the climb, Mary Anne Potts of *National Geographic Adventure Online* interviewed Alex. She asked, "Why did you smile at that moment on the wall?"

Alex's characteristic answer: "I have no idea since I haven't seen the film, but I'd assume because I was happy." To underline the point, he appended a happy face.

Indeed, in the makeshift register on the summit of El Toro, with a pencil stub Alex scribbled a note that a later visitor photographed. It read:

> 1/14/14
> Solo!!
> In two hours
> Alex Honnold
> Great day out!!

(Two hours on the fifteen-pitch climb, another hour to scramble to the summit of El Toro.)

The Camp 4 film closes with the bald statement: "It could be the most difficult rope-less climb in history." Almost two years later, no one has come forth to dispute that claim—except Alex. In outtakes filmed by Renan just after the ascent, he insisted, "It's not like this is the physical limit of my climbing. Not like the hardest thing I could do. It was well within my comfort zone." ("No Big Deal" Honnold at his deadpan best!)

Others weighed in less equivocally. On Supertopo.com, post-

ers expressed their awe. Wrote one, "The dude is so scary good.
. . . All you can do is shake your head in wonderment and amaze-
ment." Another: "Compartmentalizing fear is a very real thing, and
he excels at it. Or is he just so good that he's not afraid?" Yet another,
tongue in cheek: "I'd be way more impressed if he was human."

Jeff Jackson, editor of *Rock and Ice* and the author of the first
(roped) free ascent of El Sendero Luminoso in 1994, editorialized,
"What do I think? Well, honestly, I try not to think about it. . . . The
Sendero free solo is a different realm entirely—so bad it makes me
wonder if Honnold will ever get another visit from Santa."

Less ironically, Jackson—one of the strongest rock climbers of
his generation—analyzed the feat by comparing it to his own experience on the route. "To my knowledge," he wrote,

> no one has ever soloed a wall with such sustained technical
> climbing—11 pitches rated 5.12a or harder. The pitches are long
> (the first five are 50 meters or longer) and unrelieved by big fea-
> tures where you can chill and shake out your feet. The wall is a
> slab, mostly just under vertical, and if you've ever climbed a difficult
> slab you know how mentally trying that kind of climbing can be. To
> me, climbing a 5.12 slab is a little like pulling a rabbit out of a top
> hat. There are elements of magic at work. Though it has been 20
> years since I climbed the line, I clearly remember the feeling of get-
> ting away with something when I redpointed [climbed free without
> falling] the second pitch. I skated through on updraft, sticky rubber
> and whispered petitions to demons. . . .
>
> And Honnold soloed that pitch! And all the others! Shit me! How
> is that even possible?

Alex was not about to rest on his laurels. Less than a month after
his Mexican triumph, he was off to a part of the world he had never
visited, to try a climb of the sort he'd never before attempted.

CHAPTER **EIGHT**
FITZ

The Fitz Traverse was Tommy Caldwell's idea. As soon as he mentioned it, I said, "That sounds rad! Let's do it!" I was on board, even though I'd never been to Patagonia. I didn't even know anything about Patagonia.

Though it stands only 11,168 feet above sea level, Fitz Roy is the tallest peak in a tight cluster of amazing granite spires in southern Patagonia, on the border between Chile and Argentina. It's named after Robert Fitzroy, the captain of the Beagle on the famous 1830s voyage that gave Charles Darwin his first inklings about the theory of evolution. The first ascent, by the great French mountaineers Lionel Terray and Guido Magnone in 1952, may have been the most technical big-range climb performed up to that date anywhere in the world.

That cluster of peaks, which also includes Cerro Torre, Torre Egger, Aguja Poincenot, and many other agujas (Spanish for "needles"), probably comprises the ultimate collection anywhere on earth of steep, soaring, and breathtakingly beautiful mountains. The granite is shockingly good—as good as Yosemite—but Patagonia is notorious for bad weather, for shrieking winds that don't let up for weeks, and for humongous mushrooms of rime ice plating nearly vertical slabs and cracks.

Tommy first climbed in Patagonia in 2006. Even though most of his prior experience had been on rock, he put up some formidable lines that season. As mentioned in chapter five, Tommy, with Topher Donahue and Erik Roed, freed the Línea de Eleganza on Fitz Roy. Tommy and Topher also tried another massive route, Royal Flush, on the east face of Fitz Roy. The peak was pissing wet that February, and other climbers gave up on the climb, declaring it hopeless, but Tommy went up there in the same conditions and damn near freed the route onsight (on his first time on the route) before he and Topher had to back off.

By 2014, Fitz Roy had really gotten under Tommy's skin—so much so that the year before, when his wife, Becca, gave birth to a boy, they named him Fitz.

Though a formidable peak in its own right, Fitz Roy doesn't stand alone. It's the centerpiece of a chain of seven connected towers, starting on the north with the Aguja Guillaumet and ending on the south with the Aguja de l'S. The obvious challenge was to connect them all in a single continuous ridge climb—the Fitz Traverse.

In 2008, Freddie Wilkinson, who would be my partner five years later in the Ruth Gorge, and Dana Drummond completed the first half of the traverse, linking Guillaumet, Mermoz, Val Biois, and Fitz Roy, but then rapping off Fitz Roy and hiking out. They called their half-traverse the Care Bear Traverse, because they were stuck in the clouds so much of the time that they started joking with each other, "I bet all those other climbers are thinking, 'Those stupid Americans are up in the clouds!'" (In the children's cartoon series Care Bears, the ursine heroes live in lairs among the clouds.)

Freddie and Dana took three days for the traverse, with two exposed bivouacs. The Care Bear was repeated numerous times *after 2008, but nobody had gotten beyond Fitz Roy. The problem for all those teams was that because the second guy did so much jugging, by the time they got up Fitz Roy their ropes were pretty core-shot from rubbing against the rock.*

Tommy and I arrived in El Chaltén, the gateway town to climbing in the Fitz Roy region, on February 1, 2014. For the first nine days, the weather on the peaks was horrendous, so we climbed down low, bouldering and doing sport climbs on small crags. There's a ton of good climbing all around El Chaltén. Sweet! I thought. I'm gonna get strong! But I also thought, Wow, these peaks are so intimidating, I'm not sure I'd really mind if the weather never gets good.

We climbed every day, and ate out every night in El Chaltén. It was a pretty nice lifestyle.

CALDWELL WOULD LATER WRITE about the Patagonia adventure for *Alpinist* in the winter 2014 issue. In his thoughtful piece, he talked about how much harder it was to climb with all-out commitment once he had become a father. "I'd had this Romantic idea," he wrote, "of pulling my family into my life of constant travel. So they followed me from Colorado to Argentina. Then, after two blissful weeks together in El Chaltén, the wind had calmed, and I'd packed."

Saying good-bye to Becca as he headed for the Fitz Traverse, Tommy minimized the danger. "Don't worry, baby, we'll be careful," he told her. "It's just a rock climb."

But privately, "I remembered that I wanted nothing more than to live to be an old man."

In the same essay, Tommy recalled meeting up with Alex in the Valley in the spring of 2012 and being taken aback by his nonchalance. "Anyone could daisy-solo the Regular Route of Half Dome," Alex claimed. "It's not that big of a deal. . . . You know you're not going to fall on 5.11."

Drawn to Alex by his skill and amiability, Tommy puzzled over his friend's almost blasé attitude about risk.

How could Alex talk about his climbs in such a cavalier way? . . . [H]e described free solos of routes like the Regular Northwest Face of Half Dome as if they were nothing more than particularly scenic hikes. His conversation never drifted to places of death, love or even innate beauty. *It's as if he thinks everything is either badass or boring,* I thought. *That's probably part of the reason he is so good at what he does.* I found Alex's apparent indifference toward risk both exciting and terrifying. In an age of technology, he reminded me of a lost instinct. A hunter, a warrior.

Whatever Tommy's doubts, he soon realized that he and Alex made a superb two-man team. On their Triple Crown linkup in 2012, in the middle of the night on Freerider on El Cap, Alex had been deeply impressed by Tommy's stemming a pitch in the dark that he normally would have liebacked. But Tommy was equally impressed by Alex's nerve and aplomb.

He rarely stopped to place gear, only a few pieces per pitch. Somehow, that boldness, that confidence that he wouldn't fall, was contagious. . . .

   Tied to the upper end of the rope, Alex was simul-climbing out of sight and earshot. Above me, the cord arched past a dark off-width—clipped to nothing. My arms quivered with fatigue; my head pounded with dehydration. I hoped to God that he had some gear in. Best not to think too much about it.

Even while they simul-climbed at a nearly perfect level together, Tommy and Alex engaged in a friendly debate about free soloing, with Tommy voicing his doubts. As Tommy would later comment, "Alex is as solid as anybody I've ever met on technical rock. But I worry about him. I've never tried to talk him out of free soloing—I just express my doubts. But he'll turn around and try to talk me *into* free soloing.

"We climbed Velvet Tongue at Red Rocks together, roped. Leading the 5.12+ crux, Alex slipped. But he hung on by one finger. Anybody else would have fallen off. I said, 'Wow, that was impressive!' But of course I was thinking, *What if he were soloing when that happened?*"

In the *Alpinist* piece, Caldwell explains how completing the Triple Crown with Alex gave him the idea for teaming up to attempt the Fitz Traverse. On the summit of Half Dome, after climbing some eighty pitches in twenty-one hours,

> I'd expected the trifecta to be a test of human will and endurance. I'd wanted to see that place of survival again, where we're reminded that human capabilities are nearly limitless and that our world still contains mysteries. But Alex was just too good. The big walls seemed to shrink to only half their size. . . . I wondered what we would be able to climb if we took these techniques to Patagonia, where the big storms and bigger mountains made fast and light climbing a necessity—rather than merely a cool trick.

When the weather finally cleared on February 12, with a forecast of a good window during the next few days, Tommy and I headed up. The big advantage we thought we had over previous parties that had tried the Fitz Traverse was that instead of having the second jug every pitch, we'd simul-climb almost everything. That ought to mean less wear and tear on our rope.

Just as we had on the Triple in Yosemite, we each led huge blocks at a time, upwards of 800 feet. Part of what makes climbing with Tommy so great is that we can lead interchangeably, though on this traverse he would get all the ice and mixed pitches, since he had vastly more experience with that terrain. We got up the first tower, Aguja Guillaumet, in only two very long pitches, taking a mere two and a half hours to climb the thousand feet of the Brenner-Moschioni route.

It turns out that Rolo—Rolando Garibotti—and Colin Haley were trying the Fitz Traverse at the same time we were. Rolo's the man when it comes to Patagonia—not only its tireless chronicler, but the guy who's put up more routes on more different peaks than anyone else. He's also become a kind of steward of the range, improving trails and assembling route guides. We met up with that pair on the summit of Guillaumet, since they'd climbed a different route. Rolo had had hip surgery the previous year, and now his hip was really bothering him, so, reluctantly, they abandoned their effort. Rolo was kind enough to lend me his aluminum strap-on crampons, which would turn out to be extremely helpful for the traverse.

We went really light, figuring speed would mean safety. Our rack was seventeen cams, a handful of nuts, and fourteen slings. No pitons. We were counting on finding fixed anchors and even fixed gear along the way, to supplement the pro we'd place as we led. The real question mark was whether we could find the rappel anchors left by other parties, so we could rap most of the big descents from each tower as we moved along the ridgeline.

We had one sixty-meter climbing rope, and a skinny eighty-meter tag line—a rope to use not for leading but for rappels. By tying the tag line and the lead rope together end to end, and feeding it through the anchor sling, we could make a rappel on the doubled rope as long as sixty meters, then pull the ropes down to use on the next rappel. For the ice, only one ice screw and a single ice tool—a Black Diamond Cobra, a short metal axe with a curved shaft and a sharp, notched pick.

We did most of the climbing in approach shoes, or tennies, as we call them. Rock shoes only for the hardest pitches. No mountain boots. We strapped our crampons onto our tennies, which doesn't make for the most stable configuration, because the soles and edges of the shoes are too soft and flexible.

One sleeping bag between us, and one big puffy (down jacket). A stove and three gas canisters. We originally planned not to bring a tent, but on one of our "training" days during the bad weather, we'd spent the night in our Black Diamond First Light tent and realized how comfortable it was. It's a pretty amazing shelter, because it weighs only one pound. At the last minute, we decided to take it. It turned out to be a godsend.

We were determined to go light enough that all our gear, stove, fuel, and food could fit into one fifteen-pound pack (for the leader) and one twenty-five-pound pack (for the second). For a multiday alpine traverse, that's pretty frickin' light!

Afterward, some clueless journalist asked us if we'd had a film crew along. As if! But Tommy had been given a very light camera, so we tried to take video clips of each other as we moved along the traverse—footage that might eventually be spliced together into a film documenting the climb. We also had iPhones to shoot photos with. Actually, my iPhone was one of my most important pieces of gear, because I had about sixty topos of the various routes on the various towers loaded onto it.

From the summit of Guillaumet, we ridge-traversed over to the Aguja Mermoz, topping out at 5:00 p.m. Four hours later, we set up the tent right on the crest of the ridge and settled in for our first night's bivouac. I got the puffy that night, and slept nice and warm. It was only a few days later that Tommy confessed that he'd basically shivered through the night. In fact, I hogged the puffy for three nights, thinking that as a suburban California boy I needed it more than a Colorado hardman did. At last, Tommy's reluctant admission of how cold he was made me stop being selfish and give him the puffy.

We got off at 8:30 a.m. on February 13. It took a long, long day to climb over the Aguja Val Biois and up the Goretta Pillar via the Casarotto route. There we found some of the finest rock climbing on the whole traverse, with free moves up to 5.11d. That stretch, which I led, was one of only a few passages on the whole traverse where we switched to rock shoes. We French freed whenever we could, either grabbing and pulling on fixed gear or popping in a cam or nut and pulling on that. Still, we did very little aid on the whole traverse, nothing that we'd rate harder than A1.

It wasn't until 7:45 p.m. that we stood at the base of the final headwall on the north pillar of Fitz Roy itself. We were pretty darn tired after more than eleven continuous hours of climbing, but this was no place for a bivouac, so we decided to try to get up the head-wall and camp on the summit. We also thought that the colder snow conditions of evening would be safer than waiting till morn-ing, when sun on the wall might send all kinds of stuff falling down on us.

We could see at once that there was way more ice and snow on that headwall than we'd expected, thanks to one of the wettest summers in recent years. It was Tommy's turn to lead. As he forged his way up into that mess of ice, snow, and rock, we faced what would turn out to be the crux of the whole traverse. And here the climbing got really scary.

. . . .

Crusted up with rime ice, that headwall would have been tough enough to lead with a pair of ice tools, a good supply of screws, and crampons firmly strapped onto mountain boots. For Tommy, with only the one screw and the Cobra as his sole tool, and crampons wobbling on his tennies, it was a nightmare. As he worked his way up into the rime, he uncharacteristically shouted down, "I don't know about this."

I tried to encourage him. "Dude, you got this," I shouted up. "You're a total boss." But I had my own doubts and fears.

A waterfall was springing out of the ice, as Tommy put it, "from a hole in the mountain that resemble[d] the mouth of a dragon." He later captured that incredibly dicey lead in his Alpinist piece:

> I let the pick of my single axe pierce the sheet of flowing water and strike the new-formed ice beneath. The point glides around for a moment and then sticks in a small slot. I have to move now. In another thirty minutes, that cascade will freeze and coat everything in verglas. Our few cams will skitter, useless, out of the cracks, and the aluminum crampons strapped to our tennis shoes will be more like skates. My hand trembles. . . .
>
> I enter the waterfall, and I gasp as the cold flow seeps into every conceivable opening. I slot my single tool in a fissure, pull up and place a nut. . . . I look down: a large, dry ledge extends like an island below me. A growing chill reminds me that it's already too late to retreat. The only option, now, is to keep moving. I'd wanted us to have an adventure, but this is a bit too much.

For the next half hour, Tommy flailed around, as he described it, "like a hooked fish in a rapid." Finally he leaned off his tool placement far to the side and got a tiny cam partly slotted in a crack. He wasn't sure it would hold, but he grabbed it with both hands and swung over. Soaked to the skin, he was shivering, on the verge of hypothermia, but at last he was on dry rock.

The sun had set a while before. Tommy switched on his headlamp and aided up the crack. At last he took off his crampons and free climbed beyond. As he later wrote,

> Coarse rock grates my skin. Blood splatters on stone. My clothes freeze. With each move, ice cracks off my jacket and chimes down the wall. The rope becomes as stiff as a steel cable. I climb faster, trying to create more body heat. . . . Occasionally, my only option is to chop through the rime that blocks our passage. Debris showers on Alex's head. Large chunks hit his back and shoulders with a guttural thud.
>
> "Are you OK?" I shout down.
>
> "Yeah, man, you're doing great," Alex says, but the words sound forced.

All this time, I was wearing both of our jackets, the big puffy in addition to Tommy's light puffy. He was leading in just his hoodie and hardshell. It was amazing because after he got soaked, he climbed a lot farther, then eventually dried out and got warm again. Since I was doing nothing but belay for forty-five minutes at a stretch, then jugging for fifteen minutes, I was getting kind of chilly. It was impressive that Tommy could keep it together in such cold temps. Total hardman.

Finally the angle of the headwall relented. But now, in the dark, Tommy led a 600-foot pitch of snow and mixed steps. You're just scrambling, except that it was really snowy. Since we only had the one ice tool, he was leading with it, which meant that I wound up simul-climbing in strap-on crampons with no tool. Since the rope just disappeared into the night and I didn't know if he'd gotten in any pro, I was seconding with only Tommy's pick marks to show me the route. And just generally clawing at the mountain with my hands. It was scary.

We didn't get near the summit until 2:00 a.m. Just below the top, we found a nook shaped by a cornice that gave us a lee space to set up our tent. "What a day!" said Tommy.

We got ourselves inside the tent and shared our single sleeping bag. Once again, since I had the puffy, Tommy shivered through the night without complaining.

I'll have to admit that, on that headwall, I was way outside my comfort zone. That was one of my hardest days of climbing ever.

After only three hours of fitful sleep, we packed up camp and hiked to the summit of Fitz Roy. We didn't spend long there, shooting a few photos, still dog-tired. But from here on, we were pushing beyond the Care Bear Traverse that Freddie Wilkinson and Dana Drummond had established in 2008.

To get off Fitz Roy and down to the col between it and the Aguja Kakito, we had to make twenty rappels down the Franco-Argentine route. The route was like a waterfall. Three days of sunny weather on a south-facing wall had melted everything in sight. The ropes were like sponges and we got massively wet—not that that was a big problem, since it was sunny and nice out. An acquaintance of ours, Whit Margo, had just successfully guided a client up one of the ice routes on the other side of Fitz, and we ran into him near the summit. He gave us good beta for how to find the rap anchors, which was really helpful. But then, as we were rapping the face, his client's ice axe came tomahawking past us at about a million miles an hour. He'd accidentally dropped it and it went the whole distance down the wall. It was kind of a weird encounter.

From the col between Fitz Roy and Kakito onward, though,

we were in largely uncharted terrain. We managed to weave our way over and around the various spiky summits of Kakito. But it was 6:00 p.m. before we stood at the base of the north face of Aguja Poincenot. Here we faced our second major rock climb, as we started up the route pioneered by Dean Potter and Steph Davis in 2001. It's a serious, 1,000-foot route with some bad rock and poor protection on a few pitches. Dean and Steph rated it 5.11d A1.

Our three days of nonstop climbing were starting to take their toll. The skin on Tommy's fingers was starting to be really painful, it was rubbed so raw. On Poincenot, I led the whole wall, but instead of simul-climbing, Tommy jugged up second to save his fingers. I short-fixed—tying off the middle of the rope to an anchor so he could jug while I soloed on—as often as I could to make it less arduous for him.

For one of the few times on the traverse, I switched to rock shoes. Then I managed to lead the whole thousand feet in only three and a quarter hours. There was only one pitch of truly bad rock, up at the top, but it was easy. And there was some semi-unprotected face climbing at the bottom that was spicy. But basically the route followed nice splitter cracks and I just charged along. I really felt like I was at home in the Valley. Really comfortable climbing.

Wasted as we were on the summit of Poincenot, we were still getting along great and climbing as efficiently as we knew how to. Throughout the traverse, we'd found time to take short breaks as we shot video clips on Tommy's camera. For voice-over, we added commentary about the whole undertaking. At one point, for instance, Tommy said, "This has gotta be the most scenic thing in the universe." On the summit of Fitz Roy, I'd seen other climbers maybe five hundred feet below us on a different route, and I couldn't help blurting out, "There are humans down there! We're going to go down and hug them!" Now, with the camera rolling, Tommy said, "Tell us where we are." I dutifully answered, "We're on the summit of Poincenot!" Corny, maybe, but who knows what a good film editor could do with that stuff.

We pitched our tent again just below the summit of Poincenot on the south side and managed to get another few hours of sleep. That night, Tommy tried to build a little tent platform out of rocks so we'd have something level to sleep on while I cooked dinner. He finally gave up about halfway through because he couldn't make it work. The ledge we were on was just too rocky and misshapen. So we wound up sleeping with our legs hanging over this big drop and a bunch of rocks sticking into our backs. There was always a junk show inside the tent. But we slept well enough. Fatigue does wonders. Still, I remember that bivy as the worst of the traverse.

By now we looked pretty haggard. We weren't eating nearly enough food to match the calories we burned, and our meal breaks were pretty on-the-run. I remember at one point both of us eating polenta with Tommy's broken sunglasses because we couldn't find our spoon. We were able to stay hydrated, however, by using straws we'd brought along to suck the standing water out of little huecos (natural pockets) in the rock. Or we'd eat snow while we were belaying.

By now, our gear and clothing were in tatters. Our shoes were falling apart, and our tent floor was full of little holes from pitching it on uneven rocks. Our pants had rips and tears in them. We'd managed to burn a hole in our sleeping bag. Our packs were trashed from dragging them through chimneys. Somewhere along the way, Tommy dropped one of his climbing shoes. We didn't even see it disappear into the abyss—it just suddenly went missing. On the Fitz Traverse, you could say that we product-tested a whole line of equipment.

Getting down the 3,000-foot south face of Poincenot proved to be the second crux of the whole traverse. That wall isn't climbed very often, but we absolutely had to find the fixed anchors left by

other parties to continue our traverse. If we couldn't find those
anchors, we'd easily use up our rack—and then some—making
anchors of our own. And then, if we could get down, we'd have
to abort and hike out. It's a scary business to rappel blind down a
wall you've never seen before, looking for those fugitive pitons. I'd
get fifty-five meters down and start thinking, Boy, I hope I find an
anchor! We downclimbed as much as we could, but we had to rap
most of the way. At one point, Tommy just picked up a stone and
wedged it into a four-inch crack for an anchor. I said, "Wow. Did
you ever do that before?" Tommy reassured me: "It's bomber."

In the end, we never got off-route. We pretty much nailed that
descent.

By now, we were sort of flying on autopilot. Tommy described
our state well in Alpinist:

> At times, a kind of mutual delirium builds like the electric charge
> of a thunderstorm. Chemicals release from our brains: dopamine,
> norepinephrine, endorphins. Our focus narrows and intensifies.
> More and more, we appear to think as one. A sixth sense seems to
> warn us of each loose block or hidden patch of black ice. . . . Each
> footstep is sure and precise. The absurdity of our situation makes
> us giddy.

We were beginning to think we could really pull off the traverse. There were only three towers to go, none as tall or as serious
as Poincenot. We tackled the Piola-Anker route on Aguja Rafael
Juárez. It's another thousand feet, rated by the 1989 first-ascent
party 5.11a A1, but the rock is mostly good. I led in rock shoes, while
Tommy alternately jugged or simul-climbed. Near the top of the
route, though, I ran into a 150-foot-long 5.10b crack that took only
number 4 cams. One edge of the crack was coated with ice. I didn't
have a number 4 cam on my rack, so I kept pushing a number 3 in

front of me and pulling on it. Because it was too small, it was tipped out, with the plates barely catching the edges of the crack. It would never have held a fall, but at least it helped with the climbing. That just goes to show that in an international arena like Patagonia, you never know what the ratings are going to wind up meaning.

Even so, we got up the Piola-Anker in two long pitches, taking only two and three-quarters hours. A little more than two hours later, we'd traversed the sharp ridge and climbed two longish pitches to the summit of Aguja Saint-Exupéry.

By now, though, our climbing rope was shredding, thanks to the countless abrasions we'd subjected it to as it rubbed against the gritty granite. One section was so badly damaged that we finally had to cut it, leaving us with only thirty-eight meters of usable rope. The other twenty-two meters we carried with us to cut into smaller pieces for slings for our rap anchors. What this meant, however, was that we could make only pitifully short rappels with our doubled remnant of rope—a maximum of nineteen meters. If it hadn't been so windy, we could have used our eighty-meter tag line to make longer rappels. We tried to use it, but it got so tangled up that it drove us insane trying to sort out the snarls. So we coiled it up, stuck it in a pack, and just resorted to shorter but safer raps on our thirty-eight meters of good lead rope.

Tommy would head down first, get to a stance, and yell, "I'm off!" I'd say, "I know, I can see you right below me"—scarcely sixty feet from my own stance. On a bunch of the gear anchors that we constructed, after Tommy rapped I would remove one of the pieces just to save gear. So I'd rappel off a single cam or nut, which can be a bit risky. (If it pops loose, you're dead.) I did that a few times in random places. It was all about preserving the rack for as long as possible.

On the ridge between Rafael Juárez and Saint-Exupéry, we were simul-climbing with the twenty-two-meter section of our lead line. (We were trying to save the longer part for climbing later, and twenty-two meters is long enough for ridge climbing.) In the lead, I got up to a little tower that dropped off maybe eighteen feet. No place to get in any pro. So I told Tommy to hang back a bit, and I climbed over the tower and rappelled off the other side, using his body weight as my anchor. Then, when he got to the tower, he just looped the rope around a little horn on top and rapped off the other end. So we were each tied into one end of the rope, rapping off each other's body weight. There was no actual anchor, just a little natural horn that the rope ran behind. When we were done, we just flicked the rope loose and it fell down.

It was a really weird configuration. We did all kinds of improvising like that. Which is what made things go fast.

The rappel off the south side of Saint-Exupéry is down a major wall. But here we were in luck. A few years earlier, there'd been a serious accident on this wall, so it was covered with trash from the massive rescue effort. Anchors, fixed ropes, junk all over the place. It seemed as though it took us an endless number of nineteen-meter rappels, and we were so tired it felt like a nightmare, but we got down it.

It was late evening. In the col below the last tower, the Aguja de l'S, we pitched our fourth camp. This time Tommy finally got the puffy, so he was warm. I did okay myself, since we were at a relatively low altitude. That night, we got a solid six hours of sleep. But the alarming fact was that we didn't feel at all recovered in the morning. By this point, we were just crushed.

On the fifth day, we got really blasted by the famous Patagonian winds, blowing out of the west, at our backs. It was so gusty as we pushed up the Aguja de l'S that we had to wait and time our bursts of climbing around the gusts. The wind was threatening to blow us off our feet. But we got over the Aguja de l'S and down to the glacier by 10:00 a.m. The relief was tremendous. All we had to do now was hike out. *The only trouble was, my vision was blurry. Apparently I'd developed a minor case of snow blindness.*

That five-hour stagger back to El Chaltén, crossing the glacier by postholing through knee-deep slush, was a real trudge. Once off the glacier, we stripped off all our wet clothing. Tired as we were, I was pretty frickin' happy. Later, other climbers would hail our Fitz Traverse as "cutting-edge alpinism." Rolo Garibotti himself, a man of few words and high standards, saluted us in print: "Respect, respect and more respect."

It didn't feel so cutting-edge to me. Tommy was always in good spirits, and we always got along. It felt like a really fun five-day camping trip with a good friend. I was proud of the fact that on the whole traverse—three and a half miles of travel, gaining and losing 13,000 feet of technical rock, snow, and ice—neither of us took a single fall.

• • • •

The first climber to greet us in El Chaltén said, "Man, we were starting to worry about you guys." Something was wrong. Then we heard the news. Just two days earlier, Chad Kellogg, an extremely experienced forty-two-year-old American climber, had been killed on the descent from Fitz Roy, after climbing the Supercanaleta route. On rappel, he'd pulled loose a huge block that hit him on the head. He died instantly, with his partner, Jens Holsten, hanging right next to him. Holsten then had to complete the long descent alone.

Tommy knew Chad better than I did. In fact, I'd only barely met the guy. The tragedy hit Tommy hard. As he later wrote in Alpinist:

> We can tell ourselves that we minimize the dangers. Pick objectives that we're relatively certain we'll live through. Alex can cal-

culate every ropeless move with precision. I can choose to use a rope. We can approach our climbing as a series of athletic goals or as a quest for enlightenment. But the truth is, this kind of accident could have happened to any of us. For the next few mornings in El Chaltén, a hush appears to weigh on our little community of climbers. People wander the streets as if unsure of what to say. Each night, we still congregate under the dim lights and rustic tables of La Senyera and drink red wine. Gradually the laughter returns. But when we talk about our climbs, it's with our heads down, our voices low. The night seems to press against the windows, and the wind shakes the door.

Kellogg's death also seemed to make Tommy reconsider extreme climbing. He was thirty-five years old, and during the traverse he'd thought often about Becca and one-year-old Fitz waiting for him to return. As he concluded the essay for *Alpinist*,

On one hand I am still a kid, full of wonder at the world, chasing dreams of distant summits. But I'm also a father—and this means I am no longer allowed to die.

CHAPTER **NINE**
INTERLUDE: 2014–15

Note: *The writing in chapters 9 through 11, new for this edition, is all by Alex Honnold. For ease of reading, it is published in roman rather than italic text.*

ABOUT SIX WEEKS after I came home from Patagonia with Tommy, I found myself on a different kind of expedition, this time with Cedar Wright, climbing desert towers and bicycling between them. He went on to make a short film about our adventures (or mostly misadventures) called *Sufferfest 2,* which toured with the Banff Mountain Film Festival and is easily found online.

But notably absent from the thirty-minute film was possibly the most meaningful part of the whole trip: the moment when Cedar and I heard about the death of our friend Sean Leary. We had just finished rappelling down from the Titan, the biggest of the Fisher Towers, when Hayden Kennedy, who was working on the film, told us that he had some bad news: Sean's body had been found in Zion National Park. He'd died in a wingsuit BASE jumping accident a week earlier, but his friends and family had only now realized that he was missing, owing to an unfortunate confluence of events.

Cedar was immediately devastated by the news; Sean had taught him how to climb twenty years earlier, while they were both in college. I was also shocked—Sean was one of my best climbing partners. Even though we weren't close friends the way he and Cedar were, we'd shared many outrageous climbing experiences. Together, we held the speed records on several of the most classic aid-climbing routes in Yosemite. And he'd accompanied me and filmed throughout the hardest parts of my solo Triple a few years earlier. And now he was gone, just like that.

Cedar and I considered bailing from our silly bicycle trip and driving to Zion to be with our friends and mourn for Sean. But ultimately we figured that he wouldn't have wanted us to pass up a climbing trip. He was one of the most "core" climbers I'd ever known—he would never have passed up a chance to climb!

That night we had to ride to the next destination. It was only a fifteen- or twenty-mile ride, but it was in the pitch-black desert night. We rode separately and in silence, both lost in our own thoughts about Sean and his life.

I couldn't believe that he was gone. He was only thirty-eight and happily married. And his wife was seven months pregnant with their first child. What a loss. It was my first loss of a close friend or partner in the mountains, and I didn't really know how to process it. I rode through the night wondering whether any of us were making the right choices.

Six months later, I discovered that one of my sponsors, Clif Bar, had been asking itself the same thing: Were we making the right choices? They decided no, and in a move that shocked the climbing world, they dropped five of their biggest athletes, arguing that as a company they couldn't support the risks that those athletes were taking. They dropped Dean Potter, Timmy O'Neill, Cedar Wright, Steph Davis, and me—everyone on the team who either BASE jumped, highlined, or free soloed.

The timing of the move was confusing, since it came right after the guys at Sender Films released *Valley Uprising*, about the history of climbing in Yosemite. The film featured Dean and me climbing extensively, and Clif Bar was one of the film's biggest sponsors. It seemed that if they didn't want to condone our "risk taking," then maybe they shouldn't have supported a film like that.

Even if Clif Bar's action was surprising and seemingly misguided, I wasn't too concerned by the whole thing. As I concluded in an op-ed piece for the *New York Times*: "Everyone needs to find his or her own limits for risk, and if Clif Bar wants to back away from the cutting edge, that's certainly a fair decision. But we will all continue climbing in the ways that we find most inspiring, with a rope, a parachute or nothing at all. Whether or not we're sponsored, the mountains are calling, and we must go."

I was disappointed to be dropped by one of my sponsors, though they wound up paying out my contract and continuing to send me product when I needed it. So it was a best-case kind of firing, and I respected them for taking a stand.

• • • •

A much more difficult firing came later in the month, when Stacey and I broke up in a much more final way. We'd been struggling with all the normal issues—commitment, lifestyle, family, etc. She'd finished a master's degree in nursing and was looking forward to a real career, which meant a slightly more stable lifestyle, preferably in one place. I was vacillating between finding a place with her and settling down a little bit or just splitting up and hitting the road in a more serious way for the next year.

I made two separate plans for 2015. One was a program of pure climbing and traveling, the other a more subdued version based around wherever Stacey might land.

But ultimately, she made the decision for us, pulling the plug for good at the beginning of December 2014. We'd been talking about the issues for weeks, and her decision wasn't a surprise. But it was still sad. This time, when she said it was over, it felt final in a way it never had before. I was glad it wasn't a bitter breakup. We didn't yell and scream at each other. There was no major drama. Just the sad realization that we wanted different things from our lives at this point and it was too difficult to stay together. We'd still be friends, eventually.

There was a lot of sadness on both sides. I felt the loss of something I might never find again. I'd never been in such a serious relationship—I'd always thought that we might have a family together someday. But instead it was over.

At the same time, I felt a certain liberation. Ahead of me stretched another full year of great adventures and new climbs. Patagonia, Australia, maybe even Pakistan in the summer. . . . I could suddenly travel full-time without feeling like I had to come back for something.

• • • •

My newfound freedom was first put to use with a trip to Patagonia with Colin Haley in the winter of 2015. I'd intended to go with Tommy Caldwell, but he'd just finished his lifetime project by freeing the Dawn Wall and was suddenly inundated with speaking offers and media appearances. He didn't really have the time to escape to South America for a few weeks, so I joined Colin instead.

We hadn't climbed together much at that point, though we had tons of good mutual friends. When I joined him in El Chaltén, Argentina, we didn't even have any particular plans. Well, I didn't have any plans. After ten seasons of climbing in Patagonia, Colin always has some kind of plan. He has lists of objectives for every occasion and every possible weather condition.

Our first objective, something Colin had been scheming for a while, was to climb Torre Egger in a day. Torre Egger is a slender granite spire, capped by a mushroom of rime ice that sits below its more impressive and famous neighbor, Cerro Torre. It's right in the middle of the Torre group, so climbing it meant traversing below Cerro Standhardt and summiting Punta Herron in order to get to the route we wanted to climb on Egger. Basically, we climbed half of the entire Torre range in order to climb one of the towers in the middle.

Colin had previously climbed the entire Torre Traverse, both north to south and south to north, each climb having taken four days. After our successful ascent of Torre Egger, I asked him why we didn't just do the whole traverse in a day? He was initially dismissive, since his previous ascents had taken so much longer. But on the long hike back to town, as we talked through the possible logistics, it started to make some sense. By the time we were back in town, we'd decided: If we got more good weather, we would definitely try the whole traverse in a day.

We were back below the Torres the next week, trying to take advantage of a very marginal weather window. Despite mists, wind, running water on the rocks, and lousy ice conditions, we got over Standhardt, Punta Herron, and Torre Egger in really good time. At 7:30 p.m., we started up Cerro Torre in the waning light. Halfway up, we switched to climbing by headlamp. We were only two pitches short of the summit when the storm really socked in.

For two hours, we hung off ice screws on a nearly vertical sheet of ice, huddling and holding each other for warmth. The wind raged and we couldn't see any stars, but it wasn't precipitating. We wanted to wait for dawn and see what the conditions were really like. There were no great options for retreating so we waited to make sure it was absolutely necessary before we started. The weather forecast hadn't predicted a storm like this for another twenty-four hours, so we tried to maintain optimism.

But as the faint glow of dawn began on the horizon, we were able to see the full extent of our predicament. The wind was stronger than ever and the entire sky was covered in thick black clouds. We were almost 4,000 feet above the glacier, hanging on a sheet of ice in a building storm. It seemed like a terrible situation.

Fortunately, Colin had a plan. He thought that, in these wind conditions, rappelling the north face, which we'd climbed up, was too dangerous. So instead, we started rappelling down the west face—an almost entirely smooth wall of ice all the way to the southern ice cap at the bottom. The only problem was that rappelling the west face left us on the entirely wrong side of the mountain range. We wound up having to hike another twenty hours back to town with no food, stove, or bivy gear. All told, it was a fifty-three hour adventure in the mountains, certainly the most glorious failure of my life.

As Colin wrote the next day, "It's unfortunate that we didn't quite get to finish the goal, but I'm very pleased with our performance, knowing that if the weather had held out we would've easily finished within a cool twenty-four hours of starting. Despite failing, it is probably the best day of climbing I've ever done in these mountains, and it certainly turned into the most epic experience I've had here."

· · · ·

I suppose I first started thinking about soloing El Cap in 2009, the year after I'd soloed the Regular Route of Half Dome. I have a vivid memory of hiding out in my rental car in Europe, outside an evening party, fantasizing about goals for when I made it back to the States. Soloing El Cap was the obvious next step for me, and I figured I'd do it the next season.

But when I returned to the Valley, it seemed much too daunting. One look at the wall was enough for me to realize that I wasn't quite there yet. The vague idea of soloing thirty pitches up to 5.13a seemed somewhat feasible, but when I stood at the base and looked up at the 3,000 feet of clean, vertical granite sweeping into the sky, it seemed like an alien world. No matter how much I may have wanted to solo El Cap, it didn't seem possible. I let the dream simmer on the back burner, never really talking about it or even admitting to myself how much it meant to me.

At the time, Dean Potter was super active in the Valley, as he started to integrate his vision of BASE jumping with his climbing. In 2010, David Roberts interviewed both of us for a profile of me he wrote for *Outside* magazine. When David asked me about free soloing El Cap, I admitted, "It's possible. You'd have to be really ready. You'd have to really want it. The hardest thing would be just getting off the ground. I kind of want to do it. It would be amazing."

Dean seemed annoyed by the question, telling David: "Let's talk about it after it's happened. The magazines want a race between Alex and me. But this would go beyond athletic achievement. For me, this would be at the highest level of my spirituality."

But in 2011, Dean created a new solo route on El Cap by downclimbing the top of Lurking Fear, traversing Thanksgiving Ledge, and climbing back up the last five pitches of Freerider. His climb was filmed for a television special and had the slight feel of a stunt, but it was the first step toward a complete free solo of the face. He dubbed his new creation Easy Rider, since it was a much easier version of the Freerider.

In early 2012, I heard rumors that Dean was preparing to solo the West Face of El Cap, a route that also accesses Thanksgiving Ledge. I knew that once he reached the ledge he could easily traverse across and finish on Freerider, completing a hybrid version of an El Cap solo. I say *hybrid* because the West Face isn't typically considered a "true" El Cap route, since it's so far to the left that the character of the rock is different. But I knew that to the casual climber it would be hard to understand the difference. I considered a potential free solo of El Cap to be the Holy Grail of climbing. I didn't want Dean to taint it by traversing in and completing an easier variation.

In one of the few overtly competitive acts of my life, I decided to solo the West Face before Dean could. By doing it first, I could make sure that it wasn't considered a true solo of El Cap. I wanted to preserve the real thing for someone in the future, whether or not that someone was me.

Two days after the free Triple with Tommy, I took a lap up the West Face with my friend Kate Rutherford. I saw Dean's cache at the base and his fixed lines on the first two pitches. They were well ticked and chalked, and I could tell that he had certainly done some preparation. We simul-climbed most of the route, with me stopping to repeat each of the hard sections. I memorized some moves and inspected most of the holds. We topped out in about five hours—a suitably mellow day. Which was good for me, since my fingers and toes still hurt from my twenty-eight-hour mission with Tommy.

The next morning, I was back at the base of the West Face, alone this time. The first pitch includes a slabby 5.11 boulder problem that I death-gripped my way through. I wasn't really warmed up yet and I was quite sore, but I managed to bear down on the tiny granite edges and squeak by. I wasn't feeling particularly "on"—I just wanted to get it done. An hour and fifty minutes later, I was on top, delighted to be finished.

I told few people about the climb. To be honest, it was overshadowed by the free Triple with Tommy a few days earlier, and then even more so by my solo Triple a week and a half later. I'd done the West Face only to ensure that Dean wouldn't claim it as the first solo of El Cap. In a strange twist of fate, I actually wound up bouldering with Dean four days later in Telluride, Colorado, during a

break from the Banff Mountain Film Festival. At that point in my
life, I was still more afraid of him than anything else, so I never
mentioned any of my recent climbs in the Valley. He didn't either,
and we ended up having a great bouldering session together. I never
did find out how he felt about me swooping in on his project, or if it
even bothered him. Maybe he'd decided he was never going to do it
anyway. I'll never know. But at least the first free solo of the *real* El
Cap had been saved for the future.

• • • •

On May 16, 2015, only three months after I got home from climbing with Colin in Patagonia, Dean Potter and his partner, Graham
Hunt, died in a BASE jumping accident in Yosemite. The first edition of this book was headed to the press at the time, but I hurried
to add an afterword that did justice to the influence Dean had on
my climbing. I wrote:

Though we were never close friends, news of Dean's death shook
me in a profound way. Especially when I was younger, Dean had a
powerful influence on my own climbing, and I looked up to him as
a role model. I'd always thought that he would live to an old age
because, despite how his deeds may have looked to others, he
was actually fairly conservative. But accidents happen, especially
in BASE jumping, and although I was shocked I couldn't say I was
completely surprised.

The most striking thing about Dean was his uncompromising
approach to his arts: climbing, BASE jumping, and highlining. He
devoted himself to the perfection of his craft, pursuing each aspect
with limitless passion. Never one to follow the herd, Dean was
always out in front, forging a new path. His vision took the sport
of climbing in entirely new directions, from speed soloing in the

1990s to freeBASE a decade later. He was the true nonconformist, devoted to his art but unconcerned about legality or other people's opinions.

At the same time, I couldn't help but think that maybe Clif Bar had been right: Maybe our sports were too dangerous. I've always considered BASE jumping to be much riskier than free soloing, but then everyone always thinks the sport they don't do is the sketchy one. Maybe we "experts" should be the last ones to judge.

CHAPTER TEN

FREERIDER: THE BUILDUP

IN THE SUMMER OF 2015, Peter Mortimer, the Sender Films director who'd launched my screen career with *Alone on the Wall* in 2009, started talking to me about making a major feature film about me. By coincidence, Jimmy Chin and his wife, Chai Vasarhelyi, approached me at almost the same time with virtually the same idea. They were fresh off the successful release of their film *Meru*, which documented Conrad Anker, Renan Ozturk, and Jimmy climbing the legendary Himalayan peak of the same name. *Meru* was acclaimed by climbers and the general public alike, and was even short listed for an Academy Award. A full-on feature about my climbing represented a once-in-a-career opportunity, and I knew that I had to take advantage of it. Being a professional climber has always been a relatively fickle thing—sponsors can drop you at any moment, as I'd found out the previous year with Clif Bar. A major motion picture would certainly be good for business.

The dilemma was choosing whom to work with, since they were all friends. I'd filmed with the Sender guys for years and considered many of them buddies. But of course I'd also traveled with Jimmy for many months on various expeditions. It all felt extra complicated because of financing and agents and wrangling over contracts, but ultimately I chose to work with Jimmy and Chai because I admired their work and they were different. I'd already made so many films with the Sender guys that I felt like I should try something new and see where it could lead.

But regardless of whom I wound up working with, I knew that the only objective worthy of a feature film was El Capitan. It was the one wall I'd dreamt about for years, the only thing so big and inspiring and yet simultaneously terrifying that it held me totally captivated. And I also knew that if I ever managed to solo El Cap, it would be something to be lastingly proud of—something I would be happy to share with the public. It's the most beautiful wall in the world.

In my mind, it was always the only possible choice. To me, the idea of shooting a film was inextricably tied to the idea of soloing El Cap—without El Cap, the film would feel hollow. There was no point in shooting a whole movie about a homeless man who traveled around climbing on rocks unless it was all building up to soloing the most magnificent rock in the world.

Jimmy and Chai both insisted that they would make a great film either way—there was no pressure to climb El Cap if I didn't feel comfortable. Which is of course what anyone would say. No one's ever going to say, "Please risk your life so that I can make money off the images." It's always more like, "Do whatever you feel comfortable with (I'll just be recording over here . . .)." But I knew that it would obviously be better for everyone if I actually did succeed in soloing El Cap, even if no one was asking me to. That was fine with me—I wanted to solo it more than anyone else could have imagined. I wanted the extra pressure.

. . . .

The first edition of *Alone on the Wall* was published in November 2015. As soon as it came out, I was launched on an extensive book tour, giving talks at bookstores and climbing gyms all over the country. I'd done plenty of events for my sponsors by then—showing up at various festivals and stores to schmooze with fans, show slides, and generally talk climbing. But the book tour was more intense than anything I'd done before. I was in a different city every night, speaking to crowds that were sometimes close to a thousand people. I would do interviews for radio and television all morning, give a presentation and sign books in the evening, and then travel to the next venue. It was as close to the life of a movie star as I ever wanted to get.

November also marked one year of being single, so I looked forward to the book tour as an opportunity to meet women and mingle a bit. I'd just finished a monthlong media tour of South America that was spent in largely the same way—climbing as much as I could, presenting at events, and trying to talk to women. I was hindered by my limited Portuguese and Spanish and my general lack of charm. I figured that in the US I would at least have a little less of a handicap.

As it turned out, the schedule was so packed that it was all I could do to survive. The endless cycle of interviews, talks, and travel left me permanently exhausted and somewhat overwhelmed. I was constantly half a step behind, trying to catch up.

Midway through my month, I presented at the Town Hall in Seattle. The gathering of about 900 people was the biggest crowd I'd yet attracted. At some point during the book signing, a pretty girl left a note on the table that read: "Because you made me laugh. And why not? Sanni." It included her phone number. It barely registered at the time, since I was signing as fast as I could, but I remembered the note as I walked back to my hotel. I texted her that night, saying I was sorry that I was leaving at 5:00 the next morning, so I couldn't hang out. I figured I might as well plant the seed, even though nothing would ever come of it.

A week later, I got another text from her reminding me that I had a second event in Seattle. Maybe we could meet up before or after? By happy circumstance, it was my last obligation of the month—a sponsored event for Goal Zero and REI, and it would be much mellower than the town hall talk, leaving me time to pursue my own interests. I asked Sanni to pick me up at the climbing gym before the talk and we could go to dinner. That day, I was climbing with my old friend Cedar Wright, since he was cohosting the event. He decided that he was hungry too, and he would tag along on our date. I didn't really mind, since it made the whole thing seem more casual. I couldn't remember what Sanni looked like, since I'd had only a brief glimpse of her two weeks earlier. As the appointed time neared, I started looking around the gym anxiously, hoping that whoever showed up to collect us would be cute.

She was. Petite, with blue eyes and medium-length blonde hair, she showed up from her marketing job in downtown Seattle wearing a classy little dress. She had a friendly and cheerful presence that filled the room. I was charmed.

We made our introductions and she asked what we wanted for dinner. Cedar and I both replied, "Asian food, or noodles of some kind." She paid us no mind and took us to her favorite pizza place instead. We didn't complain. She was the party—we were just along for the ride. And Cedar was probably just happy to be going out with a beautiful woman other than his wife.

The event that night was forgettable, as Cedar and I rambled on about climbing. But afterward, Sanni threw a little bonfire-centered party at the house where she lived with four other girls. This time, Cedar let me go by myself. Sanni was a beginner climber, and all of her friends were somehow connected to the outdoors via climbing, skiing, or running. It was like a gathering of the tribe, except that they were all attractive and single. As Sanni said later, "I didn't really think it through that well. I don't know why I invited you to a party of all single women. . . ."

It didn't matter; my eyes never left her. She was an energetic sprite who spread happiness everywhere she moved. The party was just the kind of silly cover that people use when they aren't sure how they feel about each other. But we both knew—we just had to wait for everyone else to leave so that we could be alone. I spent the night. When we both went to brush our teeth that night, I stood behind her and held her while we looked at each other in the mirror, a strangely intimate gesture for two people who didn't technically know each other that well. But it felt right. We dove right in.

I left Seattle the next morning and returned to my normal life. The book tour was over, and all I had to do now was climb. I got back in my trusty van and hit the road, rallying to Las Vegas to sport climb for the season. Sanni and I kept texting, wondering about the next time we could hang out. It was a difficult situation, since we would never see each other again unless one of us traveled specifically to see the other—the kind of thing you do for a committed partner but rarely for a casual date. We hardly knew each other, but we both wanted to see each other more. I invited her to Vegas for a three-day climbing weekend. It was a nice way for her to escape the Seattle winter, which made getting together seem more casual.

Some people like to woo a prospective partner with a lovely excursion. Not me. I just gave Sanni exactly the experience she would have if we were dating long term—life in the van and sport climbing at some random crag where I had a project. In this case, it meant the Virgin River Gorge, which is quite possibly America's least pleasant sport crag. The VRG is a north-facing limestone wall known for its razor-sharp rock and microscopic holds. A freezing wind blows through the canyon the entire winter. And the climbing is a few hundred feet above Interstate 15, so it's impossible to hear your partner over the roar of nonstop truck traffic. But the VRG is home to some of the hardest routes in the country, and I was working on one of them. I figured Sanni would love it.

Anyone at the VRG is there because he or she is a serious sport climber, the kind who cares more about the latest project than comfort or happiness. Sanni was not that kind of climber. She liked climbing with her friends in beautiful, sunny places. She hadn't been climbing that long and didn't really know how to lead or lead belay yet. I figured it would all work out fine.

For my third warm-up, I tried a thin 5.13d face route that I'd been working on as a side project. Up high on the route, I fell and must have dropped at least forty feet. Sanni wasn't that familiar with a grigri and had been standing away from the wall. She shot up like a rocket as I plummeted. I quickly realized that someone else should maybe belay me on my project, and that climbing with Sanni should be limited to more casual objectives.

But even at the VRG, Sanni managed to maintain a positive attitude and enjoy herself. She was a delight, even at the most hateful crag in the country. We spent the next two days climbing more pleasant routes on the sunny, sandstone walls outside Las Vegas. We'd go out for dinner and talk for hours. When she flew back to Seattle, I knew we had a problem.

There was no easy way for us to date, since she had a full-time job in Seattle and I was living in a car in the desert. But Christmas was two weeks away, and she was spending hers with her family in Mammoth Lakes, California, for a ski vacation. I would be driving by there on my way back to Sacramento for my own family's celebration. Our third date would see me spending three days with her parents, sister, and sister's boyfriend in the rented family condo. It was quite an accelerated program.

But again it felt easy and natural. Her parents were easy to get along with—they were both more focused on living a full life than acquiring a lot of things, an attitude I could certainly relate to.

We'd ski all day (quite poorly—none of us were any good at skiing) and play board games all night. Her mom cooked amazing food and they all made me feel like part of the family, even though I'd spent a total of only five days with Sanni.

On our respective drives home, we took an afternoon to climb together as a family in the Owens River Gorge. By the time we parted ways, Sanni and I were already planning the next trip. She'd join me in Vegas again as soon as it seemed feasible with work.

For Sanni's second trip to Vegas, I decided to try to show her a good time. We rented a hotel room on the Strip for a night and went to see a Cirque du Soleil show (in addition to climbing fun, classic routes in the sun at Red Rock). I must have really been falling for her to wind up in a hotel on the Strip. But I wanted her to like me. She livened any space she entered, including my dingy old van. Our farewell at the end of the weekend seemed particularly sad, since I was leaving for Patagonia at the end of the month. We made vague plans for me to stay with her in Seattle when I got back, but I knew that she was returning to a busy city and social life. It's hard to wait for someone for a month when you've only been on three dates.

· · · ·

In January 2016, I arrived in El Chaltén, the little town that's become the center of the Patagonia climbing community. Although I still didn't consider myself a real alpinist, this was the third year in a row that I'd headed south to tackle the fierce, glaciated granite spires outside of town. I joined Colin Haley, who'd already been there for several months, to give the Torre Traverse another attempt. We'd failed the season before by such a slim margin that we felt obligated to return and finish the job.

Because we had the route dialed from our last attempt, I was sure that with the right weather window, it wouldn't be too hard to finish the Traverse in under twenty-four hours. But even as I left the States for a month in the mountains, I was more motivated by sport climbing and took a hangboard with me so that I could keep working out between stretches of good weather. I was glad to be climbing with Colin again and knew that it was a great opportunity to redeem ourselves, but I secretly would have preferred to hang out with Sanni and climb in the gym. That's always the tension on expeditions—wanting to climb big objectives in the mountains but loving life at home as well.

As soon as I arrived, we got a half-day weather window in which we climbed a new ridge up Cerro Huemul. It was a scrappy route but the perfect way to get back into Patagonian hiking shape. As Colin and I hiked in and out of the mountains, we caught up on life and chitchatted endlessly. I told him about book touring and the whole crazy process, but I focused on Sanni. I was smitten. He told me that if I was really psyched on her, I should make things exclusive. Either way, I was stuck in the mountains for the next month and would be focused on climbing, but he felt like it was always better to have an open conversation with a prospective partner and lay it all out there.

In addition to wise insight, Colin also happened to have a sat phone with unlimited minutes of calling time. I'm not sure how he swung it, but I took advantage of the situation to call Sanni as often as I could. The next time we chatted, I mentioned that I would happily be exclusive. She felt the same way, and just like that it was official. We were dating! But I was in Argentina.

On January 29, we got another weather window and hiked into the mountains to attempt our main objective, the Torre Traverse in twenty-four hours. Our speed depended almost totally on simul-climbing and short-fixing. We'd already discussed who would lead what—mostly

Colin on mixed ground, while I'd lead on the harder stretches of pure rock. On all but one rappel, we would simul-rap—each of us sliding down one strand of the doubled rope at the same time.

We started our timer at the base of the first pillar, Cerro Standhardt. It was 1:42 in the morning. Despite the darkness, our climbing went like clockwork. We were over Standhardt and at the base of the second pillar, Punta Herron, in under four hours. For the first time, we changed into rock shoes, as I led off up Herron. Near the top, where the tower was capped with bulging rime ice, we had to awkwardly change from shoes to crampons at a hanging belay. Colin reminded me that dropping a boot would be disastrous.

We reached the summit of the next-to-last pillar, Torre Egger, only nine and a half hours into our traverse. We were making great time, and the weather was holding. At the notch between Egger and Cerro Torre itself, we took our first rest break. Then I took the lead up the north face of Cerro Torre. For the first time all day, the cracks were running with water and chunks of ice from the summit mushroom were plunging down around us. I moved as fast as I could, with long runouts and huge gaps between belays. Just below the last rock pitch, I brought Colin up. He asked if I still wanted to lead. "Fuck that," I said. "I'm done." He aided up the last ice-filled crack and got us to the base of the pure rime ice. We switched modes and wrung out our soaked jackets, preparing for a long, cold night as we finished up the route.

We reached the top at exactly midnight. Our timer read twenty hours and forty minutes. We'd beaten our deadline by more than three hours. We were pretty tired but exuberant. I don't remember much about the descent, as we rappelled Cerro Torre's southeast ridge. Colin later recalled "a blur of anchors and dehydration and shivering."

It was gratifying to finish in such a smooth style what we'd so nearly accomplished the previous year. Our partnership was almost perfect. Colin later called it the best day of climbing in his life. Even I admitted to *Alpinist* magazine, "The traverse was certainly my big dream. Cerro Torre is a lifetime summit for me—one of those mountains you have to climb eventually in your life." Though it was unfortunate that we'd summited in complete darkness and couldn't bask in the beauty.

After only a few days of rest, the forecast looked promising again. We considered skipping the weather window, since we were still pretty tired from the Traverse, but Colin has a hard policy against ever skipping a window. We packed up to hike back in.

This time we had our sights on the Wave Effect, a linkup of Aguja Desmochada, Aguja de la Silla, and Cerro Fitz Roy. The first ascent in 2011 had taken place over three days—we hoped to do it in a single push. It would be basically all rock climbing, much more my style than what we'd been doing across the valley on the Torres. We camped right at the base of Desmochada and blasted off at first light.

We did everything right out of the Yosemite Valley speed-climbing playbook—simul-climbing the entirety of all three routes. We completed the Wave Effect—without any crises or glitches—in only seventeen hours.

Back in town, we reevaluated. I'd been in Patagonia for only two weeks of my potential monthlong trip, but we'd already completed our two main objectives. I wasn't sure whether I really cared to climb anything else. The ten-day forecast looked terrible and I wanted to get back to Sanni. I changed my ticket and flew home.

• • • •

When I got back to the States, I flew to Seattle for a week or so, anxious to see my newly official girlfriend. Fortunately, she hadn't forgotten me while I was away. Her friends and housemates welcomed me as I moved into her tiny room in the basement.

On my first afternoon in Seattle, I made plans to join Sanni at the climbing gym on her way home from work. I've slowly gotten comfortable with being stared at and approached by strangers when I go to a gym, particularly a gym I don't usually frequent. I knew that going to Vertical World, a popular gym in downtown Seattle at the end of a workday, would be a shit show. It didn't bother me much, certainly not enough to stop me from going. But it was Sanni's first time dealing with all the stares, and it unnerved her. Since she wasn't a particularly experienced climber, having everyone in the gym staring at her definitely didn't help calm her down. On her first lead, she got all pumped, skipped a clip, and punched it out on a small roof until she exploded off the route. She fell probably half the length of the wall, making an enormous *thud!* as she swung back into the wall. If only a third of the gym had been watching her before, now everyone was. We created an utter spectacle.

I spent the next month loosely based out of Seattle, spending as much time with Sanni as possible. Toward the end of the month, we spent a weekend at Index, an amazing granite crag outside of Seattle, with her entire family. Sanni and I were breaking in my new, bigger van and her parents had their own van. Her sister and sister's boyfriend were camped out, as well as her cousin/housemate and her soon-to-be-husband. It was a classic example of her whole clan coming together to enjoy a family outing. It was my last time to see everyone together before leaving for a few weeks in China on an expedition for The North Face. I'd been training quite a bit in the gym because the objective in China would be the hardest multi-pitch I'd ever tried. I was feeling really strong and spent the day repeating a few of the hardest routes on the Lower Town Wall at Index.

We were back at the wall the next morning, ready to put up a toprope on a classic 5.9 called Godzilla. I was all tied in and ready to climb when we decided to switch to her parents' rope so that we could leave it up for them after Sanni had a go. I climbed the route in my approach shoes, not really taking it very seriously. Sanni's whole family was gathered around chatting with her as she lowered me back down. The mood was quite jovial and fun.

Until she accidentally lowered me off the end of the rope. Turns out her parents' rope was thirty feet shorter than mine. I was about twelve feet above the ground when Sanni felt the end of the rope pop through the belay device. I dropped like a stone, landing on one butt cheek on an enormous jagged rock. I flopped over the rock and came to a stop, crumpled among the talus. I didn't really know what had happened—I just felt pain all over my body.

Everyone at the base was horrified. Sanni's mother helped me lie down in a flat spot to collect myself. Sanni's sister and her sister's boyfriend were both part of Seattle Search and Rescue, so they both knew first aid. They evaluated my neck and spine and didn't think anything was broken. I was dazed, feeling absolutely crippled. Not much was bleeding besides a gash on my arm, but I felt like I'd been run over by a bulldozer.

After a little while, I started to feel slightly more alive. I was able to sit up and drink a little bit. We decided that I should head out of the mountains and down to the ER. It seemed that I should at least check to see whether anything was broken. I think it was Sanni's dad who helped me hobble back out from the crag, though I can't be sure. I could barely walk. But at least I was walking!

As soon as Sanni got into the van, she broke down in sobs. She was terrified that I was crippled and that it was all her fault. I just lay in the back of the van trying to find a position that didn't hurt. I didn't really blame her—I should have asked how long the rope was, tied a knot in the end, and been generally more attentive. It was obviously her fault, since the rope went through her hands. But as the vastly more experienced climber, it was really my responsibility to make sure we didn't get into that kind of situation. It was ironic, though not entirely surprising, that the most serious injury in all my years of climbing would happen on something so casual.

Sanni's dad drove us to the hospital. There the medics X-rayed me and decided that I'd compression-fractured two vertebrae in my spine, but otherwise I was fine. I was uncomfortable in pretty much any position, but I was still functional. It wasn't that serious after all.

The next day, I was able to drive us home. It was somber in the van. I wondered if I could still fly to China. I wondered if I should even be dating Sanni. I've always wanted to be a good climber— my whole life is focused around that seemingly simple desire. I've always wanted a partner who helps me toward that goal, a partner who brings out the best in me. I worried that by crippling me, even by accident, Sanni was holding me back. I'd certainly ended plenty of other relationships because I felt like the woman might be holding me back.

Sanni and I stopped for burritos on the drive home. I started trying to express my feelings in my own halting, painful way. I told her that even though I thought she was great and I really liked being with her, I wondered whether it was really the best choice for my climbing.

She said, "I know you're hurting. I know this is terrible. But is being single really going to make you feel any better?"

She had a point. But I just sat there in sullen silence.

"This sucks," Sanni went on. "I'm so sorry. But this doesn't mean you have to be alone. You can be a good climber and still be in a good relationship. You can have it all."

I hadn't ever really considered that. Could I have both?

We collected our roadside burritos and continued chatting. Over the next twenty minutes, she made it clear that I was not allowed to break up our promising relationship. I was relieved. I hadn't really wanted to break up anyway, I just thought I was supposed to, as part of my commitment to sending the gnar. But I preferred to have both, just as Sanni said I could.

· · · ·

I had two days in Seattle to lounge around and heal before boarding a plane to Shanghai to meet Felipe Camargo, one of South America's strongest climbers and a fellow North Face athlete. Our goal was to climb Corazon de Ensueño, an eight-pitch 5.14b in southwestern China that tackles a 500-foot-tall limestone arch called Getu, via a route that crawls up the underside of the span through one outrageously steep pitch after another. The route had been put up in 2011 by the Spanish climber Dani Andrada, who led the whole thing in one push without falling. By 2016, it still awaited a second ascent.

In my injured state, success seemed unlikely, but I didn't want to cancel the trip and leave Felipe in the lurch. I figured I could support his attempt and just see how things went. When we met up in China, I told him about my accident—he was obviously shocked and worried for me. But he also happened to know a physical therapist in Shanghai who specialized in working with professional athletes. He made the introductions and I managed to go in and get evaluated while we were in the city.

Eric Yue was a fellow Brazilian who'd spent his life working with athletes of all kinds and had recently opened his sports clinic in Shanghai. It was the first time I'd been to a physical therapist, and I immediately saw the benefit in having a trained professional set me on the best path back toward fitness. He told me that my problem was that I'd sprained a ligament in my hip and that certain stretches and gentle exercises would speed my recovery.

As someone who's always lived in a car and never really regarded myself as much of an "athlete," it was eye-opening to see how the right kind of help can make a difference. I knew rationally that every other serious sport had trainers and coaches and PTs and masseuses and a whole gamut of support staff, but for whatever reason, I'd always felt that climbers could just live in the dirt and somehow recover naturally. This was my first time embracing the help.

After a few days of media events for The North Face in Shanghai, we arrived at Getu, a national park in the Guizhou Province. The film that Jimmy and Chai were making about me was going to follow me around the world as I trained on different kinds of rock toward a possible free solo of El Cap. I hoped that Corazon de Ensueño would be a good test of pure fitness and stamina—a checkpoint along the way to El Cap.

The route required a fair amount of prepping, both to climb and to set up for filming. We got to work hanging the quickdraws and cleaning the holds. The whole inside of the arch is completely sheltered from the elements, so dust settles on the holds, making them super slippery. Felipe and I settled into a routine of toiling on the route all day, then staggering back to our little hotel, eating rice and vegetables, and going to sleep.

In a lot of ways, it was a perfect rehabilitation routine for me—I could do as much or as little climbing as I could handle, knowing that Felipe would take up the slack. And I had plenty of time in the evenings to stretch and do my exercises. When we'd arrived at our hotel, we'd discovered to our chagrin that the bedspreads that looked like mattress covers were actually just placed on wooden boxes. We were literally sleeping on boards. But I think that helped my back. Or at least it didn't hurt—I slept like a rock every night.

Our approach up to the arch involved almost a thousand concrete steps angling straight up a jungly hillside. It was still challenging for me to climb stairs, especially so to descend them. But I found that I could slide down the handrails instead. It felt extreme—sliding at near-terminal speeds down very steep beams through the jungle—but it saved me quite a bit of pain. In some ways, it was the highlight of each day.

During the first few days on the route, I could barely lift my right leg out to the side, which was a serious problem for climbing big limestone tufas and stalactites out a horizontal roof—pretty much the most gymnastic and dynamic style of climbing there is in the whole sport. But as we kept working on the route, I saw quick and steady improvements.

After a week of work on the route, Jimmy Chin showed up to start filming. By then, Felipe felt ready to send, so we rested a day and blasted up the route. He crushed the whole thing, demonstrating why he's possibly the best climber in South America. I fell on a few pitches. I just didn't quite have the grrr—the try-hard that was required to dangle my way out the roof.

That night we celebrated for Felipe, who'd been dreaming about the route for years. He'd made the second ascent of one of the hardest multi-pitches in the world. We all decided to rest the next day, and then I'd try to lead the route with him supporting.

This time, I had the grrr. I felt healed enough that nothing was really holding me back. The fitness I'd had before the accident on Index showed through, and I managed to send the whole route as well. We were all delighted that despite my showing up in China feeling totally crippled, we'd managed to stick to the plan and complete our objective. And even get some good film footage to boot.

I flew back to Seattle almost three weeks after I'd left, feeling like I had a new lease on climbing. I felt strong and healthy again and more committed than ever to sticking to my program. Stretches and core exercises had become an important part of my nightly routine. I was starting to think of myself as more of an athlete. But maybe the most important part of the trip was that I felt that it boosted my confidence. I hadn't climbed anything significant in more than a year—I'd taken some time off, published a book, toured around the world, and generally done things other than send the gnar for far too long. It felt good to work toward a specific goal and achieve it. I hoped that it boded well for the coming Valley season. For the first time, free soloing El Cap seemed within the realm of the possible.

• • • •

I spent the summer of 2016 in Europe with Sanni. It was a combination of work and play—a lecture series in the UK, a climbing festival in Ireland, a few events promoting the French translation of my book, and a lot of amazing sport climbing with my girlfriend. For a few weeks in the middle of the trip, we shared a rustic chalet with a few other American climbers in the Swiss town of Interlaken, which wound up being very near the home of Ueli Steck. I hadn't climbed with him since 2010, but I'd seen him at a few events. We weren't close by any means, but I felt like we shared a certain connection. He joined Sanni and me for a few casual days of sport climbing—he would have already done thousands of vertical feet of mountain running for his real training, and then he would swing by the crag in the afternoon to do a few pitches with us and socialize. It was amazing to see his dedication to training and to see firsthand what it did for his performance.

One day I went over to Ueli's house to accompany him on a "rest day hike" up his backyard mountain. It was 5,000 feet of ascent over only a few miles—steeper than nearly any trail you can find in the States. Ueli had already done his training run that morning; he was only hiking to keep me company and enjoy a paraglider flight back down. I found it all very next-level—he'd already trained, now he was charging up a huge mountain before dinner just to fly his ultralight wing back down. It was like nothing I'd ever experienced.

As I panted up the hill behind him, we got to chatting about El Cap. By now, I'd decided that if I was going to try to free solo the Captain, the route I would choose would almost certainly be Freerider. I had done it many times over the years, notably as the second route of the free Triple with Tommy, and it's the "easiest" route up the wall, though still pretty hard. I was really curious about Ueli's views on training, since he was one of the few truly elite multisport climbers out there, and probably the only one who also free soloed at a very high level. In one year, he'd set the speed record on the north face of the Eiger (solo, of course), climbed the 8,000-meter Gasherbrum II in the Karakoram, and almost onsighted El Cap via the route Golden Gate (only one fall on a wet crack!). Probably no other climber has ever had that kind of versatility. I wanted his advice on how I should craft my fitness program for potentially free soloing El Cap.

At first we just talked about fitness—how many pitches to climb each day and at what grade. (He had trained for Golden Gate by climbing ten pitches a day up to 5.13b/c.) But the interesting part of the conversation came when I asked him how close to the limit he'd ever soloed. He said that he'd soloed 5.13b when his most difficult climb had been only 5.13d, meaning that he'd soloed very close to his physical limit. I've never really done that, preferring to keep my soloing within a wider margin of error. But part of the reason that I hadn't yet soloed El Cap was that it was so challenging to make it feel easy. I'd never become such a strong climber that the route just felt trivially easy. And I wasn't sure that it ever would. I wondered whether I should adopt something closer to Ueli's approach, which seemed to be to choose the day and make it count. It seemed like a few of his solos had as much to do with timing and motivation as they did with his mastery of the routes. That's never been my style— or at least I have never wanted it to be—but I definitely considered it an option for El Cap. If I could just squeak it out once, I would be happy. I didn't have to feel 100 percent on it, I just needed to make sure that one day really counted. In some ways, it was an appealing strategy, since it meant I didn't have to make it feel secure, I just had to psych myself up enough—somehow.

I'd always thought that in order to solo El Cap, I should be climbing at least 5.14d—that I should be such a strong climber that the moves felt piss-easy. But the reality was that years had passed and I wasn't even close to being that strong a climber. Maybe I needed to consider different approaches. In July, I said good-bye to Ueli as we continued our tour of Europe. I could hardly have imagined that I would never see him again.

. . . .

Taghia is a remote gorge in the High Atlas mountains of Morocco— a rarely visited climber's paradise. There were several reasons why the place seemed like the perfect pre-Valley fitness trainer for me: The climbing is in condition in early autumn, when it's still too hot in Yosemite, and the walls are of a similar size and difficulty. Even though Taghia is mostly limestone face climbing and Yosemite is mostly granite crack climbing, both areas require big days out climbing a lot of rock.

But one of the chief reasons I wanted to go back to Taghia was that I'd been there before my Yosemite season in the spring of 2012, the year I'd sent the free Triple with Tommy, soloed the West Face of El Cap, soloed the Triple, and set the Nose speed record. It had been my best season ever, and I felt like part of that was because I showed up in great shape after a productive trip to Taghia. In addition, there were two perfect objectives—an enormous free-climbing linkup to attempt with Tommy Caldwell and then the possibility of soloing one of those routes.

Tommy was fresh off a year of writing his own book, *The Push*, and doing tons of speaking events. Since he'd sent the Dawn Wall, he hadn't been on any pure climbing trips, choosing instead to focus on work and family. Coming to Taghia and trying a big linkup would be the perfect motivation to whip himself back into cutting-edge climbing shape.

We hadn't really done anything big together since the Fitz Traverse, but Tommy was the perfect partner for simul-climbing hard routes quickly. And he was also willing to put up with the film crew and deal with interviews, something not many climbers have experienced. Mostly, he was a good friend and I trusted him. He was someone I could talk to openly about my El Cap aspirations without too much fanfare. I knew that he was personally opposed to free soloing, but that didn't stop him from being a good sounding board for ideas about strategy and training. And he knew El Cap and what it takes to free climb up there better than anyone else ever has.

There's no road to Taghia. When the road ends, you hire a donkey to carry your stuff up to the village. The two-hour hike through sinuous limestone canyons passed quickly because there was so much stimulation. Everywhere we looked, there were green fields cut into the steep hillsides or young children herding goats. It was like a journey back in time.

Tommy and I set to work on the linkup in the same way we'd worked other projects in the past—we climbed each route individually, then rested and tried them all together. The only difference was that these routes were a bit out of our element. They were the same size as things we'd climbed in Yosemite, but a totally different style—they required slower, much more thoughtful climbing. And they were scarier in some ways, since we couldn't just put a piece of gear into a crack anywhere we needed it. We had to stick to the bolts that were already drilled in the faces, but because we were trying to simul-climb long sections, we were forced to skip a lot of bolts to make our gear last. The challenge was knowing which ones to skip—we didn't want to wind up thirty feet above our last piece of gear while struggling through the crux of one of the routes.

Each route took us slightly longer than expected. The style of climbing was technical and involved, and there was very little chalk on any of the holds. We had to search for all the holds and try to mark key hands and feet with chalk for our next time. But overall, things went smoothly. In fact, we simul-climbed through 5.13 terrain, which was a first for me. Tommy likes to say that he's a careful family man and that I'm the daredevil risk-taker forcing him to go fast and take chances, but the reality is that half the time he is the one saying we should do something and I'm looking at him blankly and saying, "Really? Can we do that?"

I valued the time we spent approaching and descending each route almost as much as the climbing itself. We passed the empty hours of hiking by chatting about anything and everything. Tommy would talk about his family and all the work he'd been doing recently; I tended to drift back to Freerider, since El Cap was never far from my mind. Tommy would complain about his wife buying a new furniture set he didn't think they needed. I would wonder whether it was worth looking for a different route around the Freeblast slabs. We'd talk about the new training zone he'd built into his home garage and then seamlessly transition into training for El Cap. What had he done for his hardest first ascents on the wall? What should I be doing? It was good to chat about everything openly.

We'd return to our *gîte* in the village each night and have a big communal dinner with the film crew. Then we would retreat to our shared room and each dive into our laptops. He was finishing the final draft of *The Push*, though there was no title at the time. I was reading his book in sections on my own laptop and offering the occasional feedback. We brainstormed possible titles, stymied by the overlap of all things Dawn Wall with the *Twilight* books. *Breaking the Dawn Wall? New Dawn? The Dawn of Man?* I didn't help much, but I deeply enjoyed his book. He also had Andre Agassi's memoir, *Open*, which he'd been using for inspiration. I knew nothing about tennis but found the book mesmerizing. Agassi was a gifted and

driven athlete who hated his own sport. Much of the book was cra-
ziness to me (dating models, jetsetting, drugs, multimillion-dollar
contracts), but his commitment to training and his dedication to his
craft struck close to home. Between living with Tommy, possibly the
hardest-working climber of all time, and reading about Agassi, I was
feeling pretty light-duty. I needed to up my game.

After a week of work, we were ready for the linkup. We climbed
Babel, an almost 3,000-foot 5.13a, in six and a half hours. From
the summit we descended a drainage to the east and wound up at
the base of L'Axe du Mal, a 1,500-foot 5.13a that we climbed in
four hours. From that summit, we headed due north into a different drainage that led us down to the base of Rivières Pourpres, a
1,600-foot 5.12c. Even though this was by far the easiest route, it
took us four and three-quarters hours to climb it through the night.
We were both slowing down and getting tired. We made it back to
the *gîte* twenty-three hours after we'd left, having climbed the three
most iconic routes in Taghia in one long day.

After a few more days of hard climbing, Tommy set out for Mar-
rakech to return to his family. I took a much-needed rest day and
vegged out watching mindless TV shows on my laptop. I needed
a break from the constant filming and climbing. Throughout the
Morocco trip, I was working my way through a TV show on my
laptop called *Spartacus*, a fictional account of gladiator slaves rising
up in revolt against their Roman masters. It was mostly sex and vio-
lence, but I saw something familiar in the ceaseless bouts in the
arena. The gladiators spent their whole lives training for the brief
moments in which they could determine their fates through their
own poise and skill. Fear was not an option—at least not if they
wanted to survive. It might have been a stretch, but I started to
think of soloing as modern-day gladiating—a chance to prove my
skill when my life depended on it. And with the film crew there, it

was entertainment for the masses, just like in ancient times. Blood sport had evolved to wearing sticky rubber shoes and a chalk bag.

After a full day of *Spartacus* episodes, I went mini-traxioning on Rivières Poupres one more time to make sure I had it all dialed in. Thinking of the potential solo in the mythical terms of ancient Rome made it seem that much more rad. Not that it needed to be more rad—1,600 feet of overhanging, technical limestone was plenty. Maybe it was that imagining myself as a gladiator made *me* feel more rad—and feeling rad certainly helps with confidence. But imagining doesn't make something so, and there's nothing more dangerous in soloing than misplaced confidence. All that is to say that watching a lot of epic TV got me way overstoked. But after a few casual mini-traxion laps, I knew I had the route memorized. My confidence was founded—I would have my day in the arena.

I rested the next day, finishing yet another season of *Spartacus*. In between episodes, I spent time thinking through all the crux sequences. I imagined what it would be like to shift my weight onto the small footholds and how it would feel to climb out overhanging roofs more than a thousand feet above the narrow canyon below. I loaded up my backpack and went over the plan with the film crew— who would be where on the wall and when I could expect to hear the drone flying behind me. The fewer surprises the better.

Finally it was time. I woke up the next morning feeling rested and strong. The film crew had left the *gîte* extra early to get prepared, which allowed me the pleasure of strolling to the base of the route alone with my thoughts. I was ready to do battle with the over-hanging red wall. Not that it was really a battle—it was more like a personal test. I was getting the privilege of testing myself against one of nature's most impressive creations. It was utterly pointless in many ways. But I hoped that the test would bring out the best of me, at least for a little while.

The first pitches passed quickly and easily, and I was soon in the overhanging meat of the route. There was a crispness in how I grabbed the holds—an edge that hadn't been there when Tommy and I had simul-climbed the route through the night in a state of exhaustion the previous week. Now I had energy to spare and I used it to grab each hold with purpose. I savored the feeling of my fingertips squeezing behind the tiny limestone edges as I worked my way up the wall.

As I continued up into the middle of the wall, I started hearing a consistent bleating. I assumed it was some young goats in distress, or something to do with the Berber shepherds who called the region home. Unconcerned, I continued crimping my way up the face. I heard the telltale whine of a drone taking off—the film crew on the rim of the canyon behind me was starting to get aerial footage. When the bleating got louder and more insistent, I began to think that it was actually someone yelling my name. As I started to look around, I suddenly realized that suspended in space midway between the summit of the peak I was climbing and the edge of the adjacent canyon was a French highliner. He had fallen off his high line and was dangling from his leash, at least 1,200 feet above the ground. The bleating had come from him—yelling, "Allez!" at himself. Suddenly I felt like I was part of a carnival act. Jimmy Chin and Mikey Schaefer were dangling above me on the right, jugging fixed lines and filming as much as they could. The highliner was having his own epic experience in the middle of space. And there was a drone hovering behind us, watching it all.

It all felt vaguely silly, though I was still tiptoeing my way up 5.12 slabs. This was not the pure soloing experience that I wanted. I knew that filming soloing always changes things a little. And I'd had no way of knowing that there would be a random dude screaming at himself and whipping off a high line above me over and over. But it all felt a bit wrong.

There was only one more hard pitch above me, a severely over-hanging 5.12c face with big moves between big holds. I waited for everyone to get into position and then climbed it efficiently, exactly as I'd practiced. It felt mechanical and joyless, as though I had been performing for the crowd instead of for myself. I didn't feel rad, I felt like I was just getting it done. I wasn't a gladiator from ancient Rome, I was a worker commuting to the office.

Our trip was almost over, and I knew I'd be in Yosemite in about a week, finally ready to start working on Freerider. During my last two days in Taghia, I onsight soloed two more routes in an effort to get ready for the Valley. One of the routes, a 1,000-foot 5.11b named Canyon Apache, felt very similar in scale and difficulty to the Rostrum, my first difficult solo from so many years ago. The thought that I could now onsight solo a route of that difficulty was energizing. I was ready to take it to the next level.

. . . .

On October 3, 2016, Sanni and I rallied the van into Yosemite, all ready to settle in for two months of climbing. It was my first time coming to the Valley with the intention of actually working on a potential free solo of El Cap. I was still agnostic about my chances of doing it, but I was ready at least to do the prep work.

We pulled into El Cap meadow midafternoon and immediately prepared for a lap up the Freeblast, the bottom ten pitches of Freerider, which end on a prominent ledge a third of the way up the wall. I'd always considered the Freeblast to be one of the scariest parts of a potential free solo because it's so insecure. It's rated only 5.11b—not terribly difficult by modern standards, but it's so low-angle and slippery that it demands a certain respect. The hardest parts are maybe only 60 degrees, but they are as smooth as a mirror. Sanni had never climbed on El Cap before, and I was excited to start practicing the moves on the slabs and share the experience with her.

It was uncharacteristically cold and windy as we hiked quickly to the base. Normally, I might have been annoyed by the conditions, but I was so excited to be back in the Valley that I just called them "sending temps"—the cold would help the friction with the rock. I figured the season would only be getting colder and it would enhance performance (up to a point, anyway).

We climbed the first four pitches quickly and efficiently, with me taking tons of pictures of Sanni and writing notes on my phone to remember specific moves. I figured I should take my preparation seriously—notes, photos of the rock, memorizing moves, etc. But we were having a good time, laughing our way up the route. I was delighted to be back on El Cap.

The Freeblast mostly follows thin crack features, but the crux of the route comes when the cracks run out—400 feet off the ground. The next 150 feet are basically a blank shield of granite. There are almost no handholds; it all comes down to how delicately you can balance on tiny footholds and tiptoe your way upward. Because it's less than vertical, your whole weight can stay over your feet, but it's the most insecure style of climbing imaginable.

The route is protected by bolts, but I was clipping only every second or third one in an effort to simulate the feeling of soloing. I was tied into a rope, so I couldn't really die, but the gaps between protection were long enough that they demanded that I really pay attention. Suddenly, moves that might have felt trivial if I were on toprope required a lot more care.

The crux of the second slab pitch is surmounting a tiny roof. It's really a small overlap in the rock, but it feels big enough on such a slippery, low-angle wall. The moves are normally protected with a piton, but I chose not to clip it, relying instead on a bolt a few feet below. I tiptoed carefully across the wall, knowing that I was getting farther above my gear. I surmounted the little roof and made several more moves, when suddenly I slipped off. I don't know what happened. The easy answer is just that I wasn't paying enough attention. I was wearing a backpack and multiple jackets. It was very windy and drizzling on and off. I was chatting with Sanni. The climbing felt pretty easy and I was doing well. But suddenly I was flying through the air. I think I pushed out—often a good instinct, because it creates separation from the wall and reduces the risk of hitting rock features, but probably the worst thing to do in this case. I cleared the small overlap and hit the wall fifteen feet below, then continued sliding for another ten feet before the rope came tight and stopped me. Had I not pushed off and just slid down the wall, I wouldn't have had such a traumatic impact, though I might have been more scraped up. But at least Sanni was paying close attention, or else I would have gone much farther.

As soon as I stopped, I knew I was fucked. I couldn't weight my right foot. It was instantly swollen like a balloon. This wasn't a "walk-it-off" kind of injury. Sanni gently lowered me to the anchor, where I switched back into my approach shoes. We started rappelling to the ground, with me hopping one-footed. I was embarrassed and ashamed of myself—how could I have fallen off the Freeblast slabs?! Why was I skipping bolts? What the fuck?! Had I really just ended my Valley season before it began? And of course I wondered about more pertinent things, like "Is it broken?" I wasn't in *that* much pain—I was mostly just upset with myself.

We arrived safely back on the ground and packed up our things. I realized that what was normally a ten- or fifteen-minute hike to the road was going to be an immense challenge. Sanni found me a stick that I could use as a crutch, though it wasn't enough on the steep and rocky terrain. After only a few minutes, I was exhausted from jumping one-footed, and I'd barely made any progress. Sanni was too small to carry me.

At that moment, another climber came strolling down the trail. I sheepishly asked if he could help me hike out. It was embarrassing to plead for his aid, but I didn't think I'd make it out alone. Sanni took our packs and hiked out ahead to move the car close to the trailhead.

Through a combination of leaning against the Good Samaritan and using my "crutch," I was able to hop for long sections at a time. We would sit down to rest when I couldn't go farther. The fellow told me that he was from Australia and that he was in the process of rope-soloing the Muir Wall. He was positive and kind—happy to help but low-key about it. I appreciated his calmness, because I felt very fragile. The thought that I'd just ruined my season in such a stupid way made me want to burst into tears. I couldn't even think about the idea of calling Chai and telling her the bad news. To ruin a season of climbing was bad enough, but there were supposed to be fifteen-odd people coming to Yosemite in another ten days to make a movie. Through one moment of inattention, I'd managed to fuck things up for everyone.

We made it to the van, then Sanni drove straight to the Yosemite Medical Clinic. They put me in a wheelchair, which didn't help my morale. But I was treated quickly and efficiently, and the X-rays showed no breaks. I started to hope that I might be able to salvage my season. Maybe I wouldn't even have to admit to anyone that I'd fallen! Maybe it'd all be OK. . . .

• • • •

Despite my desire to keep the setback to myself and hope I healed quickly, I knew I had to tell the film crew. They were all scheduled to arrive soon to start production in earnest. I felt terrible calling Jimmy and Chai, since I knew how much trouble it would be to change plans for the whole team. I was worried that I'd let them down. But, to their credit, they were understanding and tried to be supportive of whatever I needed. Ultimately, we decided to push everything back a few weeks and hope that I'd be healed.

Before coming to the Valley for the season, Sanni had planned several side trips with girlfriends in order to make herself scarce for some periods of filming. For her first excursion, she'd decided to spend the next two weeks hiking the John Muir Trail, the iconic 210-mile journey through the High Sierra from Yosemite Valley to the summit of Mount Whitney. But now the timing felt very unfortunate. Sanni and her friend set out hiking, while I stayed in the van, crippled and alone.

Instead of two weeks of intense filming, I spent two weeks watching movies alone in the van. I tried to hangboard a little, but I was so afraid of falling off the board or weighting my foot that I couldn't try very hard. Wearing a boot, I bicycled a little bit. After a week or so, I tried climbing on super easy routes with a mountain boot on my bad foot. I couldn't yet imagine putting on a climbing shoe—my ankle was still much too swollen. The black-and-blue bruising radiated up my leg and all around my foot. It looked terrible. But I still tried to hobble around and enjoy the Valley.

I maintained optimism that in another week or so I'd be able to start working on projects. I was rehabbing nonstop—RICE-ing like it was my job. But my daily recovery was barely perceptible. From all indications, it was going to be about six weeks until I could do any real climbing. I ignored the discouraging signs and kept doing what I could.

Sanni returned from her John Muir adventure a few days before the crew arrived in the Valley. I wanted to be useful, but I still couldn't do much. We got lifestyle and beauty shots around the Valley. We did some interviews and filmed some van life. But we all knew that a documentary about free soloing El Cap was going to require some climbing, and I still couldn't put on a climbing shoe.

I started mini-traxioning on some side projects with my right foot in an approach shoe. I wanted to feel productive and actually work on some climbing goals, even if they might be a long way off. El Cap was out of the question—the sheer scale was too massive. Even with two good feet, it's incredibly tiring to climb the face and walk down. Simply walking up the back side takes hours of difficult hiking. I needed something closer to the road that was still inspiring.

•   •   •   •

The Excellent Adventure is a 5.13a variation finish to the Rostrum, one of the more historic routes in Yosemite. I'd onsighted it many years earlier and always thought about soloing it. The Rostrum is closed for peregrine falcon nesting in the spring, so timing was a factor. And one of the years when I wanted to work on it, I was recovering from a hamstring injury and couldn't do one of the crucial moves. For various reasons, I'd thought about it a lot but had never quite done the work or made it happen.

The beauty of the Rostrum is that you access it from the top via a fifteen-minute stroll from the highway. And the crux is that last pitch, which meant that with only 200 feet of rope and a short walk, I could be working on a personally significant project.

The classic images of Peter Croft soloing the Rostrum in his white painter's pants were an inspiration as a kid. Later, Dean Potter soloed a harder finish called the Alien (5.12b) while wearing a BASE rig. I'd repeated the Alien solo as well, though it was a bit of a consolation prize for me, because I hadn't felt ready for the Excellent Adventure.

The actual climbing is almost like two separate pitches—a super technical 5.12c corner followed by a pumpy, overhanging 5.12c finger crack. They're connected, or rather disconnected, by an enormous overhang so that you have to dangle your way out. The overhang has a huge block in it that's easy to hang from, so it's not technically very difficult, but the exposure is unreal. The Rostrum's entire 800 feet drop away below you—if you fell off, it would be clean air all the way to the ground.

The challenge in soloing the Excellent Adventure was basically twofold. There was the extremely technical, thin, and insecure corner and there was the fitness factor of feeling comfortable even while extremely pumped. Both aspects seemed like good trainers for the Freerider, since both would be present there in much bigger ways. The Excellent Adventure was thin, but nothing like the blankness of the Freeblast slabs. And it was pumpy, but nothing like the deep fatigue that sets in after 3,000 feet of climbing. But it was probably the pumpiest route I'd ever considered soloing; it felt like a step forward.

Splitter cracks are notoriously hard on ankles, since they force you to bend your foot sideways to slot it into the crack, then put all your weight on it. Fortunately, the Excellent Adventure leans slightly to the right, meaning that my left foot would be in the crack but my right foot—the bad foot—would be on the blank face to the right. Normally, a leaning crack is somewhat harder, but it was a boon in this case.

I got into a routine of hiking down to the top of the Rostrum and doing a few mini-traxion laps. I'd tie my rope around the big pine tree on the summit and drop it down the north face of the Rostrum. Then I'd rappel in at my leisure—chalking, brushing, and fondling all the holds. The steepness of the crack forced me to place directionals—pieces of gear that held my rope closer to the wall. Otherwise I would have wound up hanging out in free space. It all felt pretty relaxing, spending as much time as I wanted working on a very simple project, figuring out how to make the Excellent Adventure feel secure enough to solo.

I tried various sequences over and over in subtly different ways—every combination of footholds and handholds. And when I occasionally found something that felt secure, I would tick the holds with chalk and commit the sequence to memory. The difficulty was linking all the sections together. Sometimes a good sequence would get me to a certain hold with my left hand but the section above required my right hand on that hold. That would require a compromise—could I climb the section below wrong-handed in order to make exit climbing easier? Or should I switch? Time disappeared as I pondered each possibility.

From the beginning, I could climb the Excellent Adventure every try without falling, but it didn't always feel secure. But after two weeks of sporadic effort, it was starting to feel pretty solid. I'd dialed in a sequence up the corner that felt reasonable and that I could do exactly the same way each time. My fitness had improved and my skin had thickened—the sharp, overhanging crack felt locker. I was physically capable of soloing the route, but was I ready mentally?

I'd always wanted to solo the route; I'd been thinking about it for years. It was beautiful, historic, and badass. The desire was definitely there. But was it too scary? Could I keep it together? Would the exposure be too much? I always prefer keeping my weight on my feet when I'm soloing, and the Excellent Adventure would force me to fully hang over the void. There was no way to avoid cutting my feet loose and just swinging in space by my arms. But as I felt more ready physically, it started to seem less scary and more fun. Excitement started to displace fear, until eventually I knew it was time to just go up there and make it happen.

The film crew would be on hand to document the solo, the first real climbing I'd done in weeks. We were in the Valley to make a movie about me free soloing El Cap, but so far it was mostly about me elevating my ankle and resting. I was starting to feel bad about holding up the whole show, though it's not as if anyone was complaining but me. The film crew had made the most of their time by capturing the scenic beauty of Yosemite. But I felt frustrated and impatient—I was just annoyed that I'd injured myself.

By chance, Tommy Caldwell happened to be in the Valley with his family the same week that I was ready to solo the Excellent

Adventure. I hadn't seen him since Morocco so I was excited to hang out and catch up. It was also a good opportunity for the film crew to shoot a sort of joint interview between the two of us—a casual chat about soloing and risk. But the only time we all had available was the afternoon before I was planning to drive up to the top of the Rostrum and actually go soloing.

We sat in the meadow below El Cap and talked about why Tommy thinks that free soloing is too risky. He's never pushed his opinions on me. He certainly knew what I was getting into in Morocco after he left, and he knew what I was hoping to do in Yosemite. But I've always known that he disapproves of the "dark arts." He explained that he sees soloing as irresponsible and disrespectful to his family, since he knew the pain he would cause if something happened. I understood his point of view, but disagreed.

There's something vaguely off-putting about having a childhood hero explain why he thinks that soloing is a terrible idea right before you go free soloing. Fortunately, I had a fifteen-minute drive ahead of me to crank some music and find my proper mental state.

In some ways, doing the interview with Tommy was a good check to make sure that I was actually prepared for the route. I still felt ready and psyched, despite what anyone else might think. In some ways the whole process of filming served as the same kind of check. It killed some of the spontaneity of my free soloing since it required a bit more planning, but that actually made the whole experience feel safer in some ways. I couldn't rush into anything—filming forced me to really evaluate my motivations and preparations.

I showed up at the pullout above the Rostrum to half a dozen parked cars. The whole crew was already there in position on the wall. There was a long lens set up on an adjacent cliff where Chai and some crew were posted up to watch. I strolled down through the forest and joined Cheyne Lempe for the rappels to the base of the formation. He would film me starting up the first pitches and then hike back to the summit. I appreciated his quiet competence. We didn't talk much. I just laced my shoes and chalked up.

The Rostrum is relatively easy compared to the Excellent Adventure finish. The normal route is rated only 5.11c, and even that seems generous—which meant that the first six pitches to access the Adventure were quick and easy. I didn't get pumped or even slow down at all. It felt good to be really climbing again—this was the first thing I'd climbed in a month that I could be proud of. The pitches of crack climbing flowed by effortlessly. At least I hadn't lost too much.

But the peril of the easy approach was that I wasn't very warmed up for the main event. I stood on a small ledge at the beginning of the technical corner and felt like I hadn't even pulled with my fingers yet. I didn't want to get flash pumped—the kind of debilitating deep pump that occurs when you haven't warmed up properly before a real effort. But it was too late to worry about that kind of thing. I was here and it was time to execute.

My brain turned off and I started climbing the corner exactly as I had rehearsed it during the previous two weeks. My feet worked up tiny edges on each wall and my fingers crimped down with precision. Between my legs was a 700-foot drop, but I didn't notice. I shifted my weight from one leg to the other as I moved between the tiny footholds. Twelve moves later, I was through the corner, nestled into a tight little perch under the roof. I shook out my arms and prepared for the second half of the pitch.

I reached out around the roof and let my weight swing out beneath my arms. I was now hanging from a big block over the abyss. My friend Mikey Schaefer was manning a camera above me. There was a remotely operated camera in the roof. I didn't really notice. I threw my left heel onto the block and used it to lever my body upward, reaching as far as I could above the roof to a sharp, inch-wide crack. I slotted my knuckles into the crack and ratcheted my elbow downward to lock my fingers in place. It was probably the most exposed position I'd ever experienced while soloing. I was hanging above the void by the tips of my first two fingers. Not that I noticed that, either. I just brought my right hand into the crack and started cranking my way up the splitter.

Generally, when I climb finger cracks, there's a delicate balance between pain and performance. I crank on my fingers just enough to stay on the wall, but no more. Fingerlocking can be quite painful and there's no need to crush my fingers more than necessary. But as I jammed my way up the second half of the Excellent Adventure, it seemed as though pain did not exist. I felt nothing; I just executed.

The last few feet of the crack ease back, and I pulled onto the summit of the Rostrum. I was met by cameras and people and ropes—the whole film experience. I felt extremely happy but also fairly relieved. I'd spent the last month worried that my moment of inattention on the Freeblast slabs had cost me a whole season of climbing. I was delighted to find that I could still climb at a high level despite my ankle. I'd thought about the Excellent Adventure for years and even worked on it before, but it had always seemed like too much. But now it had felt pretty easy, even while injured. I was back on track.

• • • •

I spent the day after my Excellent Adventure in Sacramento doing a home solar installation and speaking for the nonprofit group GRID Alternatives. The installations are performed by volunteers such as myself and by groups in need of job training. It's a perfect win-win situation, in which underserved communities are helped in a way that also helps the environment—exactly the kind of project that we try to support through the Honnold Foundation.

I often struggle to talk publicly about my foundation. I'm typi-cally asked about climbing and fear and death, all the normal stuff.

Hardly anyone asks about energy access in the developing world or why I think it's important for the world to transition to renewable energy as quickly as possible. But I'm just as passionate about those kinds of issues, and I figured that while I had a film crew following me around I should highlight some of my other interests. I might be shy talking about the foundation, but I still wanted to make sure that it appeared in the movie.

We spent the afternoon laying photovoltaic panels on a roof in South Sacramento and wiring the whole system together. It was a great opportunity for me to see firsthand what my foundation had been supporting: Two of the crew members working on the install had come from a job-training program financed by a grant from the Honnold Foundation. It was fitting that they would be the ones to teach me how the microinverters worked and how to attach everything smoothly.

I found the evening gala surprisingly inspiring, particularly after working on the install all afternoon. At the job site, I'd spoken to the homeowner—an elderly man who lived on a fixed income. For him, saving eighty dollars a month on his electric bill would mean a real and substantial improvement in the quality of his life. Hearing about the rest of GRID's work for the year just reminded me that my foundation can make a difference in the world in a way that my climbing cannot. Soloing the Excellent Adventure made me extremely happy for a little while. Supporting GRID Alternatives would wind up saving some forty low-income families $1.4 million and offsetting 2,900 tons of carbon emissions over the twenty-year life of the systems.

Being a public figure has several notable downsides, the biggest being a lack of privacy. Knowing that people are watching and judging anytime I climb takes a toll. I'm a naturally private person who winds up posing for pictures with strangers whenever I'm in public. But the big upside is being able to use my public persona to do something positive for the world. I might not love having a lot of eyes directed my way, but I do appreciate being able to steer those eyes toward issues that really matter, like energy access and poverty. Spending a day working with GRID made me appreciate the film project. A bigger media presence would, I hoped, allow me to do more good in the world.

· · · ·

Right after the gala, I drove back to Yosemite, feeling all energized. It was time for El Cap. Even though my ankle wasn't doing great, I was boosted by my success on the Rostrum. I was ready to start working on the main prize.

The next morning, November 4, I hiked up to the summit of El Cap and rappelled the whole wall, spending time on the way down to work on the upper corners and the crux Boulder Problem. Normally I would have rappelled in, climbed out, and hiked back down, leaving all the ropes and material on top. But with my ankle injury, I didn't think I could handle the hike down, so it made more sense to rappel the whole wall instead.

It turns out that there are two options at the crux for Freerider— both equally hard but in completely different styles. The one I'd always climbed in the past is called the Boulder Problem. It was found by the Huber brothers, Alexander and Thomas, when they first established the Freerider variations to the Salathé Wall. But when Todd Skinner and Paul Piana first free climbed the Salathé in 1987, they had climbed a system to the left that they'd dubbed the Teflon Corner, so named because it was slippery as hell. The corner has no holds at all; it's all about palming and smearing your feet. Imagine climbing the inside corner of a concrete parking garage strictly by pushing as hard as you can. It had always felt vaguely impossible to me, so I'd climbed the Boulder Problem on the right.

The Boulder Problem is a twelve-move sequence up the smooth

face to the right of the corner. The holds are small and rounded and almost none of them are down-pulling, meaning that tension is always required between your feet and hands. Which is a challenge, since the footholds are even smaller and more slippery than the handholds. But the benefit of the Boulder Problem is that it has a very specific sequence that I could follow exactly the same way no matter the conditions. Whether it was hot or cold or in the sun or not, I'd always grab the same holds in the same order, which made the sequence very easy to rehearse and memorize. By contrast, every time I'd tried the Teflon Corner, I'd used different techniques and never really succeeded—it always felt like some good luck and a little magic would be required to actually climb it.

I did three laps on the Boulder Problem, pausing between efforts to brush the holds and memorize every intricacy of the surface. I inspected and considered each grain. If even the slightest fragment of rock broke or crumbled, it could mean death. The margin for error really was that thin. In a lot of ways, the Boulder Problem embodied how most people think about free soloing—any mishap of any kind would probably mean death. Most of the free soloing I do is on climbing easy enough for me that if a foot slipped or if I grabbed a hold incorrectly, I could probably recover. But there was no margin for error on the Boulder Problem.

The pitch was originally rated 5.12d by the Hubers, but a few years later, a key hold that had marked the end of the crux had broken off. I have an old photo of me hanging on that key jug from my first time up Freerider in 2006. When I freed the Salathé in a day in 2009, I pioneered a new sequence that involved jumping from where the jug used to be all the way into the aid climbing corner to the left. It was an outrageous maneuver that I knew could never be free soloed—I considered a six-foot horizontal jump completely off the table, even if it wasn't *that* hard. But other climbers had found an alternate way of doing the sequence involving a karate kick with the left foot into the same corner. Instead of jumping with both hands, one could instead lead with the left foot, stem into the corner, and reach over with more control.

The karate kick became the standard method. When Tommy and I did the free Triple in 2012, we both used that method, and to my knowledge no one has repeated my double-dyno technique. Nowadays, everyone does either the Teflon or the karate kick on the Boulder Problem. The difficulty is probably closer to 5.13a now, considering that the hardest moves come after the end of what used to be considered 5.12d. But topo maps still typically call Freerider 5.12d. Rating aside, it's quite a difficult section of the wall, no matter how one climbs it.

I'd been doing nightly stretches for the previous six months in an effort to make the karate kick easier. I needed to be able to stick my left leg straight out at full extension with relative ease. The tighter my hamstring was, the more I had to fall into the move, and conversely, the more flexible I was, the more static the move became.

Now, as I rappelled down the wall on this initial reconnaissance, I was encouraged to find that I could do the Boulder Problem multiple times in a row, on command, with relative control. It was an encouraging first step. It still seemed outrageous to consider being in that position ropeless, but at least I knew it was possible.

The next day, I climbed the Freeblast again with Sanni, more than a month after our botched initial attempt. This time, I clipped every bolt and was glad I didn't fall off. The slab still felt wildly insecure, but it was a first step. I was starting to piece Freerider together.

I spent another two days rappelling the wall and climbing the Freeblast, and then we all decided to camp on the summit in order to better film the process of working on the route. Normally I prefer not to camp, since my van is so much more comfortable than freeze-dried food and a sleeping pad, though it made sense in this case, since the hike down was still too much for my ankle. We spent the next few days living on the summit of El Capitan.

One of the great things about filming was that they could help with a lot of the rope and rigging work. In this case, they fixed the ropes down the wall; all I had to do was rappel in and climb back out, which saved me a ton of effort. The first morning, I dropped into the Boulder Problem, climbed it roped four times in a row without a warm-up, and climbed back to the summit. It took me about an hour and a half to climb the upper 1,100 feet of Freerider, a time that I repeated an hour later after a lunch break on the summit. It was encouraging to know that I could romp up the steep upper third of the route with relative ease. I was certainly noticing my ankle in all the pitches of crack, but it wasn't stopping me. Being uncomfortable was a lot better than being incapable.

We spent the afternoon shooting scenic interviews on the summit and classic camp cooking photos. The next morning, I repeated the process, running two laps on the upper third of the route. By my fourth lap, I was starting to feel like the rope was superfluous—I was just running up the cracks anyway. I didn't really need the harness and micro-traxion attaching me to the wall.

It was now November 12. Winter was coming. Despite California's typically sunny conditions, we were still in the mountains of the Sierra Nevada. Once it started snowing, the season would probably be over. The forecast was starting to show hints of rain and snow on the horizon. I worried that the season would end just as I was starting to feel a bit of confidence.

After two days on the wall, I took a much-needed rest day back on the Valley floor. The forecast had not improved. Even if it didn't snow and end the season, one day of heavy rain would be enough to wash off all the chalk and tick marks, which would set my process back quite a bit. If I was going to free solo El Cap this season, my window of opportunity was narrowing.

I climbed the Freeblast again the next morning with my friend Brad Gobright. We continued past the normal finish and did the two pitches above Heart Ledge, dialing in a few more sections. It looked like it was going to rain in two days. If I was going to give Freerider a shot, it would have to be the next day. I didn't feel 100 percent prepared, but I felt great about the final third of the route. I could repeat the crux Boulder Problem on command and knew the upper cracks quite well. The middle of the route was more of a question mark, since I'd only rappelled over it a few times (and of course climbed it something like fifteen times over the years). And the Freeblast was still just as slippery and insecure as ever. But if I could just get up to the crux, I would probably be fine.

The other big issue was that by mid-November the sun wasn't rising until 6:30 a.m. or so, and it would hit the crux by 8:30 a.m. The sun was so low in the sky that it was practically perpendicular to the wall, which turned the wall into a big parabolic oven. So even though it was quite chilly at night, the daytime temperatures on the wall were surprisingly hot. I knew I'd have to finish the Boulder Problem on pitch 23, before the sun baked it. I guessed that it would take about three hours to get there, so I'd need to start climbing by around 5 a.m. to allow some safety margin. That meant a lot of cold climbing by headlamp before the sun rose. Not that I mind climbing by headlamp—in some ways, it feels less scary, since there's no exposure. But the Freeblast slabs are particularly technical, with footholds so small that they can disappear into the shadows of a headlamp. It was definitely not ideal to go up there in the dark. But the rain was coming and it was time for me to perform.

I was also feeling some internal pressure to wrap up the filming. Not that anyone had asked me to free solo El Cap—I think the idea made the crew even more uncomfortable than it made me. But I was tired of people watching my every move and of the constant planning that was required. Having a cameraperson in the van was

straining my relationship with Sanni. All the time spent doing interviews and shooting lifestyle was cutting into what normally would
have been quality time. I wanted to have our normal life back. And I
wanted to undo my mistake on the Freeblast: If I managed to solo El
Cap anyway, it would make up for my inattention. No harm, no foul.

The problem was that there were too many people around. I
was constantly talking to the camera, explaining how I felt about
things or talking about my process. If there was no camera, then I
was talking to Sanni or her family—all of whom climb and most of
whom were in the Valley for various parts of the season. I never had
any time to myself just to think about the climbing and memorize
sequences. I needed time to daydream about the positions and the
exposure, and to focus my thinking on what I was going to do and
how I wanted to do it.

It was all vaguely stressful. I just wanted to be done with it all so
we could leave the Valley. I knew it was possible now. I was within
striking distance of free soloing El Cap. But I still needed to strike.
The forecast was unchanged—I could either solo the mountain
tomorrow or wait until spring.

After tons of deliberation, we made plans to shoot the solo the
next morning. I would start around 5:30 a.m. There would be a cameraman in the van with me for the drive to El Cap meadow, on the
approach to the wall, and on various parts of the route. I'd be miked,
so it would all be properly recorded. We were making a movie! I just
needed to climb the route.

The next morning, I drove to the meadow while Sanni stayed
curled up in bed, enjoying the warm comforter on a crisp autumn
morning. I knew she was deeply uncomfortable with everything, but
I had to set that aside. I kissed her on the forehead and told her I'd
see her soon. She said, "I love you. Have fun," as I left the van. She
told me later that she had tossed and turned all night, but that she
fell into a deep sleep once I left.

There were about ten cars in the meadow already, various people involved with the filming and those peripherally connected. *National Geographic* magazine was writing a profile of me in conjunction with the film. The writer was there, along with someone from the office. It all had a vaguely carnival feel again, just like Rivières Pourpres. I ignored it all and hiked to the base.

My TC Pros felt tight on my right foot. I hadn't worn my normal-size shoe since my accident. I'd tried them on the night before and been delighted that they fit again. I took it as a good sign that I could at least wear my high-performance shoes. But now, in the cold pre-dawn, the tightness felt like it was numbing my toes. Not that I'd never had numb feet while climbing before—it was certainly a lot warmer than Patagonia. I figured I'd warm up as I climbed. I fiddled with my headlamp, chalked up some more, and started climbing.

It felt good to leave the cameras behind. I was slightly nervous, though I attributed the shakiness to the cold and the dark. I just needed to warm up a bit, both physically and mentally. The first pitch, a lovely 5.10c finger crack, flowed by easily enough. But the second pitch, the short 5.11b roof, felt scary. The first move required rocking my entire weight onto my right foot, the injured foot, which now felt numb in my overtight shoe. I didn't really want to make the move, but at least I knew exactly what to do. I'd always done the sequence exactly the same way, so I just put my feelings aside and did the moves. I was overgripping and a little shaky, but I could afford to be slightly imperfect on 5.11b terrain. I knew I'd warm up as I did more pitches.

The corners above were easier, but that just meant they passed by more quickly. A few minutes later, I was at the beginning of the Freeblast slabs. It was still dark, I was still cold, and I wasn't any more warmed up. I paddled my way up the groove that guards the actual slab and rocked up into the blankness above it.

If I'd ever had a nightmare about climbing, this would be it.

Dark, cold, alone, and relatively unprepared. I could see the dark form of a cameraman hanging at the top of the next pitch above me—though having someone hanging up there didn't do anything to change the situation I was in. I was scared. I tiptoed up the first few moves of the slab and got situated for the crux, a horizontal rightward traverse with no handholds. It's all about balancing on small feet and trusting the rubber on your shoes. Except that, in this moment, I didn't trust my feet at all. I still couldn't feel my right foot properly, and I needed to trust my life to it. I hesitated a moment, scared and unhappy. I was annoyed that the cameraman was up there witnessing this debacle. I was annoyed that there were people in the meadow judging me. I didn't want to be here. They should be up here instead of me!

I grabbed the protection bolt in front of me. I didn't even really think about it, I just grabbed the bolt and pulled on it, skipping the scary move. I'd cheated, ending my free solo on the fourth pitch. I was still very much solo, but it was no longer free climbing, since I was pulling on gear. I didn't think much of it. I just wanted to be off the wall. I was a little embarrassed and didn't really want to explain this to anyone, though I knew I would have to as soon as I got down. I kept climbing, since it was not as though I had a harness or rope to rappel with. I needed to get to Heart Ledge, 500 feet above me, to access the fixed ropes and work my way down. But since I was cheating anyway, I grabbed every bolt now and did anything I could to make the climbing feel easy and secure. The cameraman didn't say much as I passed by, though he lent me a double-length sling and a locking carabiner so I could fashion an improvised harness and rappel down the fixed lines.

He radioed the rest of the crew, advising them that I was bailing. I continued on down the ropes. It was light by the time I reached the meadow, where a camera crew was waiting for me. They asked how I was feeling and asked me to explain things a little bit. I can't remember what I said—I didn't feel like talking. I poked my head into the van, waking up Sanni. She groggily asked, "Back so soon? Everything OK?"

"Everything's fine. I bailed." I closed up the van to finish talking to the cameras.

A moment later, Sanni came out to give me a big hug.

After half an hour of debriefing, we drove the van back to where I was staying on the Valley floor. It was still quite cold, but my body was hot. I'd just soloed the first thousand feet of El Cap and rappelled back down in about an hour and a half. It was actually a fairly remarkable morning of climbing, but I still felt like a big failure. I'd wasted my one shot at free soloing El Cap for the season.

The real bummer was that I was feeling quite good physically. I was warmed up now and felt strong. I just hadn't felt comfortable on those particular moves on the Freeblast. But if I'd had a harness and gear, I would have just continued up the Salathé by myself and done the speed record or something. I was ready to climb something rad, and I was hungry for it, I just didn't have any ready objectives.

I couldn't handle the crowds or the camera. I just wanted to go do something, anything. I threw together my day bag, hopped on my bicycle, and rode over to the base of Astroman. Though I hadn't climbed the route in maybe eight years, I'd climbed it many times in the past. It had been my first taste of hard soloing back in 2007. Now I wanted to repeat it just to show myself that I could. No people, no camera, just me, blasting some tunes out of my phone, by myself.

An hour and a half later, I was on top of Washington Column, convinced that even if I was a total failure when it came to El Cap, at least I'd improved a little as a climber over the last decade. I decided to solo the Rostrum again that afternoon as well, just to revisit the whole linkup that had put me on the map so many years ago. Having just done the Excellent Adventure, I knew that the Rostrum didn't add a whole lot, but it still gave me a certain sense of completion.

It rained the next day, which gave me a good reason to snuggle up with Sanni in the van and relax. Part of me felt like an abject failure. I could have been done with the whole crazy project if I had just trusted my feet on that move. But the more rational and more mature part of my brain knew that I'd made good decisions and that it was all a good learning experience. I didn't free solo El Cap, but I learned a lot more about what it would take. And I'd practiced the bottom third. And I'd done more than anyone else ever had—I'd left the ground without a harness or rope.

The season was over, but I was more motivated than ever. I knew it was possible. I knew that I could do it. I just needed to execute.

CHAPTER **ELEVEN**

FREERIDER: THE CLIMB

HAVING TO BAIL on Freerider was disappointing. But I'd definitely made the right decision. My foot still wasn't healed enough to allow me to climb at my max—and I'd definitely need my max to pull it off. The fear I felt on the thin moves on Freeblast was telling me something. I needed to heed the warning.

I could have left it right there. Nobody—least of all the film crew—was telling me I had to free solo El Cap. I'd always thought that if I couldn't rise to the challenge, I could leave it for a better or a bolder climber sometime in the future. Not that at the end of 2016 there were many other candidates queueing up in the meadow to give it a try. . . .

But the idea of it had really taken hold. I knew that if I were ever going to make another attempt to solo Freerider, I'd have to train through the winter, aiming for a go in late spring. And by now, I knew pretty well what that training would require.

I attributed my failure in November to a general lack of preparation, which I blamed mostly on my ankle injury preventing me from doing the necessary volume of climbing to feel ready. But I

didn't consider the season a total failure, since I'd learned a lot. The
short days of autumn had forced me to climb in the dark and cold;
the long days of spring would allow me to climb in warmer and yet
shadier conditions.

After a short expedition to Kenya for The North Face over
Christmas, where we climbed a few 2,000-foot walls and put up
a few new routes, I was back in Las Vegas, ready to start whipping
myself into the shape of my life. As soon as I got home, I started
a difficult hangboard routine, and I instantly started feeling elbow
pain for the first time in my life. I realized that I needed to rest and
regroup. My ankle was still bothering me quite a bit, and my body
felt worked from three weeks of nonstop adventuring in Kenya. My
mind was telling me to train hard and get ready for Yosemite, but my
body was telling me to rest.

I spent the next week eating cookies and climbing casual routes
with Sanni and her family. A lot of cookies. Too many cookies. I let
myself go for a week and a half, totally disregarding training or diet.
I knew that the pain in my elbow would only get worse if I tried to
train through it, so I had to do one of the hardest things in climbing:
listen to my body.

During this time, I also got recommendations for a good physical therapist in town. My ankle needed to feel close to perfect if I
wanted to trust my life to tiny footholds in the spring. I wound up
meeting Scott Pensivy, an extremely experienced physical therapist
who'd worked with a lot of mainstream professional athletes. The
walls of the office were lined with signed jerseys and balls and the
PT area was an open space, shared with a sports training facility.
So while I worked through various exercises designed to improve
the strength and mobility of my ankle, I could watch lots of big,
strapping ball-sport athletes train. As someone who's never had any
athletic prowess at all, it was inspiring to see how other athletes

trained. Though to be honest, it made me appreciate the fact that most of my training takes place in the mountains.

Doing physical therapy helped me start taking my body and health more seriously. Around the same time, I also met Pat Teves, a great deep tissue masseur. I figured that regular sessions with Pat would help with recovery and allow me to climb more, particularly over the long term.

I had always subscribed to the dirtbag view of climbing—just do it as much as you can, and if anything starts to hurt, ease off for a bit. As someone who'd never had decent insurance or access to health care, I'd never taken bodywork seriously. But I realized that both my desires and my circumstances had changed. I was no longer the homeless climber kicking around in a beat-up van. I was a professional athlete, getting paid well by sponsors to perform at a high level. Even writing that makes me cringe a bit, but it's the reality of my life now. I can afford to take better care of myself, to act more like a true professional.

After almost two weeks of easy climbing and family time with Sanni and her parents, I started sport climbing seriously again, trying things that were challenging for me. I could feel a twinge in my elbow, but it didn't seem bad. I figured that with bodywork and stretching, the pain would stay manageable, and I could climb through it. Motivation soared once I could actually climb again. I started doing core exercises and stretching every day.

I settled into a pleasant routine. I would finish my PT by midmorning and then drive half an hour out of town to join my friends at the sport crag for the day. We'd climb all day and then I'd do extra core work and stretching in the evening before bed. The days blended into weeks as I ground my body to dust day after day.

As my ankle improved, Sanni and I would go for progressively longer hikes on our rest days. I knew that all the wall climbing

I wanted to do later in the season would require serious hiking; after months of barely walking, I wanted to whip myself back into shape. What started as little strolls around the neighborhood and hikes around Red Rock Canyon eventually culminated in a thirty-five-mile hike across Zion National Park with Sanni and my sister, Stasia. I figured I didn't need to be in any better shape than that, unless I wanted to become an ultra-runner instead of a climber.

As the days got longer and the temperatures warmed up, I started doing some of the longer multi-pitches in the canyons. It was still mostly sport climbing, but I started adding one adventurous outing a week—one day to try one of the hardest long routes in Red Rock. I ticked my way through routes like Rainbow Country (12-pitch 5.12d), Fortress of Xanadu (5-pitch 5.13d), and Emerald City (12-pitch 5.12d). Some of the routes were up on the Rainbow Wall, the site of my 2010 solo of the Original Route (12-pitch 5.12b).

The Rainbow Wall was also home to Dreefee, a 12-pitch 5.13d, the hardest route in Red Rock. Some friends had ropes fixed on it for the season, making it easy for me to do micro-traxion laps up it each time I finished one of the other routes. It became my perfect Yosemite trainer—a big hike up to the remote wall and then a stack of hard climbing. The pitches broke down at 5.7, 5.12a, then five pitches in a row of 5.13, culminating in an ultra-thin 5.13d face pitch, then a few more pitches of exit climbing to the top of the wall. It required an extremely technical, footwork-demanding style of climbing on sandstone, very similar to Yosemite granite.

•   •   •   •

But my season of training on the Rainbow Wall did not begin well. It was February 25, and I was climbing with my friend Brad Gobright. Brad's an extremely strong and fast climber, and we planned to mostly simul-climb Rainbow Country and then work on Dreefee. The only problem was that it was thirty-four degrees when we left my van, and that was 2,000 feet below the wall. The entire approach was covered in sheets of ice, and the wall felt like a freezer. We managed to climb up to the 5.12d crux of Rainbow Country before we both fell off and gave up, unwilling to keep freezing our fingers for no real reason. But after we rappelled back down, we decided to do a quick mini-trax lap on Dreefee, since we were already all the way up there.

It was my first time on the route and Brad's first of the season. The static lines that were fixed on the route ended about seventy-five feet before the actual ground, but it was easy 5.5 slab climbing to close the gap, so we didn't think much of it. We just scrambled up to the ropes and started from there. Both of us struggled with numb fingers and the hard climbing above. As the sun started to set behind the wall, I rappelled down to get ready for the hike out. Brad was above me and followed suit, after a bit more climbing. We were chitchatting about the route while I packed up my bag. I complained that the climbing was so insecure—there were no real holds.

"Yeah," Brad agreed, "it feels like you could fall on any move."

As soon as he said that, I heard a slip and the sickening noise of something heavy sliding down rock. I turned around just in time to see Brad ricochet off a small ledge with a tree and continue sliding to the ground thirty feet below. The rock was at a low enough angle that he wasn't moving crazy fast, but it was also too smooth for him to stop. I felt helpless as I watched him crash to the ground.

I scrambled down to Brad as fast as I could. Outwardly he looked fine, but he couldn't weight his right foot. He'd broken his ankle in the past and was sure that he'd just broken his foot. The Rainbow Wall is perhaps the most technical approach in all of Red Rock, since it's set so far back and so high in the canyon. It had taken us about two hours to hike up to the wall in the morning, and we had about one hour left until dark. Of course, we hadn't bothered to bring headlamps, since we were planning on a casual day of climbing. We were in for a long night.

The beginning of the hike out was too steep and technical for me to carry him. He began to crawl downhill while I considered our options and made some phone calls. I tried the search-and-rescue number to see what would happen if we required a rescue, but I got the impression that he'd be helicoptered out. As a true climbing dirtbag with no insurance, Brad wanted to avoid involving the authorities. All we really needed was a strong friend to come meet us with food, water, and headlamps.

I tried everyone I knew who was around Vegas. The problem was that the front gate on the one-way loop road that gives access to all the climbing would close at dark, so unless someone was already in the park, it would be tough for them to come help. As Brad laboriously picked his way down the steep, icy slabs like a crab, I scouted for the easiest paths and kept making calls. Finally I reached Jonathan Siegrist, who was at dinner with his girlfriend. I asked him to enter the park through the exit when they were done with dinner and come join us out in the desert. I figured that by the time they hiked out toward us, we would have made it down out of the technical canyon and into the relative flats, where Jonathan could help me carry Brad.

As the sun set, we settled into a grueling routine: Brad would crawl or hop down everything that was steep or technical, being careful not to touch his foot against anything, and I would piggyback him on the terrain wherever I could. I used our phones as flashlights as we slowly picked our way down. We finished the last of our food and water. Brad must have been coursing with adrenaline—I'd never before seen someone hop one-footed down technical fourth-class terrain. He's a prolific soloist, and I think calm nerves served him well as we wove down the steep slabs. Once we were

off the rocky slabs, I would scout ahead on the trail, taking both of
our backpacks, then dump the bags, double back, and carry Brad
as far as I could. We were both quite tired before we'd even begun
the descent. By the time we were halfway down, my quads were
burning. But below us in the canyon, I could see the headlamps of
another climbing party trying to find their way back to the parking
lot. For a brief time, we were gaining on them, and that gave me
renewed vigor. I really wanted to pass some poor party while carrying Brad. But eventually they pulled away and we never caught up.
We needed to train harder.

Just as we'd hoped, Jonathan and his girlfriend Shaina met us
right at the mouth of the canyon with supplies. Now Shaina could
carry the bags and Jonathan and I could alternate with Brad. We
made it back to the cars with only an hour and a half more of toiling. By the end, Brad was so tired from hanging onto our backs and
holding up his broken foot that his breathing reminded me of hard
sport climbing. He might as well have been sending 5.14 as we carried him up the final hill to the Pine Creek parking lot.

We all headed back to the lot on the edge of town from which
we'd carpooled. Brad insisted that he was OK to drive himself home,
and after a quick test drive around the lot to make sure, he headed
out. I was suddenly alone in my van again, exhausted and somewhat
shell-shocked. We'd spent twelve hours out in thirty-degree temps.
The climbing had been some of the hardest I'd tried all season. And
then I'd carried an extra 150 pounds back down the mountain. I
took it as a good sign that my ankle was improving—hiking down
steep, rocky terrain with the extra load had been a serious test. But
I was pooped. I decided to skip my core workout.

But mostly I couldn't get out of my head the sound and image of
Brad sliding out of control. I've always known rationally what would
happen if someone fell off a slab without a rope. But actually seeing
and hearing it made it much more viscerally real. I couldn't help but

think of the Freeblast slabs. I'd randomly slipped off them in the fall, with a rope, thankfully, but I'd still been injured for the whole season. Slipping without a rope would mean a long, terrible slide to the ground. Plenty of time to process the fact that I was about to die and there would be nothing I could do about it.

I felt terrible for Brad, knowing how long it would take for his foot to heal. I was still dealing with my ankle, and it hadn't even been *that* serious. My injury, and now his, provided a stark reminder of how frail our bodies are, and how uncaring a rock wall can be.

• • • •

At some point during our time in Vegas, Sanni and I started house hunting. We never had a conversation about it specifically, but during our down time she would find house listings online and we would go check out different parts of town. I'd never actually lived anywhere, but it felt like it was time to have a home base. Part of the appeal of owning a home came from the example of other professional climber friends who owned property in various places. It seemed that everyone I knew who was doing OK later in life had some kind of rental property or the equivalent. Since being a professional athlete is such an unpredictable job, it seemed prudent to plan for my future a little. Vegas was affordable, had a convenient airport, and had probably a hundred different 5.14s within a two hour drive of the city limits that I'd never tried. A lifetime's worth of hard climbing, with, potentially, all the conveniences of a house. Our own shower! Room to walk around. A fridge! It all seemed a bit self-indulgent. But also really nice. Maybe I was getting old and soft. But having my own place just seemed right.

We found a place that we liked and made it happen. No major haggling or difficulties; within weeks, I was a homeowner. Of course, we didn't own anything to put into the house—for the first month or so, we slept in the van in the driveway. Sanni was away on a trip when I closed on the house. The first thing I did was install Wi-Fi. There were no appliances and no furniture, so I would just sit in the empty house to use my computer. Then I realized that the Wi-Fi worked just as well in the driveway, so I just stayed entirely in the van. But at least I knew that no one would hassle me over parking, since it was my house!

I kept to the same climbing and training schedule, but I devoted each rest day to my new home. Setting up utilities, finding cheap furniture, changing my address and my official residence. In some ways, the whole process appealed to my love of to-do lists—I had an almost limitless number of things to do to settle into our new home. Sanni wound up doing pretty much all the decorating and furniture-choosing. I was fairly useless, though I've never had any problem turning over the lead to a stronger partner. She was in her element, finding all of our appliances on Craigslist for less than $1,000 total.

The house definitely represented a small step toward normalcy—friends joked that marriage and kids would surely follow. But sleeping in the driveway outside an unfurnished house still felt a long way from family life. That would have to wait a lot longer.

• • • •

During the winter, Conrad Anker contacted me to ask whether I'd climb with him in Yosemite in the middle of April. I agreed wholeheartedly, happy to rope up with him again. We'd climbed two big free routes on El Cap back when I'd first been learning how to wall climb, but we hadn't climbed together in Yosemite since then. It'd been eight years, and a lot had changed in both of our lives.

Conrad was really excited about climbing El Cap in a day—just a fun, casual lap up the Salathé Wall. Five months earlier, he'd had a heart attack at around 20,000 feet on Lunag Ri, an unclimbed peak in Nepal, and had had to be evacuated by helicopter after rappelling back to base camp. I was worried that he wouldn't be up for big-wall climbing, but Conrad's wife, Jenni Lowe-Anker, assured me that as long as we paced ourselves and didn't get too cold or worked, he should be fine.

I was also glad to have an official start date to my Valley season. It had been a particularly heavy winter in California, the first big winter in years. The snowpack in the Sierra was twice the average, which felt extreme compared to the complete lack of winter the previous three years. It was great for California's trees and lakes, but not so great for the Yosemite walls. The melting snow on the rim of the Valley sent small rivers spilling down every cliff. Everything was wet.

It would have been easy for me to procrastinate, to assume that conditions were so bad that 2017 wouldn't be the year. But I knew that I had a ton of prep work and practice to do, and I knew that I could do most of it regardless of the conditions. I only needed dryness for the actual send, and that probably wouldn't come until June. I had plenty of time to let things dry out. The sooner I got to the Valley and started working on it, the better.

And the beauty of climbing with Conrad was that he already knew everything about my dream of soloing El Cap and the entire surrounding film project. He'd made the film *Meru* with Chai and Jimmy. He already knew what it was like to climb in front of a camera. It might not sound like a big deal, but for a casual climber who's never worked on a film project, the added complexity of shooting interviews and waiting for cameras to be set up and using a microphone can be challenging.

Coming into the Valley in April, I still felt unsure about eight or so sections of the route. Even though I'd been pretty close to soloing the route in the fall, the whole thing had felt a bit rushed. I didn't feel perfect about the climb—which is part of the reason that I never did it.

Our first day together, Conrad and I climbed the Freeblast, just the first ten slabby pitches, but a good reintroduction to the Valley.

That was the first thing I'd climbed in the fall as well, when I sprained my ankle two hours into the Valley season. This time I was more attentive, and we both cruised the route. Freeblast took us only two and a half hours, so there was plenty of time in the afternoon to boulder, all part of my plan to maintain some finger strength.

The next day, we jugged up the fixed lines that lead to Heart Ledge and started climbing from there. I free climbed the next six or seven pitches while Conrad and Mikey Schaefer simul-climbed and jugged behind me. Mikey was there to film, catching all the random banter while we hung out on the wall. My mission for the day was to clean a section of crack that led over to the Monster Off-width. I'd climbed it in the fall, but it was full of bushes and rocks, possible to climb around but pretty scary—especially since knocking a rock out of the crack could mean killing someone down below. It seemed like a perfect early season mission—there was hardly anyone around and no one was climbing on the route.

Once we were in position above the crack, I rappelled over to it and started collecting rocks in my backpack. After a bit of work, I managed to remove all the loose rocks and dirt, which made the crack a lot more manageable to climb. It no longer felt like a mine-field. Of course, I had to rappel back down the Salathé with a bag full of rocks, which felt a little ridiculous. I was grateful to be able to dump them on Hollow Flake Ledge, a few hundred feet lower. We carried on back down the Heart Ledge lines that we'd come up in the morning, ending our little day's mission in the middle of El Cap. Again, I went bouldering with Mikey in the afternoon to maintain finger strength.

Conrad and I had now climbed the first twenty pitches of the Salathé over two days. We decided to take a rest day and then blast up the whole route the day after that. We were watching the weather forecast: There were sporadic spring storms coming through, and we didn't want to be stopped by the rain.

My rest day consisted of bouldering. I chose to focus on slabs in order to practice for the Freeblast. And I used the opportunity to start breaking in some tight new TC Pro climbing shoes. But at least circuiting slabs didn't require much skin. I could rest my fingers, since there was basically nothing to hold—it was all about precise footwork. I knew that this would be an ongoing theme of my season. I needed to feel great on my feet.

The next morning, when Conrad and I blasted off up the Salathé Wall at sunrise, I discovered an important problem: All the seeps and water streaks were infinitely worse in the early morning. The whole Salathé side of El Cap stays shaded until 11 a.m. in the spring, which is perfect for staying cool in the heat. But it also means that there's no sun to dry out all the wet streaks. Our previous missions had been midmorning into afternoon, with the sun on the wall. We didn't know the extent of the wetness because we hadn't experienced it yet. Now, up there at 5:30 a.m., we realized that *everything* was wet. Some of the wet streaks extended for hundreds of feet down the wall. Entire pitches were running with water. I wasn't planning to free climb, since our goal was just to get up the wall in a civilized day, but I'm not sure that I could have free climbed anyway. The holds were all too wet and slippery. It was April 23, and it was hard to believe that so much water could possibly dry out during the next month.

I climbed in a water-treated down jacket, getting completely soaked on pitch after pitch. I worried that this was how I'd accidentally kill Conrad: drag him up a soaking-wet big wall until he had an even worse heart attack. But the headwall at the top of the route was bone dry, thanks to its extreme steepness. Conrad took over the lead for the hardest and most spectacular part of the route, and the film crew was there to capture the action. He let out periodic howls as he worked his way up the 200 feet of overhanging crack. He shouted, "I'm a contender again! I'm back in the ring!"

On the last move of the headwall, Conrad blew a piece of gear and took a twenty-foot plunge into space. He was delighted. He pulled right back up and finished the pitch. The exposure didn't seem to affect him at all. That moment made me hope that I will have even a fraction of his enthusiasm for climbing when I'm his age—fifty-four. Or just his passion for life.

• • • •

By the beginning of May, I felt like I'd made good progress on the idea of soloing El Cap, but conditions were still terrible. I had no idea how long it would take for the wall to dry out, since any storm that rolled through could set things back a week.

At this point, Sonnie Trotter showed up to work on a free-climbing variation on the right side of El Cap. I'd volunteered to work on it with him, since I figured that the Freerider was out of condition for a while anyway. I might as well get fit for long days on the wall by climbing on another part of El Cap, which also happened to be steeper and drier. That sounded good in theory, but it was hard for me to work on a different project when I was completely preoccupied with the dream of free soloing the wall.

But having Sonnie around for a week was a breath of fresh air. It was good for me to boulder with a stronger partner—a reminder that I should be training and trying harder. We spent our days swinging around on ropes on the side of El Cap, looking for holds and plotting a route. Our evenings and rest days were spent bouldering. And I was doing some extra fingerboarding on the side in an effort to stay on a program.

After three days of serious toiling, we managed to find a new passage through the middle of El Cap and hand drill the necessary bolts that would protect the climbing. We knew that the route would go, but Sonnie's weeklong vacation was over; it was time for him to return to his pregnant wife and his son. We planned to finish the new route—meaning actually climb the whole thing from the bottom—next season in the fall.

What I didn't realize at the time was how much our days of swinging around influenced my work on Freerider. I'd previously always thought of it as "soloing Freerider," meaning free soloing that exact route, the one that I'd climbed with a rope so many times. Only after Sonnie left the Valley did I realize that it wasn't necessarily the route Freerider that I cared about free soloing, but El Cap itself. I'd be happy with any variations or detours, whatever it took for me to feel secure and comfortable with the climbing. I started looking at a much bigger swath of wall on either side of the established route. Six days after Sonnie left, I found my first crucial variation.

I had to fly to Washington, DC, in May for an Access Fund lobbying effort, an event called Climb the Hill. I was pretty excited to see how government worked firsthand and lend my voice in support of public lands. But I was also conflicted about leaving El Cap for any amount of time. I compromised by taking a lap up the Heart lines and rope soloing the pitch above the Heart in the morning before driving out to the airport. I spent forty-five minutes swinging around on rappel and realized that I could climb around the usual crux of that pitch.

Normally, there's a hard (5.11c) and insecure move of slab climbing protected by a bolt at your chest. It feels totally safe with a rope, since the bolt is right there, but it would be wildly insecure without a rope. But by breaking off the normal route twenty feet below, I could turn a little roof on the right side and traverse back across above, making a big circle around the hard move. It would be crazy to lead, because there was no protection at all, just a blank face with small holds. But if I was ropeless anyway, I might as well do the easier climbing. I much preferred secure 5.10+ climbing to insecure 5.11c, even if it was only one move.

I rappelled back down to my car and drove to the Fresno Airport, buoyed by the thought that, after all these years, I'd found something totally new that was definitely better. I couldn't wait to get back on the wall and continue my search. I knew that it was unrealistic to expect to find better beta on every crux, and frankly I didn't want to make the wall *too* easy. But there were just a few moves here and there that I really didn't want to do. I hoped to work around some of them.

As soon as I got home from Washington, I was back on El Cap, spending the next several days rappelling around on the wall. An old friend, James Lucas, offered to support me up Freerider so that I could free climb the entire route in one day. He'd spent several years working up to climbing Freerider in a day, and I'd supported one of his attempts. Now he was happy to spend the day jugging to revisit old friends—both me and the wall!

I short-fixed the whole route, climbing ahead with a huge loop of slack and no belay so that I could fix the line at the next anchor as soon as James finished jugging the previous pitch. It's considered a sketchy style of climbing, but it's extremely fast and efficient, and it's still a hell of a lot safer than soloing. It was good practice for me. We chatted about beta while we climbed, and as I neared the Hollow Flake, I complained that I'd never really liked the thin downclimb to access the flake.

"Why don't you use the block out left?" asked James.

"What block?" I answered. "You must be thinking of a different section." I had rappelled into the Hollow Flake only a few days earlier, and I'd looked all around for a possible variation. I hadn't found anything new, so I'd devoted my time to rehearsing the thin and insecure moves on the downclimb.

"There's a block out left. It makes it way easier," said James.

I didn't really believe him, but when I got to the thinnest part of the downclimb, there was indeed a little block the size of a shoebox wedged underneath a little overlap. It even had chalk on it. Somehow, despite years of climbing on the Salathé and Freerider, and despite spending several sessions working on that particular section of the climb, I'd never seen that little block.

It was a good reminder to stay humble and keep asking for help. Each of my friends had something to teach me or remind me on the route. I was grateful that I now could be somewhat more open about my project and solicit opinions and advice. Keeping my dream of free soloing El Cap entirely to myself would have also meant that I'd be stuck with all my own beta. No advice from my friends, no one to help me with the work.

I was starting to feel very confident on the Freerider, but I hadn't actually been free soloing much. No matter how confident I might feel on all the moves of El Cap, I had to get back the feeling of flowing over rock without a rope. Two days later, I decided to do something that Hans Florine had once proposed to me: a linkup of all five of the Cathedrals—Lower, Middle, Higher, and Lower and Higher Spires.

The total amount of climbing was probably close to 5,000 feet. To heighten my experience, I chose routes that were new to me on four of the five formations. The film crew wasn't around either, which meant that I would be totally on my own. It was a great way to feel like a real soloist again.

Three days later, I chose to continue my transition back to soloing (as opposed to roped rehearsals of El Cap) by free soloing the Easy Rider, the variation that Dean Potter had pioneered up at the top of the Freerider. This time, the film crew was on hand to record the feat. I was free soloing on El Cap again, even if it was only the top five relatively easy (5.11) pitches. The whole excursion took only an hour and a half, but it was a great teaser. And, most importantly, it made the route seem shorter, since it took the question mark off of the top five pitches. It was almost as if the route ended lower on the wall now.

Two days later, on May 26, Tommy Caldwell dropped by the Valley to climb with me for a few days. He was actually in the middle of his book tour for *The Push*, so he had very little free time, but he managed to sneak away for a little Memorial Day weekend climbing excursion.

He arrived on Friday afternoon and we sneaked away to climb a random route on Higher Cathedral Spire that neither of us had done before. It turned out to be a terrible route, but it was good for us to rope up together again and get psyched for El Cap the next day. That evening, we discussed strategy and packed our things for an early start the next morning.

Simuling the Freerider with Tommy would be as close to soloing as it gets without actually taking off the rope. In terms of pace and sensation, being roped up with Tommy has always been pretty darn close to soloing—obviously not the same, but as close as it gets. This would be my dress rehearsal: my best chance to get a feel for timing and overall fatigue.

Tommy was coming off weeks of media events and book-tour stops; he wasn't exactly at his best. But still, no matter how many events he does, he's still the Tommy Caldwell who's put up more free routes on El Cap than anyone. And his routes are still never repeated because they're too darn hard.

We started right at first light, around 5:30 a.m., as I potentially would by myself. I led, both because I knew the route much better at this point and because Tommy was pretty happy for a scenic cruise. He had no agenda other than enjoying the ride. And what a ride it was! I took us all the way to Heart Ledge on our first block, more than 1,000 feet of climbing for our first "pitch."

We stopped briefly on Heart Ledge. Normally, he would have taken the lead at that point, since he now had all the gear on his harness, but instead he decided to turn the lead back over to me. I was eager—I reracked and proceeded to lead us on a monster pitch all the way up and through the Boulder Problem. When we'd climbed the Freerider together in 2012, as part of our free Triple, we'd climbed it through the night in six hours and forty-five minutes. But this time we were linking even bigger blocks and moving much faster.

When I say, "We simuled through the Boulder Problem," it's worth visualizing what that means. It means that while I was leading the hardest section of the route, Tommy was somewhere on the other end of the rope, probably around 150 feet below me, climbing at his own pace while he managed the slack between us with his belay device. It means that I had no idea how much slack was out while I was clawing my way through the smallest holds on the route. Falling could have been catastrophic, or totally normal, depending on where Tommy was and what exactly he was doing in that moment. I didn't know, and it didn't matter. I climbed right through.

When Tommy joined me at the anchor above the Boulder Problem, all either of us could say was, "Whoa." We had just covered a lot of ground really quickly. Tommy returned the gear to me again and told me to take us to the top. He had just toproped the first twenty-three pitches of El Cap in two blocks, something that had never been done before. He was having exactly the scenic cruise he'd hoped for.

I blasted off again, this time secretly aiming for the summit. The last twelve pitches of the Freerider include quite a few turns around corners, so friction from my rope was outrageous. It felt like a twenty-pound weight pulling down on my harness throughout all the steep upper climbing. But I enjoyed the challenge. It was training weight, but it didn't seem to matter. The crew was filming as we went by, but we didn't stop.

At certain points, I was pumped out of my mind from the extra weight of the rope pulling back at me and the nonstop climbing. Tommy was generally out of view below me, and I assumed he was just enjoying himself, though I realized later that he spent a lot of the climb trying to imagine a potential free solo. As he wrote for Outside Online a few days later:

> I went to Yosemite last week over the Memorial Day holiday and we did a practice lap on the Freerider with a rope. High on the wall, panting and sweating, feet smearing on crispy flakes that made crunching noises as I stepped on them, I looked down 3,000 feet to the ground and tried to mentally transport myself into the mind of Alex, what it would be like to not be attached to a rope? Honestly, knowing that Alex would likely soon pull off the biggest moment in free solo history, I could not fathom it.

Interestingly, even though Tommy was thinking about the potential solo, I was not. I knew that if or when the day came that I was up on the wall ropeless, I'd be in a totally different mental state. And I wouldn't be so pumped and I wouldn't be dealing with all the rope drag and gear. It would be a much better experience.

We reached the summit around five and a half hours after we started, by a wide margin the fastest the route had ever been climbed. I felt terrific. I was close.

As I closed in on the actual free solo Sanni realized that I needed more space to be alone and reflect. Though she didn't necessarily want to, she packed up her things and headed back to our home in Las Vegas. I think it was hard for her to walk away so late in the process, after having been by my side for so much of the journey, but she knew it would help me find the right mental state.

The film crew was also remarkably cognizant of my needs. After the bustle and occasional stress of filming in the fall we'd all learned important lessons. Our spring season had been extremely low key, with most of the crew kept from my view so that I wouldn't really know how much was going on in the background. The only two crew members who I routinely saw were Jimmy and Clair Popkin and they kept things very relaxed.

As I lounged around the day before I intended to free solo El Cap they idly talked about what they wanted to go climb the next day.

"Maybe we should do the East Buttress of Middle Cathedral," Clair said to Jimmy, hoping they could get away for a half-day climb.

"I dunno, maybe you guys should be ready to shoot. Just in case," I replied. Not wanting to state too explicitly that I wanted to go free soloing the next day but also not wanting them to miss the actual ascent.

"Whatever you think," Jimmy responded, "I'm psyched to go climbing but if you think you're going for it then we'll definitely be up there to shoot."

Little did I know that there were already crew members hiking up to the top of the wall, rigging ropes and getting cameras ready. Hell, Chai was already flying from New York to Yosemite. But they understood that I didn't need any extra pressure or stress so they just kept the details to themselves. I was blissfully unaware of all the preparations—I was fully focused on the climbing.

•   •   •   •

I woke up at 3:30 a.m. feeling ready to go—an hour before I intended to. When I looked at my phone and saw the time, I worried briefly that I wouldn't be able to sleep any more, since I felt so energized. But the next thing I knew, I was waking up at 4:30 a.m., a few minutes before my alarm.

It was June 3, 2017. I was alone in my van, parked outside a friend's house in the center of the Valley. I got up and put on the same clothes I'd been wearing all month—my cutoff pants, red T-shirt, and thin red hoodie. It was beginning to feel like my uniform. I'd mixed my breakfast muesli concoction the night before, the way I always do before big missions. All I had to do now was pour in the hemp milk and start eating. My bag was already packed—not that I needed much gear. About twelve minutes after I woke up, I was driving toward El Cap. I stopped at the Yosemite Lodge to use the bathroom. My previous month of early starts had reprogrammed my body to take a full morning poop at 5 a.m. As I sat on the toilet, I checked the weather on my phone. It had felt quite warm on the short walk into the lodge reception area. I noticed that the low for the day was about ten degrees higher than it had been all week. It had been overcast the night before, so the clouds had trapped the warmth. Since it felt muggy and warm, I briefly considered waiting for a better day. I knew that these weren't perfect conditions, but ultimately I didn't really care. It was go time.

I drove to the easternmost parking area below El Cap, not wanting to leave my van in the meadow and risk running into people there. I didn't know who, if anyone, from the film project was around, and I honestly didn't want to. I was there slightly earlier than normal, and for a brief moment I couldn't find the trail in the dark. The sky was brightening just enough to see the mass of El Cap looming above, though the forest below was still quite dark. I trotted along the trail, occasionally looking up at the wall. I thought to myself how enormous the wall looked, both height and width. By starting at the eastern parking, I was walking the whole length of the wall to get over to the base of Freerider. That really made the scale sink in.

Soon I was at the familiar little terrace that marks the start of Freerider. As I neared the climb, I worried that Clair, the videographer who'd been shooting everything off of the wall, must have gotten lost in the dark, because I couldn't see him at all. I wondered whether I should wait for him. But then I noticed him tucked into a little nook in the wall, filming my approach. I exchanged a few pleasantries with him, though I can't remember what I said. I laced up my shoes and started chalking up. Clair took my small backpack with my approach shoes and some extra food and water, which he would be carrying to the summit for me for my walk down. I started some music playing from my phone, shuffling a playlist of my favorite rock songs. It was quiet, the predawn stillness muting everything. I chalked up a little more and then started my timer.

The first thirty feet of the route involve a 5.7 pillar, a perfect way to ease into the climbing. A 5.10 finger crack continues above, though as I slotted into the first few pin scars, I heard the characteristic jangling in the forest of someone hiking with a rack of gear on. I really didn't want anyone watching me; it would make me self-conscious. I looked down a moment and saw three guys coming toward the Freeblast, though they seemed to stop when they saw me. I continued jamming my way upward, as the first 5.11b roof loomed above me.

Clair told me later that when the guys hiked up to the base of Freeblast, all they said was, "Oh my god. It's happening!" and then they waited until I'd climbed out of view. As I later found out, they were serious climbers about to attempt their own free ascent of El Cap, though with ropes over many days. They were probably just as uncomfortable walking up on me starting as I was with people watching me.

It was warm and humid, and the lowest pitches of the route always feel like they're still in the forest. I was sweating a little, though the trade-off was that my fingers and toes weren't at all numb.

The 5.11b roof above me marked the first *real* climbing on the route. I had to trust my feet to tiny edges and pull hard with my fingers. It was the first section of the route that required total commitment. I could climb all the 5.10 cracks with complete control— if a foot slipped or I broke a handhold, it might not matter because I felt so solid. There's a big mental difference for me between *real* soloing, meaning total commitment, and easy soloing, which I can overpower if I need to in order to make it feel secure. *Real* soloing requires me to climb exactly as I normally would with a rope; it's climbing that has only one solution. But on easy terrain, I can vary my technique to make it more secure—I can pull harder on the holds or avoid the little footholds or whatever else it takes to make it feel good.

The first move of the 5.11b roof was a rock-over onto my right foot. If the foot slipped off, I'd die. But fortunately it's a pretty good edge, at least by the standards of El Capitan. It was a perfect way to force my mind into the right gear—a move that's totally committing but not too hard. Once my weight was over my right foot, I tiptoed across a few tiny chips while underclinging up into the roof above me. The holds were small and insecure, but the sequence was only six moves. It was basically a short boulder problem to get me warmed up in the morning. Except that I was almost 200 feet off the ground.

Once I pulled around the roof, I got to enjoy almost 250 feet of easy climbing before reaching the Freeblast slabs. Some of the climbing was up a thin finger crack in a corner, a style that often feels fairly insecure. But compared to the roof below, the holds felt huge, and wearing my tight, perfectly broken-in shoes made the footholds feel crisp and precise. I cruised up the corner and found myself in the groove that marks the beginning of the slab pitches. I didn't slow or hesitate, I just kept climbing at an even, measured pace. After months of practice, I knew every hand and foot movement. I just had to do them. I tried to climb exactly as I had with a rope, rocking my weight fluidly back and forth between my feet. Good posture, hips up away from the wall, keeping my weight pushing straight down onto my feet. Not overgripping. Actually, not even worrying about the handholds—they were just for balance anyway. There isn't a single hold on the entire Freeblast slab that you could actually hold onto if your feet slipped and you started to fall. The holds aren't really for holding onto; they're just to help you balance your weight on your feet. The slab is entirely dependent on foot-work. I placed my feet precisely and balanced over them evenly.

Had I stopped to think about it, I might have been nervous, or anxious that I was on the least secure part of the route. But that's why I didn't stop—I'd done all my thinking over the last six weeks as I worked on the route. I was fully prepared and knew exactly what to do. This wasn't the time for apprehension. It was the time for execution.

I've always felt that the slabs require a certain amount of momentum, for lack of a better word. Soloing slabs is similar to skiing or mountain biking: Once you get started, you just have to see it through to the end. You can't stop and think about your posi-tion. Any hesitation could lead to disaster. Free soloing the Free-blast slabs required me to keep moving upward. There are no great stances or places to truly rest your mind—it's 200 feet of the blank-est, most slippery granite in the park. Stalling out halfway through the slabs would be a disaster, which is what had happened to me on my failed attempt in the fall: I hesitated, got scared, started cheat-ing, and wound up bailing.

The crux of the first slab is the rightward traverse where I'd given up in the fall. This time, I felt solid. My ankle felt good, I trusted my feet. And I also decided at the last minute to pinch the fingers of my right hand through the bolt hanger in front of me. It was a trick reminiscent of my solo of Half Dome nine years before, or of Peter Croft's original solo of the Rostrum thirty years earlier. I knew that I could do the slab no-hands if I had to; I'd practiced it on a rope no-hands many times. So I knew that the handholds were purely psy-chological anyway. By pinching my fingers through the bolt hanger (imagine an OK sign pinched through a small metal plate), I gave myself a little peace of mind without "cheating" at all. I wasn't pull-ing on the bolt—I was putting my hand next to it just in case.

It didn't matter either way. I placed my right foot, matched my left next to it, raised my right to a tiny chip above my waist, and leaned hard right. I snatched the good finger edge that marks the end of the traverse. I was through it! I didn't think about it at all, though, since there would be another slippery boulder problem two moves above me. I couldn't stop to think about my position until I was all the way past the slabs.

The next boulder problem involved some tiny edges on slippery black rock. I'd done it exactly the same way every time for ten years and never slipped, though I always felt like I could. But I didn't think about that now. I just did exactly what I was supposed to. Left hand on the sharp crimp, right hand on the sloping nothingness, right foot to the tiny edge, left foot up high by my waist on a small smear. Left hand up to a small three-finger edge, right hand to another sloping edge, right foot up onto the initial right-hand hold, stand up, done! Simple! It was just a matter of trusting the left foot on the smear and standing up, though that's easier said than done.

The next fifty feet were a lot more featured and offered a moment of relative relaxation. I strayed right off the normal Freeblast line and followed a faint buttress feature that was quite a bit easier. At some point, I looked up and noticed a black camera on the wall below Triangle Ledge, which marks the end of the slabs. I thought nothing of it and didn't look again. I cruised up the buttress until it was time to traverse back left onto the crux of the second Freeblast slab. I'd found this variation only a few weeks earlier, so even though I'd ticked every hold and rehearsed it many times, it wasn't deeply ingrained in my memory the way the other slab pitch was. I'd been climbing it for only a few weeks instead of a decade. Even now, it's harder for me to remember the exact holds. I worked my feet across the edges that are normally the handholds. The difficulty for me proved to be stepping back down off those edges in order to get my hands back onto the normal sequence. I'd tried half a dozen different methods for rejoining the normal route and ultimately settled on a fairly simple step down, though actually doing it without a rope on was pretty scary. I find it hard to downclimb like that, because leading with my feet means that I can't see exactly where I'm placing them. It allows doubt to creep in, since I'm not 100 percent positive that my foot is where it needs to be.

The step down was the only move on the slabs where I got scared. I pulled much too hard on the tiny handholds and my whole body was too tense. But it was only two moves: Step my left foot down and bring my right down next to it, then I could reach to the left and grab the holds on the normal pitch. My body was a little shaky and tight, but I did the moves anyway. I grabbed the hold on the left, stepped to a good edge on the left, then crimped my way through the final eight moves of the normal Freeblast slab.

I was through the scariest part of the route. Even though I'd been climbing for only half an hour or so, I felt like I'd cleared one of the biggest hurdles to free soloing the whole route.

· · · ·

I stopped on the ledge to loosen my shoes, then started up the 5.9 corner. It was a filler pitch, just an easy commute up to the Half Dollar above it. The Half Dollar is an awkward flared chimney that's always a bit heinous with a rope. It's super slippery and hard to get your body inside, even though it's rated only 5.10b. It was the first time that being ropeless really felt like a big advantage. Without rope drag or a harness pulling me down, it was much easier to slot myself into the wall. The V-slot felt easier and more secure, since I could wedge myself deeper inside the wall. I cruised up the chimney, enjoying how easy it felt compared to normal rope climbing. The two 5.7 pitches above were equally delightful. Normally, they feel like a bit of a chore because you can only climb them at the same pace as your partner climbing the chimney below. Simulclimbing is much faster than pitching something out traditionally, but you're still limited to the speed your partner is climbing below. For once, I didn't have fifteen pounds of rope pulling me down, and I wasn't limited by someone else's speed.

A few feet below Mammoth Ledge, I heard someone yell, "Alex!" just above me. I was startled but replied, "Yeah?" As I pulled up onto the ledge, I realized that there was a party of three aid climbers camped on the wall, and one of them happened to share my name. They were just beginning to get moving, packing up their camp and getting their bags ready to haul. I exchanged a few words with them while I scrambled across the ledge, but I didn't want to stop or chat. They seemed relaxed about my passing, but I didn't even make eye contact. I still had 2,000 feet of climbing above me, and I didn't feel like being sociable.

Now on the opposite side of Mammoth Ledge, I could see a different party of three still snuggled up on their portaledge on Heart Ledge, 150 feet below me. And another party of two on Lung Ledge above them. I knew there was no one higher on the route, because I'd rappelled down it two days earlier, but I was a little surprised by how many people had started up from the bottom. I would have preferred to be alone on the route, but at least everyone was still low on the route and still in bed. I downclimbed the 150 feet to the Heart, careful to turn down my music and not make too much noise. I didn't want to wake the folks on the ledge. I had food and water stashed at the anchor on the Heart, brought up that morning by the cameramen. I decided to leave the light sweatshirt I had tied around my waist, because I was already too warm. I realized I wouldn't be stopping for any significant amount of time, and I doubted that I'd get cold. If anything, I worried that I was sweating too much and that I might wish I had a little more water with me. But I couldn't do anything about that now. I just pounded the liter of water that was stashed, ate a small energy bar, and retied my shoes.

I'd never technically climbed the pitch above the Heart, at least not the way I was intending to solo it. The normal route involves a single move off a foothold that feels like glass. Though I'd never fallen on the move, it always felt incredibly insecure. A few weeks earlier, I'd discovered the small variation that circled around the insecure move, and though I'd done it on toprope a few times and had checked it out with Tommy while rappelling, I'd never actually led it. My solo would be a small first ascent! Because I didn't have it that dialed, I was particularly reluctant to have people watch. I was glad the three guys were still in bed.

I cruised up to the small roof where my variation branched right and then started tiptoeing across the slab under the roof. After pulling over the lip of the roof using surprisingly good little crimps, I then tiptoed back left across the top. It was classic featured face climbing with nice diorite knobs, the black knobs in perfect contrast against the smooth white granite. I set my feet up and made the big reach back left onto the normal route. One more question answered! I'd known rationally that my variation was quite easy; I'd certainly done it on a rope enough times. But I'd never actually sent it. Now, as I romped up and across Lung Ledge, I knew for sure that it actually was quite easy.

The party on Lung was still fully in bed, though awake. I said some kind of "hello" but didn't stop. I still had a lot of mountain above me and didn't want to slow my progress. The easy scrambling above Lung leads to a small face traverse on tiny holds and then something like 150 feet of downclimbing in a corner. A few days earlier, I'd found a crucial new foothold that made the face traverse easier, though the corner was always a little challenging. Normally, the downclimb was somewhat assisted by the weight of the rope pulling you back up; being ropeless made it a little harder. Additionally, I chose to jam the corner instead of the usual liebacking, opting for the added security of my hands wedged in the crack at the expense of getting a lot more pumped. It was the first time on the solo that I worried about getting fatigued. Up until that point, all the climbing had been on my feet—I never got pumped at all.

After downclimbing for an entire pitch, I was able to face traverse left about fifteen feet on good ledges until I gained the bottom of the Hollow Flake—so named because it's a flake that's hollow, a huge piece of rock exfoliating away from the main face, leaving a wide crack between the two. It's a laborious pitch of climbing because it involves wedging your whole body behind the flake and wiggling upward. But at least it felt secure, since I was slotted into the rock. But often the trade-off for feeling secure in one position is not being able to move upward.

The ledge at the top of the Hollow Flake marks the end of the leftward traversing on the route: From there, it's basically a straight line up to the summit. I popped off my shoes for a moment and gazed up at the remaining route. I'd been climbing for about an hour and a half, and the sun had barely risen on the other side of the wall. Everything above me was in deep shade, so I knew that conditions would stay good for the remainder of the route. I peed off the ledge, retied my shoes, and settled in for several hundred feet of commuter climbing.

The 5.10 cracks between the Hollow Flake and the Monster Off-width have always been fun and easy. They're quite secure and fast to climb, one of the rare sections of the route where I can relax my mind and cruise on autopilot. Of course, that also means that they're over quickly. After ten or fifteen minutes, I was at the traverse left into the Monster.

Normally, the Salathé continues straight up a feature called the Ear, an enormous flake of rock that protrudes away from the main wall much like an actual ear, and then tackles a very difficult thin corner above it. The Freerider avoids that thin corner by downclimbing left off of the Ear and accessing a fearsome wide crack called the Monster. Both the thin corner on the Salathé and the downclimb left seemed a little too hard for me to free solo, so I'd chosen to traverse into the bottom of the Monster below the Ear. It was physically much easier but a little more complicated, particularly because it's not a very popular variation. Earlier in the season, I'd rappelled down the route to clean a bunch of loose rocks and dirt out of the crack. But once the crack was cleaned up, it was a much more secure variation.

The Monster is a notorious and widely feared pitch of climbing. Though rated only 5.11a, it has reduced many a climber to tears and ended many a free-climbing attempt. My good friend Chris Weidner, an experienced 5.14 rock climber, once spent nearly two hours toproping the pitch. When he emerged at the top, covered in blood and sweat and completely exhausted, he no longer cared about sending the route. He just wanted to survive and get down.

It's difficult because it's wide—too wide for your hands, fists, or even both your fists stacked together, but not wide enough to get your whole body inside. It's maybe one foot across, though the width varies enough throughout the 150 feet of climbing to keep you constantly on edge. No one technique works the whole way; there are several tiny roofs or pods or alcoves that force you to change styles. The end result is that virtually every part of your body gets exhausted in the Monster. It creates a deep ache all the way into your bones. In fact, that's always been the worst part about the Monster to me: It makes my joints hurt in a totally unique way.

I'd been training opposition muscles and core all winter specifically for the Monster. I wanted to feel fresh when I got out the top, not crippled and exhausted. The hard climbing on Freerider starts up high, so it was important that I not be too pooped when I got there. And the hardest pitch, the Boulder Problem, requires a lot of tension between your hands and feet. Basically, I needed my body to still feel strong and tight when I finished the Monster.

The crack gradually widened from finger size to fist size; when it got too wide for my fists, I settled in for the long grovel ahead. The Monster was actually physically easier to free solo—without a harness, my hips could slot ever so slightly deeper into the crack. Not only did that make me feel more secure, since I was deeper inside the mountain, it allowed me to flex my hips to rest the remainder of my body whenever I wanted. I set a steady pace and inched my way upward. It was better not to look up at how much crack remained and just carry on slowly and steadily. I was breathing heavily but trying not to go *too* fast and overexert myself. Then, almost before I knew it, I was on the sloping ramp that marks the end of the crack. I wasn't even that tired. And it was probably the fastest the Monster had ever been climbed, which I found heartening.

I popped out in the Alcove, a big, jumbled ledge tucked into the wall where I've camped in the past. Chris Weidner and I had weathered a storm in the Alcove many years ago, spending a night shivering in our bivy sacs as we were lashed by rain. But today I didn't even stop, knowing that my next stash of food and water was only three easy pitches higher, below the Boulder Problem.

· · · ·

I sat on the sloping ledge below the crux and rested for a moment. I felt strong and somewhat impatient, but resting seemed like the smart move. After maybe two minutes of stillness, I began preparing. I peed off the ledge, slightly hunched over myself so that I wasn't in full view of the camera above. I systematically tightened my shoes, pulling on each row of laces until they creaked. I quieted my music and chalked up. There were ten moves of climbing above me. It all came down to ten moves. My life could be distilled down to ten moves.

I pressed up onto the starting ledge and chalked again. My left hand found the sloping crack that marks the beginning of the Boulder Problem. My right hand crimped down on a sloping ripple on the smooth wall above me. Both hands flexed hard, as if I was trying to crack my knuckles. Game on!

I raised my left foot to a tiny chip, a hold so small that it was really just body tension holding my foot in place. My right foot matched next to it on an equally poor foot, taking only enough weight for me to throw my left foot up onto a small tooth below my left hand. My left foot and hand were now in opposition, allowing me to raise my right hand up to a higher spot in the same sloping crack as my left. My thumb spragged across the crack to push off the opposing wall. Right arm and left foot were in opposition and I pushed up so my left hand could grab an undercling above. My right foot stood onto the opening crimp and I was able to rock my weight onto it. Just like that, I was done with the first three moves and able to rest again. My right hand went up to a good crimp, though really it was just a placeholder. All my weight was on my right foot and I would have been able to stand with no hands, even though the foothold was maybe an inch wide.

I chalked both hands and took a few breaths. I didn't think at all about my position or how I felt, I just carried forward on autopilot. Left hand crimped another side pull. Left foot jammed into the lower crack, somewhat sideways. Right foot came up high by my waist and toed into a tiny scoop. The tension between my left hand and my right foot created stability, and I raised my right hand up to a very small but downpulling crimp. My left hand palmed down on the wall below me and I raised my left foot extra-high onto a very sloping shelf. As soon as the foot was placed, I drove down with it and stood up into the "thumbercling" with my left thumb. The hold was an upside-down ripple, maybe an inch long and a few millimeters wide—so small that it would never qualify as a handhold except for the fact that most of my weight was on my feet. I placed my hand perfectly, my thumb going onto the more sloping part in order to leave the better inch of space for my index and middle fingers to curl over. My right foot sneaked in and matched next to my left, and my left foot kicked out leftward to a slippery black knob.

The whole route came down to the next four moves, the hardest of the whole sequence. My right hand came in to my left and I removed my index and middle fingers, which had been stuck to the wall only by the tension between my right big toe and my left thumb. My right thumb took the fingers' place on the good part of the ripple and my left hand shot out left to grab the sloping loaf. I squeezed it for all I was worth and moved my right hand back to the initial down-pulling crimp. I was in an iron cross, fully spanned between the two holds. Right foot through to a sloping dish, hips open, left foot across to a tiny chip, chalk my right hand, bring it in to the top of the loaf. Now I was set up for the karate kick, though I spent no time thinking about it. My right foot came in to the crucial small edge, perfectly placed to provide counterpressure when I kicked my left foot across. I subtly switched the position of my left hand, making it feel slightly more secure as I squeezed my two hands together and crushed the loaf.

As if on autopilot, my left foot shot out perfectly perpendicular to my body, full extension, three feet to the left. It hit the far wall of the corner exactly where it needed to be. What used to feel like a desperate, falling kick now felt like an easy foot placement. My feet felt welded to the wall. Months of stretching paid off, as I brought my left hand to the crack next to my foot. My right hand switched to palming downward and I felt secure, balanced between my left foot and my right palm. I reached my left hand up to a big edge and I was done. I was through the Boulder Problem.

I felt a flood of elation, or maybe just relief. I was suddenly aware of the world around me again, including the cameras fixed to the wall on either side of me. I said something like, "Oh, yeah!" into the camera in front of me. I started laughing. I romped up the final few easy moves to the faint ledge above. I stood on the ledge for a minute, breathing hard, exultant. I knew that somewhere in the meadow 2,300 feet below, Mikey was watching me through the long shot. I pumped my fists over my head, facing the meadow, wondering whether they saw me. For once, I was somewhat glad that I had an audience. I felt like a hero. I still had ten pitches up to 5.12b above me, but I felt like I'd cleared the final hurdle. Now it was just cruising to the finish line.

I loosened my shoes, letting my toes rest for the next several hundred feet of easier climbing. The Sewer was relatively dry, a clear sign that the seasons were slowly changing. But either way, the conditions didn't really matter to me: I jammed and slithered my way up the wet chimney with ease. That got me to the Block, a big sloping ledge the size of a picnic table where people usually camp. I didn't stop. The pitch above it was one of my favorites on the route, delightful face climbing on good flakes, leading to a perfectly cut crack.

As I traversed the flakes, the Enduro Corner came into view above me. I could see my friend Sam Crossley dangling on the lip of the Salathé headwall, looking straight down the barrel of the corner, and Jimmy Chin dangling in space out to the left. They were simultaneously close and far—only a few hundred feet away, but in a totally different world. They were filming everything, though I thought nothing of it. I stopped on Sous le Toit ("Under the Roof," because it's below the Salathé headwall), the ledge below the corner, to tighten my shoes for the next 200 feet. Several backpacks were attached to the anchor on the ledge—all the controls for the cameras down below. I asked if there was any water, but Jimmy said no. I'd have to wait until I got to the Round Table. I rested for a moment, more because I felt like I ought to than anything else. I felt strong and wanted to sprint to the summit. But I was trying to be responsible and pace myself.

The corner represented the last real difficulty on the route, a 5.11+ pitch into a 5.12b corner into a 5.12a face traverse without any great stances in between. I tried to climb at an even, measured pace to control my pump. Not that it really mattered—by this point, I felt indestructible. But I still wanted to do it right. The first half of the corner is predominantly jamming, probably my best strength as a climber. It felt fun and secure. I stopped for a moment at the anchor, balanced with one foot on one side of the corner and my back on the other. I took a few deep breaths and started up the second pitch. It's normally liebacked, but that technique always felt wildly insecure to me. I chose instead to chimney it, my left side pushing inside the faint groove and my right foot on the outside wall. It was a much less elegant way to climb, but it felt safe, and that's all I cared about. Much like the Monster down below, it was hard work to move upward, but it felt secure. And sometimes it's nice to rely on the big pushing muscles instead of tiny fingerholds. I knew that Jimmy and Sam were still filming behind and above me, but because I was facing into the corner, I couldn't see them and thought nothing of their existence. My world consisted entirely of a grainy granite crack and my chalky hands.

The upper corner pinched down at the crux, forcing me to lieback off two fingertip-wide piton scars for a few moves. I did exactly what I was supposed to do: lead with my left hand, right foot up into the corner, left foot up higher onto the face, bring my right hand to a small intermediate crimp in the crack, shuffle my body higher, then reach right hand up to a good fingerlock. It was all executed mechanically, my body doing exactly what it had practiced. The final jamming to the anchor felt the easiest it ever had, probably because I had no rope drag and was up there much earlier in the day.

At the anchor, I rested in a faint stem, feet splayed out on either side of the corner and hands alternating on a good little horn. Jimmy said something to me; it didn't register. I think he started moving upward on his fixed ropes in order to be in position on the summit. I didn't care. I took a few breaths and started the distinctive Freerider traverse.

The main difference between Freerider and the Salathé is that Freerider cuts left below the Salathé headwall and avoids the 200 feet of overhanging crack climbing that make the Salathé one of the most iconic routes in the world. The traverse is the sneaky way to bypass the headwall, climbing four pitches up to 5.12a instead of the wild 5.13c Salathé headwall.

The traverse always felt like sport climbing, specific moves between distinct holds. Because of that, I found it much easier to remember than the cracks, which all look about the same. And because the holds are mostly down-pulling and quite positive, it felt quite safe to me. Seven moves into the traverse, I reached high and left to an enormous hole right on the edge of the corner. As my weight swung around to the left, the entirety of the southwest face of El Cap swept below my feet. There was a full 2,500 feet of exposure below me as I dangled from the hole, yet I felt perfectly safe. The hole was positive and I felt strong. Cheyne Lempe was hanging above me, shooting this side of the corner. I didn't really notice and neither of us said anything. A few moves on big holes led me to a faint stance in a corner. I took a few breaths, chalked up, and executed the final seven-move sequence that guarded the Round Table. I was truly elated. Ecstatic. Effusive, even! I babbled to Cheyne as he jugged up to get onto the ledge with me and give me some water. We high-fived. I felt like giving him a bear hug. I still had 500 feet to go, but it was in the bag. Finishing was just a formality. But still, I popped my shoes off for a minute and ate some energy blocks.

I checked my timer. I'd been on route for about three and a half hours! Outrageous! I could break four hours if I hustled. I'd expected to be climbing for closer to five hours. Four felt amazing. I turned up the volume on my tunes and tied my shoes. Back to work.

Since I'd soloed the Easy Rider a few weeks earlier, this all felt like revisiting an old friend. Except that before, I was breaking some mental barriers and I wasn't well enough warmed up. This time I was on fire. I felt unstoppable. I climbed the corner crack above the Round Table in minutes, not bothering to stem or rest, but just jamming it straight on. I felt like I was swimming upward—long moves between good jams. I was locked into the mountain. There was no one filming, though I could hear Jimmy around the corner from me jugging upward as fast as he could. I occasionally bird-whistled so he could keep track of my progress. I'm not sure whether he could hear, but it was fun to think that we were racing.

As I climbed the Scotty Burke Offwidth, named after a former Yosemite Search and Rescue member who was a prominent climber in his time, I thought, "This is the best this pitch has ever been climbed!" I was moving so quickly and easily that it felt like a different route. But then, just as quickly I thought, "Humility! Stay focused!" I didn't want to fall off just because I got sloppy.

Either way, I was done in minutes. I met Jimmy and Josh Huckabee, the team's rigger, on the ledge above and gave more high fives. Jimmy kept jugging as fast as he could. I teased him to go faster. I gave him a brief head start by chatting with Josh, but I couldn't resist long. I wanted to be done.

The 5.11 finger crack above felt trivially easy. Secure jamming up a vertical crack was a delight. And I was still in the shade! I'd climbed so quickly that even the uppermost parts of the route were still shaded, the first time I'd ever experienced that. It was a pleasant surprise. The 5.10d boulder problem above it felt like a formality, just a few more moves keeping me from the summit. I caught Jimmy again on the ledge above as he switched from one rope to the next. He was winded from his long commute. I gave him another fifteen-second head start, but I couldn't contain myself. All that remained was 100 feet of 5.6, basically walking to the summit. I charged! Moments later, I was on top. I'd free soloed El Cap!

Clair Popkin was there to meet me, video camera in hand. Jimmy had also just crested the summit and started shooting pictures. I don't know what we said. We hugged. We took pictures. I've never smiled so big for so long. I was overwhelmed with happiness and gratefulness. So many people had helped me on my journey, and I wished they were all there to get a huge hug. I took off my shirt to bask in the morning sun. I took off my shoes and chalk bag and stood on the summit, soaking it all in. Jimmy moved around me snapping pictures. I didn't notice, I was floating.

I wanted the rest of the film crew to make it up the fixed lines so we could celebrate together. They had been such an integral part of the process and given me so much over the past two years—it was as much their ascent as mine. I appreciated that Sanni had given me the space to make this happen, but now I wished that she was here for the summit experience. It had been an incredibly long road, and I was filled with gratitude for all the friends and partners who had helped me along the way. But after an hour of savoring the moment, I packed up my backpack and started jogging back down to the Valley. It was still early. The day awaited.

Acknowledgments

From Alex Honnold

My biggest thanks must go to David Roberts, without whom this book would not exist. He did all the heavy lifting in trying to shape my climbing trips into a readable form. I wouldn't have trusted anyone else with the job, and I appreciate how much he helped me throughout the whole process.

My sister, Stasia Honnold, also helped me immensely with the editing process. I'm very lucky to have a sister who knows me so well and is always willing to help. And, most important, she's always inspiring me to try to live a better life.

The climbing and travel in this book wouldn't have been possible without the support of my entire extended family. I'm grateful that everyone has always encouraged my adventures and not questioned my decision to take a different path.

Thanks also to my sponsors—The North Face, Goal Zero, Black Diamond, La Sportiva, and Maxim Ropes—for providing me with the opportunities to push my climbing all over the world. Without sponsorship, I would just be a dirtbag climber living in a van. Oh, wait. . . .

The guys at Sender Films and Big UP Productions deserve thanks for so well documenting my climbing. Without their storytelling, I would not be on the same path.

And, of course, thanks to all my climbing partners over the years. I feel uncomfortable singling anyone out, since I've climbed with so many people over the years and learned something different from each of them. But a few partners have been formative to my climbing:

- Josh McCoy, for teaching me how to trad climb, and for still adventuring with me whenever possible.
- Chris Weidner, for many great climbing trips and for always providing a home base for me.
- Cedar Wright and Tommy Caldwell, for participating in some of the biggest climbs of my life and for always being good friends.

And finally, thanks to the general climbing community, which makes this entire life possible. I'm grateful to be part of such a big and inclusive family.

From David Roberts

I'd like to acknowledge a number of people who contributed vitally to *Alone on the Wall*. Our editor at W. W. Norton & Company, Starling Lawrence, not only saw the potential appeal of the book at once, but skillfully guided it through the many bumps from proposal to finished text with his usual deft erudition and wry commentary. This is Alex's first but my third book with Star, and I couldn't be happier in our teamwork or more confident of his wisdom as editor. Star's assistant, Ryan Harrington, got deeply involved in the gestation of our book, and went out of his way to fix more potential snags than most books run into. Thanks, Ryan, for your calm and canny work. Our copy editor, Kathleen Brandes, performed a careful and intelligent job of catching the typos, redundancies, contradictions, and omissions in our text.

We're grateful to the several photographers whose excellent images grace the two photo inserts in this book, capturing Alex's genius in a way that words are often incapable of. They include Jimmy Chin, Ben Moon, Andrew Burr, Peter Mortimer and Nick Rosen at Sender Films, Renan Ozturk, Tommy Caldwell, Cedar Wright, Rolando Garibotti, and Alex's mother, Dierdre Wolownick.

The parts of the book written in my voice depended crucially on the commentary of others. For their insights into what makes Alex tick, I thus salute Chris Weidner, Tommy Caldwell, Cedar Wright, Renan Ozturk, Alex Lowther, Peter Mortimer, Mark Synnott, Jimmy Chin, Freddie Wilkinson, and Stacey Pearson.

Our literary agent, Stuart Krichevsky, contributed an extraordinary range of judgments, negotiations, and even interventions to make this book better than it otherwise might have been. In a professional life as busy as Stuart's, it's almost a luxury to lavish such care and affection on a single project. This is my fourteenth book with Stuart, and it not only never gets old—I often pinch myself in gratitude to have such a stalwart and *engagé* manager and pinch hitter in my lineup. The same goes for Stuart's tireless and always accessible colleagues, Shana Cohen and Ross Harris.

Several friends who read the book in manuscript offered valuable suggestions. For that, I heartily thank Bill Briggs, Ed Ward, Molly Birnbaum, and Matt Hale (who also helped me immensely with the photo selection and procurement).

Finally, I owe my deepest debt and gratitude to Alex Honnold himself. When I first hung out with him at Smith Rock in 2010, as I researched a profile for *Outside* magazine, I was at once taken aback by Alex's brashness and obsessive focus and charmed by his wit, intelligence, and compassion. It's not always a good thing for a feature writer unstintingly to admire his subject's achievements—the writer's job, after all, is partly to poke holes in the subject's persona—but I was blown away by Alex's climbing.

From that initial week together, a friendship grew. It felt awkward at times, given the age gap between us, and given the fact that my own best climbing lay decades in the rearview mirror while Alex's gleamed through the windshield ahead of him. But we worked out a kind of teasing camaraderie that would fuel our collaboration.

Alex is a good writer—good enough, as I told him in the early spring of 2014, that he could have written this book by himself. But writing, he confessed, was slow and painful for him—and besides, it threatened to take time away from climbing. I was deeply flattered when he agreed to work on *Alone on the Wall* together. Whatever the virtues of our book, they spring directly from Alex's character—not only as a climber but also as a human being.

Index